PRAISE FOR *OUTSTANDING TEACHING. TEACHING BACKWARDS*

"Vintage Griffith and Burns: an impressive melding of anecdote and outstanding classroom practice, which provides countless strategies for ensuring that busy teachers see learning through their pupils' eyes. Simultaneously compellingly readable and rigorously research-informed, this book is the unlikely but deeply attractive love-child of Wilbur Smith and Hilary Mantel."

Barry J. Hymer, Professor of Psychology in Education, University of Cumbria

"Griffith and Burns have provided classroom teachers with a thought-provoking insight into 'teaching backwards'. They have achieved a highly accessible balance of philosophy and practical approaches, which are totally credible since they are based on years of fieldwork with outstanding and improving practitioners. This variety of fieldwork in a variety of settings means their thesis is clear, coherent and credible and will make sense to all teachers looking to improve their pedagogy. Their practical suggestions range from quick-fix templates and techniques to deeper approaches, but all are explained in a down to earth, real-life fashion, which makes them all the more appealing to a time-poor practitioner. Their prose is good humoured and has the learner at its centre. Teachers are encouraged to see learning from the perspective of the learner, and, by developing the techniques outlined in the book, provide them with the clearest support possible in how to succeed. The graphics and layout help make the ideas accessible and of practical use, especially through the summaries at the end of each section. References to works and ideas by other writers offer the opportunity for the reader to explore concepts in greater depth.

"The accessible, real-life nature of *Teaching Backwards* will undoubtedly encourage many practitioners to experiment with its techniques and produce better crafted and more stimulating lessons."

Graham Aldridge, Head Teacher, Range High School

"*Teaching Backwards* is another superb demystification of exactly what outstanding teaching looks like. Griffith and Burns have the clearest vision of how to describe outstanding teaching that I have yet come across and the book is littered with practical tools to use in the classroom the next day. To suggest to a teacher that they 'start with the end in mind' is the easy bit. The book goes on to give a step-by-step approach of how to do it. I particularly like the use of humour and metaphor and I will be looking for more Hobnob teachers and more black belt assessors.

"Enjoyed it and still learned things. Always a great sign."

James Kerfoot, Principal, Childwall Sports and Science Academy

"All teachers want to improve their practice and this book is essential reading. It is practical, practical, practical! And packed with ideas you can immediately implement in the classroom alongside little pearls of wisdom in the form of memorable stories. Based in evidence, *Teaching Backwards* will make a difference to school leaders and teachers alike. A must-read."

**Carel Buxton, Executive Head Teacher,
Redbridge Primary School and Snaresbrook Primary School**

OUTSTANDING TEACHING

OSIRIS
EDUCATIONAL

THE OUTSTANDING
TEACHING SERIES

ANDY GRIFFITH
AND MARK BURNS

Crown House Publishing Limited
www.crownhouse.co.uk
www.crownhousepublishing.com

First published by

Crown House Publishing
Crown Buildings, Bancyfelin, Carmarthen, Wales, SA33 5ND, UK
www.crownhouse.co.uk
and
Crown House Publishing Company LLC
PO Box 2223, Williston, VT 05495, USA
www.crownhousepublishing.com

Teaching Backwards figure and chapter start illustrations © Jayne Strahan

Images page 17 © rgbdigital.co.uk - Fotolia.com, page 46 © michelaubryphoto - Fotolia.com, page 124 © Claudio Divizia - Fotolia. com, page 145 © Steve Schapiro/Corbis, page 152 © Sunset Boulevard/Corbis, page 219–220 © magann - Fotolia.com, © countrylens - Fotolia.com, © demarfa - Fotolia.com, © Syda Productions - Fotolia.com, © destina - Fotolia.com, © thawats - Fotolia.com, © beeandbee - Fotolia.com, © Giuseppe Porzani - Fotolia.com, © RAM - Fotolia.com

First published 2014. Reprinted 2014, 2015, 2017, 2019.

British Library Cataloguing-in-Publication Data
A catalogue entry for this book is available
from the British Library.

Print ISBN 978-184590929-1
Mobi ISBN 978-184590933-8
ePub ISBN 978-184590934-5

LCCN 2014948800

Edited by Nick Owen

Printed and bound in the UK by
TJ International, Padstow, Cornwall

To Joe, Anna, Gracie May and Ruby Rose

CONTENTS

ACKNOWLEDGEMENTS

Andy Griffith:

First and foremost, thanks to my wife Clair for all her support. Thank you to all those who have helped us to research this book, especially Carel Buxton and Caroline Creaby.

Thanks also to Wendy Brown, Michelle Carter, Frank Lawell, Janine Lockhart, Alison Martin, and Tony McGuinness for their input and advice. Thanks also to Nick Owen for his superb editing.

Mark Burns:

Thanks go to my wife Kerry for your support and help in testing out new ideas in the classroom for me. To the many teachers and school leaders I've worked with – your growth mindsets and enthusiasm for learning have been so energising. To Nick for your patience, expertise, and advice. Thanks also to all those who read over the draft of the book and gave us such useful feedback. Finally, a heartfelt thanks to my parents, and all of the other teachers in my family who inspired me so much.

To Stephanie Smith, thanks for all your hard work behind the scenes.

A FOREWORD TO BACKWARDS
BY PROFESSOR JOHN HATTIE

So many lessons start with an engaging activity, move to the explanation, and then provide practice and 'doing'. There are many variants of this 'tell and use' or 'chug and plug' form of lesson, but they are the norm. Students are expected to work along with the teacher; in time all will be revealed and knowledge will be gained. Many students are quite happy with this approach: it is predictable – just wait and the teacher will tell you what to do next. Is it not the case, after all, that students come to school to watch the teachers teach! Certainly, by the time they get to tertiary study, the die is cast – just tell me what to do, I will do it, and then you can tell me how well I did. Indeed, many students rate lessons poorly if there are unstructured problems, if there is an expectation of creativity and initiative, and if the number of words in the assignment does not appear in bold up front.

Andy Griffith and Mark Burns ask us to turn this thinking backwards – to start by revealing the destination ('What does success in this lesson look like?') and then work backwards to where the students are now. They ask us to have high expectations, to plan, to watch for where students might go off route and where they may misunderstand, and to provide multiple opportunities for feedback, autonomy, challenge, and engagement. Based on Grant Wiggins and Jay McTigue's *Understanding by Design*,[1] this book provides the methods, the meat and vegetables, for the journey and lots of practical advice about how to understand success, work backwards from success to where the students are now, and then plan how to navigate (with all the usual twists and occasional wrong turns) the route to this success.

When we were developing our assessment and reporting engine for New Zealand schools, we developed a report based on target setting. We allowed the teacher to see a

---

1 Grant Wiggins and Jay McTighe, *Understanding by Design* (Alexandria, VA: Association for Supervision and Curriculum Development, 2005).

progression from the students' past assessments, which used a polynomial regression to predict into the future (the tool followed students from Year 4 to 12), and then said to teachers, 'If you keep teaching as you are, and the student keeps learning as he or she is, then this is where they are likely to end up in three, six, or twelve months' time.' The tool then allowed teachers to adjust the target (hopefully up) and pointed to lesson plans and assessment items for this new target. What was fascinating is what happened next. Teachers said, 'Aha, so this is where the student is now and this where I need to go, and I can work out how to make this link.' They then resolved this developmental progression and helped the student along this trajectory. But the students said, 'Aha, so this is where you want me to be, and these are items and lessons that indicate what I need to do. Let me try these items and lessons now – oh, I cannot do them. Will you, teacher, help me?' The students' thinking was so much more successful than the teachers' thinking.

This understanding of what success looks like highlights four factors. First, helping students to set high expectations of what they can achieve is a powerful incentive to action if they know what success looks like. Second, allowing students to see what they do not know and cannot do up front is a powerful motivator, if they also realise that there is expertise available to help them attain success. Third, teachers' models of development may need to be adjusted as learning rarely progresses smoothly along trajectories, but is up and down – there are many wrong turns and misconceptions. But as long as the participants do not lose sight of success then we may still get there. Fourth, we need to allow teachers rather than students to set the expectations, as young people often have major difficulties in calibrating success appropriately and need professional help in setting suitably challenging targets.[2]

Andy Griffith and Mark Burns have a detailed section on setting high expectations for teachers *and* students, and they show how the various dangers on the way to success can be turned into exciting opportunities for learning (e.g. the pit of exploration, teaching resilience, stuckness routines, celebrating mistakes, deliberate practice). They note the importance of pre-assessment to discover the students' starting points. This may seem obvious, until we recall Graham Nuthall's finding that students already know 60% of most lessons – which is rather too much scaffolding and certainly not very challenging![3]

Chapter 3 (Defining and Demystifying the Destination) is the critical chapter of this book, as it highlights such factors as clarity, exemplars and models, 'what a good one looks like', and emphasises that it is the teacher's responsibility to determine what does and does not constitute high quality work. The key is to get learners to wrestle with different notions of quality in different ways, both before and during the learning process. This requires the teacher to be a teaching and learning detective to help track progress, but

---

2   See Graham Nuthall, *The Hidden Lives of Learners* (Wellington: NZCER Press, 2007).

3   Nuthall, *The Hidden Lives of Learners*, p. 35.

with the goal so clear, this is much easier to get back on track than the alternative – starting everyone off on the journey without really knowing where they are going and what the destination is.

Finally, the importance of challenge. Experts differ from experienced teachers, particularly in the degree of challenge that they present to learners and, most critically, in the depth to which learners learn to process information. Without challenge, feedback becomes less important as there are then no gaps to close!

Many computer games understand how to get young people to learn. There is no secret to what the target is – often the next level. Games designers know the Goldilocks principle of challenge – not too high and not too low. These criteria of success are known to the user and they do not change (none of this, 'Dear, dear, you are not smart enough so I will make it easier for you; you only have to get half correct before you move on'). The game knows your prior achievement (your last level or score). Then it provides inordinate amounts of deliberate practice – that is, practice with feedback, with hints and cues, and sometimes with skill tips and lessons. Young people will spend hours (as will many of us adults) engaged in these games. When we succeed in progressing to the next success criteria, the game merely raises the level of challenge – and off we go again into the learning process. This is backwards learning in action.

John Hattie

INTRODUCTION

This is a book about planning and teaching outstanding lessons. Not just once in a while but consistently. We know it's possible because some teachers manage to achieve outstanding results year after year. These teachers are successful because they do something which we call *teaching backwards*.

The context in which teachers work today is unbelievably demanding; in particular, they face more scrutiny than ever before. When we both started teaching in the 1990s, the only people who came into our classrooms just wanted to borrow a bit of chalk. Now it's common for teachers to be observed on a regular basis. In principle, of course, this is no bad thing. The problem, however, is that the observers' judgements are sometimes deeply flawed, often reflecting nothing more than their prejudice or their interpretation of the latest Ofsted framework. Rather than creating opportunities for teachers to grow and develop their skills, the extra scrutiny has, more often than not, created unwelcome pressure and it has left many teachers confused, demoralised, and dreading the next observation.

This book is our humble attempt to relieve some of that pressure. We recognise that teachers don't have much spare time on their hands so we've worked hard to make this book clear, concise, and practical. It's packed with case studies from teachers we've worked with, and it's punctuated with reflective questions that invite teachers to slow down and do some thinking about how they currently teach, so that their teaching can have an even more powerful impact on learners.

We introduced the concept of teaching backwards towards the end of our previous book, *Engaging Learners*.[1] It was an idea that we first came across in the work of American professors Grant Wiggins and Jay McTighe.[2] Over the last seven years, our own take on this concept has deepened and taken shape as we've worked with thousands of teachers in our Outstanding Teaching Interventions.[3] As a result of these interventions, and our

---

1   Andy Griffith and Mark Burns, *Engaging Learners* (Carmarthen: Crown House Publishing, 2012).

2   Grant Wiggins and Jay McTighe, *Understanding by Design* (Alexandria, VA: Association for Supervision and Curriculum Development, 2005).

3   We've worked with more than 3,500 teachers (as of September 2014) in a series of Outstanding Teaching Interventions.

introduction of the teaching backwards concept to the teachers we've worked with, we've seen a remarkable transformation in the quality of teaching and learning in numerous classrooms up and down the country as teachers switch from teaching forwards to teaching backwards.

This book contains two overriding themes: first, that different learners need to be *catered* for in different ways and, second, that some teachers, in our experience, make far too many assumptions when planning their lessons. Let's explain what we mean with a couple of stories.

Imagine a family Sunday lunch. But it's not any old Sunday lunch: it's Aunt Ethel's ninetieth birthday. She's the oldest member of the family and someone has the bright idea of inviting the extended family to celebrate the occasion. It's a far-flung family with relatives living as far away as Australia, India, and the United States. Ethel must be some woman because quite a few agree to attend. The local family decide to have a British theme – after all, that's where the family's roots are. And what could be more British than good old roast beef?

When the great day comes everyone's happy to see each other, but the meal is a disaster. Nephew Brian's wife is Hindu for whom the cow is sacred; cousin Amelia's American husband has read in a newspaper back in Idaho about mad cow disease; grandson Richard, who lives in Australia, believes his body is a temple and doesn't eat red meat; great granddaughter Julie is just back from university and she's become a vegan; second cousins Rob and Josh are heavily into their rugby training and are on a carbs-only day.

If only someone hadn't made assumptions! They could have sent out an email to find out exactly what people did and didn't eat and what their preferences were. That way they could have catered for everyone. It would have been a little more work, but what a difference it would have made to a very special occasion.

It was great granddaughter Julie who had a bright idea and suggested they all go down to the local Chinese dim sum restaurant the next day instead. As the trolleys came round everyone chose exactly what suited them and a great time was had by all.

When teachers teach forwards, the educational equivalent of this scenario can happen all too easily. Assumptions are made and the real needs of the learners, and their starting points, are not sufficiently taken into consideration. Some years ago, we were observing a music teacher working with her class in the north of England. The bell rang to signal the end of the lesson and the learners filed out. We'd just finished videoing her lesson and from her perspective it had gone well. There was a smile on her face. She thought her learners had made good progress in developing their musical skills.

One boy lagged behind as we chatted to her. 'Please, Miss, I use violin, OK?' 'This is Adnan,' she explained to us. 'He's recently arrived from Albania with his parents.' Keen to nurture a love of music in one of her learners, she took a violin from the cupboard and handed it over to him.

What happened next challenged the teacher to completely revise her assessment of how well her lesson had gone. Adnan started to play. He launched into a virtuoso performance of the theme from *The Godfather*, with the all the panache of Joshua Bell and the cheeky passion of Nigel Kennedy. It earned a round of applause from all of us when he finished.

The teacher was stunned. 'I had no idea he could play like that. Had I known I'd have given him a lot more challenge in the lesson.' She paused a moment to reflect and then her eyes opened wide. 'I wonder if any of the others have got musical skills I don't know about?' At least she had a good sense of humour. She chuckled and, quoting from the movie while doing a pretty good impression of Marlon Brando, said, 'Dat lesson of mine just now; I guess you could say it's sleeping with da fishes.'

What do these two stories illustrate? In each case, it wasn't the lack of time, effort, or commitment to planning that caused the problems. It was simply *poor* planning. It was planning based on insufficient information, unchallenged assumptions, and a one-size-fits-all mindset. In both situations, the family and the music teacher were asking themselves the wrong questions. They were planning forwards. They'd have been far better off if they'd planned backwards.

This book offers teachers a multitude of ways to become more rigorous, disciplined, and investigative in their planning and delivery of outstanding teaching and learning … by teaching backwards.

WHAT IS TEACHING BACKWARDS?

The most effective teachers teach backwards. At the heart of teaching backwards is a thinking process that enables teachers to plan and teach backwards from a clear and well-defined destination. This destination could be a model of a high quality piece of work that shows learners exactly what standard they are expected to have achieved by the end of a learning module or it could be a clear and compelling description of the attitudes, skills, and habits that the class are expected to be demonstrating by the end of the school year.

Teaching backwards is a journey that starts with the end very clearly in mind. It is the destination that gives the teaching backwards process its shape, direction, and structure. The journey is supported at all times by the high expectations in which the teacher holds the learners, and his or her ability to engender and encourage the same high expectations in the learners themselves. From the destination and the high expectations everything else follows.

First, the teacher needs to establish the learners' true starting points and then to demystify and clearly explain to them how each destination will be achieved. The next step requires the teacher to plan in advance how he or she will regularly elicit proof that learning is taking place, not generally but for each student, so that the whole class can move forward together. The planning and teaching must then take account of the appropriate levels of challenge that are required to motivate learners to address and overcome the obstacles

they will undoubtedly face, and develop a real and felt sense of satisfaction from achieving results they might have previously thought difficult or impossible. Finally, the teacher needs to employ strategies that give the students quality, real-time feedback that develops their **K**nowledge, **A**ttitudes, **S**kills, and **H**abits (KASH), while also training them to give quality feedback to themselves and each other.

At the heart of teaching backwards is our philosophy that great teaching and learning rely on four key ingredients. We call them the Big Four: feedback, autonomy, challenge, and engagement (for more information see the Appendix).

The structure of this book follows the sequence of the teaching backwards steps and we strongly recommend that you read it in that order. Each step is crucially important in ensuring that learners achieve their full potential, topic by topic, as well as over time. Miss out a step and we guarantee that your learning journey will end in a cul-de-sac. We've seen many a teacher experience a 'Hindenburg moment' after missing out a step. They learned the hard way as they watched their lesson crash and burn – or worse, their classes underperform over time. They realised to their cost that teaching backwards isn't a pick-and-mix approach. It's one that needs to be embraced wholeheartedly.

WHY WE USE LEVELS

The levels we use in this book provide clarity for busy teachers. We've lost count of the times that teachers have told us how helpful they find clear, well-defined success criteria, both for themselves and for their learners. These levels enable teachers to better assess their current stage of expertise and practice, helping them to understand what they need to do to get to the next level. Only when teachers realise the gap between where they currently are and where they need to be can they implement the strategies required to close those gaps. Our own experience over the last 10 years of working with thousands of teachers is that using levels really helps them to rapidly improve the quality and expertise of their teaching.

The same is true for learners. As they understand their current level of expertise in terms of the knowledge, attitudes, skills, and habits required, they begin to see what they must do to 'level up'. Once they are aware of the gaps in their learning, supported by their teacher, they can begin to work with strategies that will enable them to close those gaps. Feedback from countless teachers we've worked with on our Outstanding Teaching Interventions (OTI) programmes tells us this process works.

The levels we use are:

Level 1a = Outstanding Secure

Level 1b = Outstanding Unsecure

Level 2a = Good Secure

Level 2b = Good Unsecure

NB The level descriptors and term 'levelling up' originated in the Osiris Outstanding Teaching Intervention booklet, visit www.osiriseducational.co.uk.

LEVEL 1A

All learners have clarity on their current position and the quality of KASH they need to develop further in order to achieve their goal. Teachers and learners are highly skilled in giving and receiving feedback on how to improve. All learners routinely reflect and act on feedback. Teachers use feedback to adapt learning within lessons and in planning for future lessons. Both teacher and learners demonstrate excellent questioning of themselves and others. Collaboration adds greatly to learning and to learners' ability to overcome challenges. The teacher and learners demonstrate high expectations in relation to quality of work and progress.

LEVEL 1B

Feedback is used to ensure that planning, both within and between lessons, accurately meets the needs of all learners. High levels of challenge predominate due to skilful questioning from both learners and teachers. All learners have clarity on their own gaps and are motivated to close them. As a consequence learners make rapid progress. The teacher uses effective strategies to develop the KASH of learners. Well-developed routines ensure learners have time to read and act on the high quality feedback given. Peer and self-assessment are developing. Learners can now identify specific ways in which to improve, and target-setting is becoming owned by them. The teacher and nearly all learners have high expectations of progress and quality.

LEVEL 2A

Feedback from and about learners enables the teacher to adapt learning, both within and between lessons. This ensures that learning is challenging for all. Support is given for learners who are struggling to progress or who require higher levels of challenge. A feature of the level of challenge is the quality of teacher and learner questions. Effective written and verbal feedback from the teacher ensures all learners are clear on their next steps to improvement. The teacher is training learners to identify these steps themselves. The teacher demonstrates high expectations of learners in terms of progress and quality of work, and this is beginning to be adopted by the class. Learners make good progress.

LEVEL 2B

The teacher plans and provides learning using evidence from some aspects of the available assessment data and other feedback. Within the lesson, the teacher reshapes tasks based on feedback in order to improve learning. Most learners understand how well they are doing and the next steps they need to take in order to make progress using the teacher's feedback. Teacher questioning helps to both extend learners and get feedback on their progress. The teacher is working to develop the KASH of learners so they can work at higher levels. The teacher has high expectations for the class.

ICONS USED THROUGHOUT THE BOOK

CATER: Throughout this book, we will be asking you to reflect on how you plan for and teach different learners with different learning needs. The CATER (community, assistance, tasks, extension, and resources) framework supports you to differentiate across a number of factors that aid in the development of all the learners in the class. Like Aunt Ethel's meal, we'll ask you to consider how you are CATERing for their different needs. We use this acronym to encourage you to think about how better to meet your learners' differing requirements.

■ **Community**. The essence of a strong community is togetherness. It's a place where people support each other when they need help. A strong classroom is no different. We ask how you are building a community where learners are collaborating and supporting each other in order to overcome challenges. For example, one teacher we know has instilled in his class the importance of being as one using the mantra, 'we leave no one behind'.

■ **Assistance**. How will teachers and other adults, such as teaching assistants, vary their approach to support the needs of different groups of learners? For example, a teacher who asked his teaching assistant to provide detailed feedback to a group of learners who were all struggling with the same maths problem.

■ **Tasks**. Teachers need to ensure that the tasks they set provide their learners with appropriate levels of challenge. If learning lacks challenge then learners make little progress, and the same will be true if the challenge level is too high. Given that learners are likely to have different starting points, this could mean that some learners are working on different tasks.

■ **Extension** (stretch). Extension refers to the raft of strategies a teacher might use to stretch learners further after they have completed a classroom challenge. Creating opportunities for learners to go beyond their current level will extend them even more. For example, a primary teacher who created a '*Mission*

Impossible corner'. When learners finish their classwork early, they go here to find tasks that will stretch them to another level. The learners see this as a challenge to rise to. In a secondary class, a teacher might invite her GCSE learners to work at an AS level task.

■ **Resources** (support). Some learners will need additional tools or resources to help them to overcome the challenge they are currently working on. Without these additional resources the level of difficulty will simply be too high for them. For example, a teacher who produced a literacy mat (or writing frame) to help his learners.

Reflection points: Here we suggest you reflect on your current practice and think about how you might challenge or change it. When you see this icon, take a little time to ask yourself whether these suggestions could improve or enhance your performance as a teacher.

Eureka moments: Here we offer inspirational ideas and case studies from other teachers' experiences. These practitioners have achieved eureka moments by trying out new ideas. Why not consider trying them too?

Level up: Here we suggest ways to 'level up' your teaching. When you see this icon, consider how you might use the idea to level up the teaching and the learning in your classroom.

To encourage you to go beyond thinking about change and actually take action, we've also included a checklist and an action plan section at the end of each chapter. It's useful to consider what you might need to stop or start doing in order to move your class up the levels. But a word of warning: we strongly advise that you don't pack the start section with too many new ideas at the expense of considering what you are going to stop doing. Our own experience, and that of the many committed, passionate teachers we've worked with over the years, confirms the wisdom of this. Teaching is a hugely demanding job and often there is little spare capacity to do much more on top of the existing workload. Consequently, we would encourage you to identify just as many things that you are going to stop doing as you are planning to start doing. As we like to remind ourselves, the road to hell is paved with good intentions. So, choose quality over quantity and settle for a small number of important changes you know you can deliver rather than overstretching yourself.

We're confident that whether you're new to the profession or a teacher with years of experience, you'll find ideas and inspiration in this book to make your own teaching even more effective and compelling, so that you can make even more of a difference to the learners that you teach.

We hope you enjoy the journey.

Chapter 1

SETTING HIGH EXPECTATIONS

'I know you can do this – you just don't know it yourselves yet'

Imagine you're walking along the corridor of a school in a socially deprived part of the UK. Outside one classroom there's a display proudly announcing one class's grades. The learners in this class are getting incredible academic results: 75% of them are achieving grades A and A*. Yet these same learners are only getting grades C or D with their other teachers. This is no one-off fluke – it's happened year after year for the learners of this particular teacher. A mystery? Not at all. This teacher *expects* these results and expertly leads learners to believe that they can get them too. As a result, they do!

The learners have really bought into this teacher's high expectations. They've not only come to believe that they can achieve these incredible results; they also believe that they deserve them. Not only do they enjoy this teacher's lessons, they've also learned from her the skills of persistence, determination, and openness that support them to succeed. These skills and attitudes have enabled them to thrive. No wonder she's feted by learners as a great teacher. By any measure (data, learner surveys, Ofsted rating) this teacher is excellent, outstanding. She's an educational black belt! She's living proof that the academic studies which time and again trumpet the value of high teacher and learner expectations are actually true.

WHAT'S IN THIS CHAPTER FOR ME?

- Have you ever wondered how some teachers get their learners to expect more of themselves and take greater responsibility for their own learning?

■ Do you sometimes dream about working with a class that believes in themselves, believes learning is worthwhile, and believes they can overcome whatever challenges lie in their way?

■ How might your credibility as a teacher take off if you took steps to raise your own game, setting higher standards and expectations for yourself and those around you?

■ Have you ever wondered how you and your colleagues could create a high expectation, high challenge culture in your school?

If you feel engaged or intrigued by the story and these questions, this chapter offers you tools, techniques, and strategies to help you to get there yourself, taking your learners with you. We explore the widely held notion that a key foundation for success in the classroom is that the teacher has high expectations of the learners and leads them to have high expectations of themselves. Of the top one hundred teachers that we've seen in action, it's their high expectations that set them apart from others. Not just the expectations that they hold of themselves but, even more importantly, the high expectations that they build with and in their learners.

WHAT'S THE THINKING BEHIND THIS CHAPTER?

This chapter addresses three key questions:

1   Why are high expectations so important?

2   How can you influence your learners to hold high expectations of themselves?

3   How can you assess whether you're a high expectations teacher yourself?

First, we'll explore why it's essential to create high expectations in the classroom, and we'll flag some of the key research that supports this claim. The evidence clearly shows that there's a very strong link between learner achievement and the high expectations they have of themselves. It also shows that teachers have a major part to play by having high expectations of their learners too. Of course, it's great when you inherit a class where all the learners want to set themselves big goals and push themselves to achieve. But this doesn't happen often enough. So, what should we do when the learners don't hold high expectations of themselves? Should we simply accept the situation or should we challenge it?

Next, we'll take you through a wide range of practical ideas and strategies which show how a culture of high expectations can be established. High expectations teachers always challenge low expectations among their learners whenever they come across them, especially around issues such as delivering high quality work and always giving your personal best. We'll suggest that the teacher has two principal roles to play here. The first is modelling; that is, teachers must personally demonstrate the qualities and behaviours they expect from their learners by consistently living those qualities and behaviours themselves. The second is through a process that we simply call 'training'. What we mean by this good, old-fashioned word is supporting learners, step by step, to develop the confidence and self-belief to take on tough challenges and to adopt their teacher's high expectations of them as if they were their own.

Throughout this chapter, we'll also ask you to reflect on your own level of expectation, both of yourself and of your learners. You might already be a teacher with high expectations, like the teacher in the story that opened this chapter, someone who makes a massive impact on their learners. If so, we're still confident that you'll find some new ideas here. But we'd also like to invite you to explore whether you might have lower expectations than you think you have. We hope the tools and case studies in this chapter might challenge you to ask yourself whether your expectations are really as high as they could be.

There are many reasons why teachers are motivated to level up their expectations of themselves and others. For some, it might be a realisation they had when they were learners themselves. For others, it might be watching themselves teach on a video recording or, as in the example below, a freak incident that ends up being a blessing in disguise.

A chemistry teacher we know had an eye-opening experience at his sixth-form college which challenged his whole concept of expectations. Each learner at the college has an AS level target grade based on their GCSE grades. One girl came to the college with high GCSE grades which translated to a target of an A grade at AS level. However, her work was below par from the outset. Knowing her previous attainment was so high, the teacher went to extra lengths to challenge and support her: after-hours sessions, one-to-one tutorials, and additional set work. The girl eventually attained a grade B. The teacher was disappointed, but the learner and her family were delighted. It turned out that the student had come to college with the minimum of five grade Cs at GCSE, but due to an administrative error her grades had been entered incorrectly! This teacher already had high expectations, but this experience encouraged him to set his expectations even higher.

Before you read on any further, how would you rate yourself, on a scale of 1 to 10, in terms of having high expectations as a teacher?

How do you demonstrate these high expectations?

Is it possible that, like our chemistry teacher, your expectations may not be set as high as they could be?

WHY ARE HIGH EXPECTATIONS SO IMPORTANT?

THE MORAL IMPERATIVE

In our opinion, Professor Mick Waters is a national treasure. His passion for wanting the best for children shines through all his work. He speaks a lot of sense about what education should be like for them: 'Education should not simply prepare children for the future, it should also give them the best present possible – a childhood on which to build the rest of their lives.'[1] But let's get real here. The promise of 'developing potential' in learners is often found in school prospectuses and on mission statements but, as we all know, it can often get lost in the everyday grind of helping learners to pass tests and exams. Nevertheless, the experience of school should always be one that really tries to create confident, successful learners, as well as helping them to become mature and responsible citizens. This should be every school's core purpose.

Moreover, most children only have one crack at education and for many it will make or break their life chances. As teachers, surely we have a duty to have high expectations of ourselves and our learners, and refuse to be limited by a learner's target grade or how they currently 'label' themselves. If we don't take up this challenge, then who else will?

In their book, *Professional Capital: Transforming Teaching In Every School,* Andy Hargreaves and Michael Fullan support the vital importance of challenge and high expectation in achieving quality. Those who manage and run schools, they say, have a 'charge to improve learning and achievement for all learners, develop their well-being and character, and

---

1   Mick Waters, presentation at the National College for Teaching and Leadership conference, Seizing Success, Birmingham, 12–14 June 2013.

close the gap between those from advantaged and those from disadvantaged social backgrounds'.[2]

versus

Comedian Peter Kay used to do a great routine on how certain biscuits compared when dipped in a cup of tea. Hobnobs, he quipped, were like commandos who wanted to be challenged. 'Dip me again! Dip me again!' On the other hand, Rich Tea biscuits were wimps. 'One dips', he called them, going floppy as soon as they were dunked.

Let's develop the analogy further. It's one thing to raise your own expectations. It's quite another to raise the expectations of others. You *might* inherit a class in September who are all Hobnobs: ambitious, adventurous, open, reflective, dedicated to pushing themselves. Or you could have a class of Rich Teas: 'But Miss, I only need to get a C to get into sixth form so I don't need to look at A grade level.'

As we argued in our book, *Engaging Learners*, you really only have two choices when work-ing with any individual or group: accept them as they are or try to change them. There is no third way – they won't change on their own. If you want to get learners to develop higher expectations, then we will explore some strategies later in this chapter. Suffice it to say, it will take time and it will challenge you as well as your learners.

Everybody needs support and encouragement to a greater or lesser degree to learn and to overcome barriers. So, can a Rich Tea become a Hobnob? Can a wimp become a com-mando? Can a person lacking in confidence become a confident, autonomous learner, and an inspiration to others? Well, we work in education, so we think the answer is a resounding yes! And we've seen it happen time and time again in classrooms and schools around the country. We see it whenever, for example, a teacher elicits stunning results from her socially disadvantaged learners by transforming their classroom from a desert of low expectations to an oasis of high expectations. In fact, teachers who can achieve results

2   Andy Hargreaves and Michael Fullan, *Professional Capital: Transforming Teaching In Every School* (Abingdon: Routledge, 2012), p. 13.

like this will do well in any environment because they have the beliefs, skills, and strategies to know how to pull and push their learners to new heights. The fact is that, in today's highly pressured educational environments, it's almost impossible for teachers to be judged as effective on a consistent basis – unless they hold high expectations that learners really are capable of going beyond their perceived potential.

TEACHER EFFECTIVENESS IN TERMS OF RESULTS

Academics such as John Hattie, Robert Marzano, and Dylan Wiliam, as well as respected organisations such as the Sutton Trust, all urge us to recognise that a high expectations culture makes a huge difference to achievement in schools. According to Hattie, the number one influence on how well learners do at school is their own level of expectation.[3] Hattie's study is wide ranging, spanning over 15 years and involving millions of learners from around the world. His extensive research into what makes the difference in schools has calculated the impact of thousands of educational initiatives and types of pedagogy on learner achievement. He has developed a chart of which factors are most likely to produce learner success. Top of his chart is the learners' own expectations of how successful they will be.[4]

The figure below shows how different teachers respond to targets. One teacher decides to teach to the target whereas another teacher, with higher expectations of the potential of her learners, makes the decision to teach way above it. The second teacher sees the target as something to beat.

Opening bigger gaps

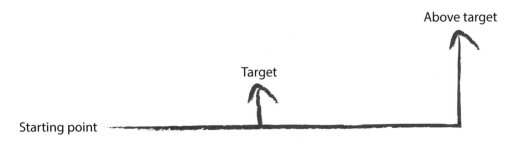

Teachers with higher expectations challenge their learners by setting more adventurous targets. They consciously and deliberately open bigger 'gaps' for learners than teachers

---

3   John Hattie, *Visible Learning for Teachers: Maximizing Impact on Learning* (Abingdon: Routledge, 2011).
4   For the full chart visit: http://visible-learning.org/hattie-ranking-influences-effect-sizes-learning-achievement/.

with moderate or low expectations. They have an ambitious destination in mind for them and understand that a key part of their work will be to motivate their learners to accept and even get excited about this challenging destination. In *Visible Learning for Teachers,* Hattie writes: 'Our role is not to enable learners to reach their potential, or to meet their needs; our role is to find out what learners can do, and make them exceed their potential and needs.'[5]

Teachers with high expectations don't teach to the target, they go beyond it. For them the target isn't a ceiling, it's a minimum! This results in higher grades and more progress for their learners.

TEACHER EFFECTIVENESS IN TERMS OF WHAT REALLY MATTERS

Our firmly held belief is that examination grades and test scores are *not* the be-all and end-all of education. We all know people who didn't do well at school but who have gone on to be really successful in life, and others who passed lots of exams but don't seem that successful. In his book, *Why Do I Need A Teacher When I've Got Google?,* Ian Gilbert refers to this as 'The Great Educational Lie': the fallacy that there's a direct causal link between exam success and career or life success.[6]

Of course, it's important to set high expectations around grades, but if teachers are to support learners to achieve high grades then something really important has to happen first. Outstanding teachers who consistently achieve great results put effort and energy into developing their learners' KASH, which means developing their well-being, their character, their sense of personal worth, and their ability to work together. It is high quality KASH that supports and enables excellent results.

When we run training courses in schools, our focus is not only on how to develop individual teachers working in their classrooms but also how the whole school can work better together to create an educational experience for every learner, so they'll have the chance to lead more successful lives. To achieve this, we believe that teachers have to work with the whole child, which means developing key aspects of their emotional intelligence (EQ) as well as their intellectual intelligence (IQ). EQ has nothing to do with subjects or topics of learning. It's about being aware of and fostering the traits and dispositions that develop healthy, mature, and well-balanced individuals. These traits and dispositions include self-awareness, self-control, empathy, social skills, and personal responsibility. When teachers create the conditions for these traits to develop in their

---

5   Hattie, *Visible Learning for Teachers*, p. 83.

6   Ian Gilbert, *Why Do I Need a Teacher When I've Got Google?: The Essential Guide to the Big Issues for Every 21st Century Teacher* (Abingdon: Routledge, 2010), p. 16.

learners, they also create the conditions in which learning can flourish so that high expectations can be achieved.

Thus, it stands to reason that if we're going to ask learners to exhibit these high standards of behaviour, we teachers need to consistently demonstrate them too. If we don't model these excellent behaviours, why should they? So, having high expectations isn't just about *what* you do in your classroom. It's also about *who* you are and *how* you do what you do. The bottom line is that everyone in the school strives to be the best they can be 24/7.

HOW TO BUILD HIGHER EXPECTATIONS

High teacher expectations are only half of the story. The figure below shows that high expectations have to be embraced fully by learners too if they are going to reach the Level 1a descriptor. In fact, getting learners not only to hold, but more importantly to own, high self-expectations is *the* key step to achieving excellent results with every class.

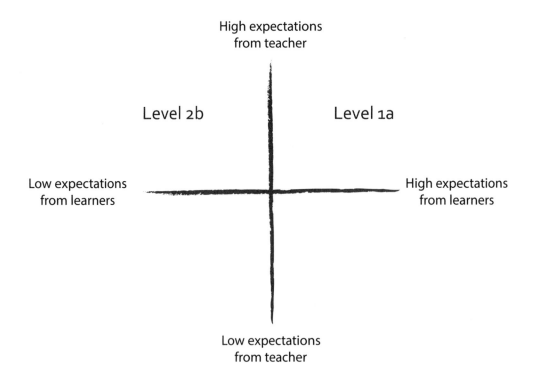

High expectations
from teacher

Level 2b   Level 1a

Low expectations   High expectations
from learners   from learners

Low expectations
from teacher

So, how can you build high expectations? By using the principle of teaching backwards from the standard of a Level 1a class. The ideal, of course, is to have our class working in the top right-hand quadrant, the Level 1a classroom. If we inherit a class in September positioned in the top-left quadrant, our task will be to build the learners' KASH so they can shift their attitudes from a low expectations to a high expectations culture. This might mean a journey from Level 2b to 1a. A teacher with low expectations simply will not be able to achieve this kind of result.

There are four key aspects of KASH that become available when learners embrace higher expectations. The first is learner resilience. These learners will be prepared to take on challenges that might previously have made them feel uneasy and uncomfortable. Second, these learners develop a greater capacity to reflect and to act on feedback. They learn to listen more actively, experiment with the feedback they are given, and go away and do something constructive with it. Third, these learners begin to develop a sense of pride in their work. They believe quality is something they can achieve if they set their minds to it. Finally, they really do believe that they have the potential to break through whatever limiting beliefs they or others have of them. Despite the high levels of challenge they face, this is a class that says, 'Bring it on! Dip me again!'

Wouldn't it be great to work with a group of learners like these? Sound impossible? Well, from our experience we know it isn't. *Teaching Backwards* can support you step by step to make it happen. In this chapter, we'll explore some ideas, techniques, and strategies that support learners to learn and demonstrate these skills and attitudes *consistently*, so that with the right modelling and training they will achieve these qualities.

TRAINING LEARNERS TO HAVE HIGH EXPECTATIONS

The best teachers, in our experience, have what Carol Dweck refers to as growth mindsets.[7] They refuse to believe that their learners can't change or that change will take too long. Instead, they have an empowering set of beliefs that with effort and the right strategies, they can support and train their learners to make positive changes to their KASH. These teachers accept that they may not get them all the way to Level 1a in the time that is available, but they harbour no doubts that with appropriate modelling and targeted training in developing their learners' KASH, they will be able to level them up *significantly*. Above, we noted three attitudes and one skill that high expectations help to elicit in learners and

---

7   Carol Dweck, *Mindset: The New Psychology of Success* (New York: Ballantine, 2007).

which powerfully contribute to the achievement of the outstanding work that is to be expected in a Level 1a classroom. They are:

1   Learners are resilient.

2   Learners have high expectations for the quality of their work.

3   Learners hold growth mindsets about their potential.

4   Learners reflect and act on feedback.

Chapter 6 is devoted to the skill of reflecting and acting on feedback, so in the rest of this chapter we'll explore ways to develop these three transformational attitudes.

 Is your class a strong *community*? Do they support each other to do well, accept each other's differences, and do they all want to beat their personal bests?

The following ideas and strategies will help you to build a strong learning community in the classroom, where every student can become more resilient, hold higher expectations for the quality of his or her work, and develop a healthy growth mindset.

TRAINING LEARNERS TO BE RESILIENT

You'll notice that many of the ideas in this section are routines. Effective and purposeful routines are helpful to student learning, giving them a powerful sense of familiarity and security. They also demonstrate that a teacher is thorough and believes in the principle that practice makes perfect.

METAPHORS FOR LEARNING – THE PIT

Choosing the right metaphor for learning can help learners to appreciate that learning necessarily involves struggle and effort. We know that for 'flow' to become embedded into a classroom culture, learners have to engage with high levels of challenge.[8] When teachers describe learning in ways that make the idea of struggle and overcoming obstacles seem both inevitable and motivating, and get their learners to buy into this idea, the chances are they're on the right track.

Guy Claxton uses a metaphor of the brain as a muscle, in that 'its intelligence grows with exercise'.[9] Another educationalist, James Nottingham, uses the metaphor of the learning pit: 'The pit encourages learners not to sit back and wait for the answer to fall into their lap; instead it requires them to think about almost every decision that they make.'[10]

We see 'the pit' as a brilliant metaphor which helps to sell challenge. We ask teachers to innovate on our courses and to come up with their own interpretation of our ideas. In the two examples below – one from a primary teacher and one from a secondary teacher – the message they're giving their learners is that to understand something they'll need to struggle with it first. The struggle may make you feel anxious, they explain, or frustrated, or even confused, but with effort and our support you'll be able to get out of the pit to a new place where clarity and confidence reigns.

The ability to cope with and overcome difficulty and challenge is one of the key elements in becoming a successful learner, not just in school but outside school too. The pit teaches each learner strategies for knowing what to do when they don't know what to do. This is why we love it. When learners successfully emerge from the pit they feel an overwhelming sense of achievement and renewed confidence. They experience that exhilarating 'eureka' moment that says, 'I've worked this out for myself. I've overcome the challenges and found a decent answer.'

Teachers adapt the metaphor of the pit in different ways. Often these become visual metaphors that help learners to realise that new learning will often involve feelings of uncertainty and insecurity that have to be worked through.

---

8   Mihaly Csikszentmihalyi, *Flow: The Psychology of Optimal Experience* (New York: Harper and Row, 1990).

9   Guy Claxton, Maryl Chambers, Graham Powell, and Bill Lucas, *The Learning Powered School: Pioneering 21st Century Education* (Bristol: TLO Ltd, 2011), p. iii. Available at: http://www.wikispaces.com/file/view/TheLearningPoweredSchool_Extract_TLOLimited_2011.pdf/241982374/TheLearningPoweredSchool_Extract_TLOLimited_2011.pdf.

10   James Nottingham, 'Encouraging Thinking Skills', *Teach Primary* (n.d.). Available at: http://www.teachprimary.com/learning_resources/view/encouraging-thinking-skills.

Here is Adele Reece's way of introducing the pit to her learners, visually inviting them to understand the metaphor as a core part of their learning. She wants them to feel comfortable that feelings of confusion and anxiety can be overcome, but not without effort. She also offers them a ladder, a metaphor for the skills and strategies she will share with them to support their success. The right-hand side of the pit promises that by taking risks, experimenting, and reflecting, they'll be able to feel amazed, ecstatic and proud.

Photo: Sue McConnell.

Secondary teacher Mark Lawlor recognises that there are different levels of understanding that learners will go through before their knowledge is secure. The metaphor of the pit helps him and his class to develop and use shared language. It also gives him quick access to feedback about where each of his learners is at any given time, helping him to differentiate and decide what needs to be done and with whom. Often, he'll ask those learners who have mastered the new learning to teach those who are still struggling with it. Mark recognises that those who have just learned something can frequently teach better than their teachers who learned it a long time ago. These teachers have often forgotten that it was difficult once, but new learners know exactly what the tricky bits are! Besides, one of the best ways to know that we have really learned something is to teach it to someone else and get feedback that now they know it too.

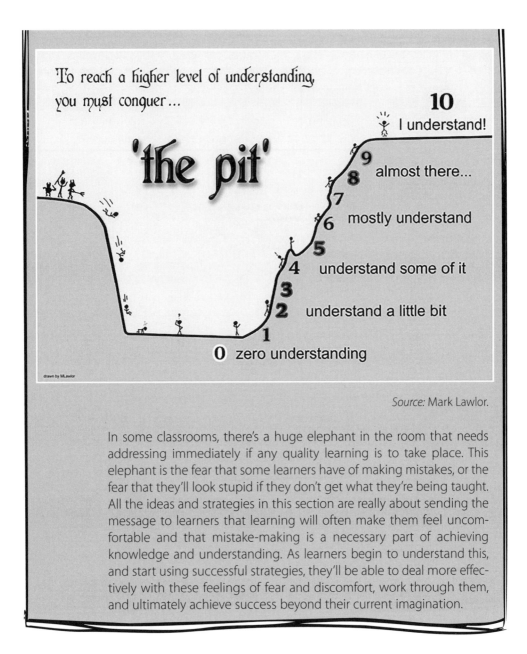

To reach a higher level of understanding, you must conquer...

'the pit'

10 I understand!

9 almost there...
8
7
6 mostly understand
5
4 understand some of it
3
2 understand a little bit
1
0 zero understanding

drawn by MLawlor

Source: Mark Lawlor.

In some classrooms, there's a huge elephant in the room that needs addressing immediately if any quality learning is to take place. This elephant is the fear that some learners have of making mistakes, or the fear that they'll look stupid if they don't get what they're being taught. All the ideas and strategies in this section are really about sending the message to learners that learning will often make them feel uncomfortable and that mistake-making is a necessary part of achieving knowledge and understanding. As learners begin to understand this, and start using successful strategies, they'll be able to deal more effectively with these feelings of fear and discomfort, work through them, and ultimately achieve success beyond their current imagination.

Maths teacher Liz Blaikie likes to get learners into the pit. However, this does not mean abandoning them in there! She gives them opportunities to get help from her during the lesson from 'hint cards' that she creates in advance. She encourages learners to work on solving the problem first, but if they find themselves well and truly stuck in the pit they can ask for a hint card – but only one for each equation.

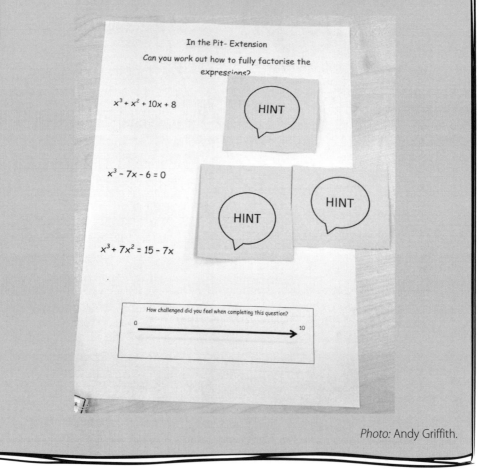

In the Pit- Extension

Can you work out how to fully factorise the expressions?

$x^3 + x^2 + 10x + 8$

HINT

$x^3 - 7x - 6 = 0$

HINT

HINT

$x^3 + 7x^2 = 15 - 7x$

How challenged did you feel when completing this question?

0 ⟶ 10

Photo: Andy Griffith.

TELL LEARNERS ABOUT YOUR OWN STRUGGLES TO LEARN

Learning is a change process. And, like all change processes, it's natural for human beings to feel uncomfortable with it. Change challenges our comfort zone. It feels safer to stay with what we know rather than risk entering into unfamiliar territory. So, it's not unusual for learners to feel they're struggling or out of their depth. They can even assume that learning comes easily to everyone except themselves. When teachers share their own stories about things that they once found difficult, it can really help learners to appreciate that struggle is a necessary part of learning – and life! When teachers tell stories about the steps they've taken to move from confusion to clarity, from mediocrity to excellence, students learn that struggle, discipline, and even mistake-making are a normal part of the learning process and key steps on the path to progress.

STUCKNESS ROUTINES

Here are a few more examples of ways in which teachers can train learners to become more comfortable with being stuck and uncertain.

Primary teachers Sue Crofton and Jelena Sloan both learned a lot about their Year 5 classes when they were reviewing their videoed lessons. Many learners seemed to give up a bit too easily for their liking, so they decided to train learners to become more comfortable with being stuck. They experimented with an idea which they found worked really well. Now, they teach their classes to sing whenever they get stuck. The class 'stuck' song might not go to number one but it certainly helps them to become more resilient.

Whenever learners find they're not making headway they sing the line, 'I've got a problem'. The rest of the class respond with, 'Can we help you with your problem?' At which point one of two things might happen: either another learner will help the stuck singer or the teacher will step in and guide the learner to work through their challenge. As well as demonstrating that being stuck is perfectly normal, acceptable, and necessary to learning, the class work much harder than before to help each other develop strategies to solve problems.

Jean Bartley encourages her learners to create a 'stuck tree'. Each leaf represents various things that they should do before they give up or go to her or the teaching assistant for help. The stuck tree offers a visual way of encouraging learners to be more creative and independent throughout each lesson.

Photo: Jean Bartley.

Teachers at Holly Hall Academy, Dudley, have trained their classes to work through being stuck by following a simple yet powerful five-step sequence.

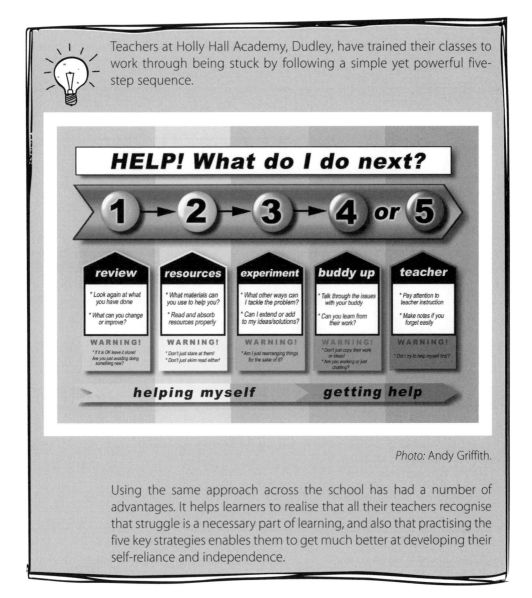

HELP! What do I do next?

1 → 2 → 3 → 4 or 5

review	**resources**	**experiment**	**buddy up**	**teacher**
* Look again at what you have done	* What materials can you use to help you?	* What other ways can I tackle the problem?	* Talk through the issues with your buddy	* Pay attention to teacher instruction
* What can you change or improve?	* Read and absorb resources properly	* Can I extend or add to my ideas/solutions?	* Can you learn from their work?	* Make notes if you forget easily
WARNING!	**WARNING!**	**WARNING!**	**WARNING!**	**WARNING!**
* If it is OK leave it alone! Are you just avoiding doing something new?	* Don't just stare at them! * Don't just skim read either!	* Am I just rearranging things for the sake of it?	* Don't just copy their work or ideas! * Are you working or just chatting?	* Did I try to help myself first?

helping myself → **getting help**

Photo: Andy Griffith.

Using the same approach across the school has had a number of advantages. It helps learners to realise that all their teachers recognise that struggle is a necessary part of learning, and also that practising the five key strategies enables them to get much better at developing their self-reliance and independence.

Here's another great idea, from Liezl Vandermerwe, a Stuck Web. The messages around the web suggest a range of strategies that learners use when they feel confused.

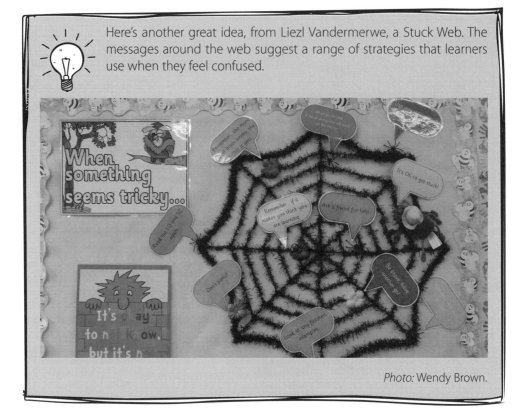

Photo: Wendy Brown.

Which *resources* could you provide that build resilience and an ability to feel comfortable with 'stuckness'?

SETTING HIGH EXPECTATIONS FOR QUALITY WORK

PRACTICE MAKES PERFECT

Whether we call it pride, quality, or even beauty, learners are more likely to give the best of themselves when teachers create the conditions and the environment for them to succeed. Some teachers create routines where learners first sketch out their work on mini-whiteboards or scrap paper before doing their 'best' version. Others expect their learners to produce several written drafts before they produce their final work for assessment. These teachers know that it takes iteration and practice to achieve quality. Not only that, it's how professional writers, artists, and scientists produce excellent work in the 'real' world.

These processes help learners to understand that their work doesn't have to be perfect at the first attempt. As they get into the routine of moving from first to final draft, several useful things begin to happen: they take more care over their work; they understand that progress is earned step by step through the process of action and reflection; and they develop competence and self-esteem by comparing the progress they have made from their early drafts to the finished work.

INDUCTING A NEW CLASS

As much as we need to start with the end in mind, we also need to start as we mean to go on! We recommend that every teacher spends some time inducting their class to instil these qualities and then build on them throughout the year. The first lesson you have with a class is the first day of their training in becoming more resilient, taking more care over quality, and having a growth mindset about their potential. Inductions need to be a part of every class's training.

Try learning to be a better salesperson! In his book, *To Sell Is Human*, Daniel Pink argues that 'each and every one of us spends a lot of our time trying to persuade others to part with resources'.[11] The most effective teachers are great at selling. They work hard to persuade their learners to invest their time and effort into developing Level 1a learning dispositions.

11   This quote appears on the inside jacket of Daniel Pink, *To Sell Is Human: The Surprising Truth About Persuading, Convincing, and Influencing Others* (New York: Riverhead, 2012).

One primary teacher we know has an excellent way of modelling the importance of making an effort and acting immediately on the feedback he gets. Every September, at the first school assembly of the term, the children observe him attempting to play a musical instrument, or perhaps it would be more accurate to say butchering it. The reason he's playing it so poorly is that it's an instrument he's never played before. In response, the children bond together as one in covering their ears in a desperate attempt to block out the din! But there's method to his madness; a serious intent lurks below the uncomfortable and unharmonious surface.

Stopping to acknowledge the reaction of his audience, he asks them if there's a problem. The children feed back that his performance is poor and needs to improve. Some of the older ones who play that particular instrument themselves are called to the front. He asks them to model for him how to hold the instrument properly and how to play some notes. The teacher then vows to go away and act on the feedback and make the effort to improve.

By the start of October, through practice and acting on the feedback he's received, his playing has improved. It's not Mozart yet, but at least some melody is recognisable. The children respond enthusiastically. They notice the improvement he's made. By December, he's reached a performance level where he can actually join in with some of the hymns during assembly.

It's a brilliant piece of educational modelling. The children get to see that their teachers are not experts at everything. They have gaps in their learning too. Through their teacher's growing musicianship, the learners realise that the way gaps can be closed is through dedicated effort, embracing the challenge, and by listening to and acting on feedback.

Other teachers, such as the ones mentioned in the section below, start training their classes in their very first lesson too.

GETTING LEARNERS TO SIGN OFF THEIR WORK

Asking learners to give their best is one thing. Getting them to sign off their work takes learner commitment to excellence and personal responsibility to another level altogether. When they put their signature to their work, alongside the statement, 'This is the very best work I can do', they are making a personal statement about themselves and their work. Remley Mann, a college vice-principal, requires her learners to do this with every piece of work they submit. She says:

I learnt it from my 8th grade American English teacher, Michael Marino, who required us to write, 'I take pride in my work', at the top of every page of homework. He also had the same phrase inscribed in large letters above the chalkboard in his classroom. When I started teaching I began to do the same thing. I remembered how taking the time to write these words at the top of every page made me pause to reflect on the quality of my work. I taught French in those days, so I'd ask the boys to write, 'Je suis fier de mon travail', and the girls, 'Je suis fière de mon travail'.

She now uses this technique from the very first lesson she has with her classes.

THE BEST BOX

One primary teacher we worked with completely understood the power of routine and ritual to establish a sense of pride and quality in her learners. Once they had completed their drafts and were ready to produce their 'best' work, she would open the class cupboard and take out the 'best box'. Inside it were stored the 'best paper' and the 'best pens'. She would ceremoniously hand these out to her learners before they got down to work.

In the next part of this chapter we'll explore how we can train learners to cope with challenge. We think the best teachers use a variety of techniques to ratchet up the level of difficulty. They do this over the academic year, over topics, and within lessons. Without specific training in how to deal with high levels of challenge many learners will flounder. Let's look at how we can help them to become more resilient.

SHOWING MODELS OF THE EXPECTED STANDARD

In Chapter 3, we will extol the virtues of building up a collection of models and examples of work. For now, all we'll say is that teachers who do this are demonstrating their high expectations by explicitly showing what constitutes quality work. Take the example opposite from teacher Gurjit Chana. She demands excellent presentation and shows the children what this entails by selecting examples of learners' work that fulfil those expectations.

Photo: Andy Griffith.

MODELLING ACCEPTABLE STANDARDS OF QUALITY

In his illuminating book, *An Ethic of Excellence*, Ron Berger writes: 'Most discussions of assessment start in the wrong place. The most important assessment that goes on in a school isn't done *to* learners but goes on *inside* learners. Every learner walks around the school with a picture of what is acceptable, what is good enough. Each time he works on something he looks at it and assesses it. Is this good enough? Do I feel comfortable handing this in? Does it meet my standards?'[12]

---

12   Ron Berger, *An Ethic of Excellence: Building a Culture of Craftsmanship with Students* (Portsmouth, NH: Heinemann Educational Books, 2003), p. 103 (emphasis in original).

In other words, learners have their own internal models of what is acceptable. Consequently, says Berger, the most important assessment goal of every school should be changing the ways learners assess themselves. The question then becomes, how do we get inside their heads and turn up the thermostat that regulates their levels of quality and effort? How do we influence self-assessment so that learners have higher standards for their own behaviour and work? How do we turn up the heat?

The first thing that teachers need is a clear idea of what quality looks like – a representation that they can explicitly demonstrate to their learners, a concrete model of what would be an acceptable standard of work. If the teacher is vague about minimum acceptable standards and what the best work would look like, many of the learners won't have a clue about what to aim for either.

BIG BOOKS

The teaching staff at Redbridge Primary School, which follows a thematic curriculum, find that it helps if each module of work culminates in the learners' production of a 'big book'. Take the example opposite from a Year 3 class. The topic they were learning about was water. Each learner has to contribute at least one piece of work to the book which will need to be better than the equivalent in the existing book from the previous year's class. This forces learners to engage in conversations about quality and what they will need to do to make their work the best it can be. They're also motivated to work harder because they know that the big book will be on display for others to see.

Photo: Andy Griffith.

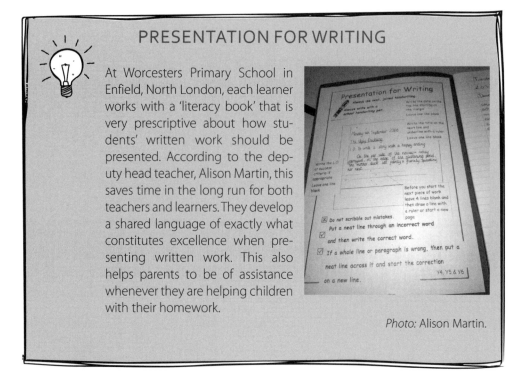

PRESENTATION FOR WRITING

At Worcesters Primary School in Enfield, North London, each learner works with a 'literacy book' that is very prescriptive about how students' written work should be presented. According to the deputy head teacher, Alison Martin, this saves time in the long run for both teachers and learners. They develop a shared language of exactly what constitutes excellence when presenting written work. This also helps parents to be of assistance whenever they are helping children with their homework.

Photo: Alison Martin.

TRAINING LEARNERS TO HAVE GROWTH MINDSETS ABOUT THEIR POTENTIAL

DEVELOPING A POSITIVE ATTITUDE TO MISTAKES

Mistake-making is an essential part of the learning process. Mistakes are a natural feedback mechanism that tells us, 'This strategy didn't work, try another!' We can also add that if a learner gets everything right first time, then the gap they were trying to close was probably too narrow. One of the key issues we have to help our learners overcome is their tendency to view their mistakes as a sign of personal failure – a failure that reflects on their perceived lack of ability in the subject. As we've argued above, this is a common consequence of a fixed mindset. Typically, these learners employ defensive strategies and are unwilling to share their answers in case they are wrong. They fear that making any kind of mistake will adversely affect their self-esteem. They haven't yet learned to reframe a mistake as a learning opportunity. Without access to this important reframe, together with feedback on the mistakes they are making, it will be much harder for teachers to help them close their gaps. If learners are too fearful to get on the horse, how can teachers ever give them feedback on how to improve their riding?

In one primary classroom we observed, we saw children wanting to tear pages out of their exercise books whenever they made a mistake. Reflecting on this afterwards helped the teacher to realise that he needed the class to embrace the power of mistake-making and the learning that can develop from high quality feedback. When we returned six weeks later, the teacher had re-inducted his class by sharing the stories of the setbacks of some of their heroes and heroines. He had also introduced a 'mistake of the week' award – the definition of 'best' was the mistake that had been the most helpful that week in aiding the class to move forward.

As a consequence, his learners had begun to view feedback in a new light and their attitude to mistakes had radically altered. There was a supportive attitude towards mistakes and mistake-makers in the class. We saw how misunderstandings were now openly shared and the class relished the challenge of unpicking how the mistake had been made and how it could be put right.

CELEBRATING MISTAKES

As Thomas Edison is reported to have said about his many attempts to invent the light bulb, 'I have not failed. I've just found 10,000 ways that won't work.' Edison is a great model of resilience. He never gave up. He saw his 'mistakes' as valuable feedback, ways to close his knowledge gaps, and information that he could use in order to get closer to his goal step by step.

Encourage learners to see mistakes as useful feedback and an important step towards overcoming a challenge. Then create ways for them to celebrate any important mistakes that lead them to a new insight or understanding. This could include a section in the back of their exercise book, folder, or learning log where they reflect on what they have learned from it.

How about awarding merits or stars for the most illuminating mistake of the week? You could also share some mistakes of your own to add a touch of personal humility!

Mistakes are crucial to learning. The chances are that if a learner gets everything right first time then the level of challenge is too low. Some learners are fearful of starting work until they get reassurance that what they are about to do is correct. When they make a mistake, a crucial and recognisable learning point has been reached. For many, however, this is the time when they feel a sense of failure and employ defensive strategies. The examples above show that it is possible to train learners to think about mistakes very differently.

MISTAKES BOARD

There's a famous Chinese saying: 'He who asks a question is a fool for five minutes; he who does not ask a question remains a fool forever.' A teacher we worked with inherited a class that were extremely reticent about sharing their own mistakes. Indeed, several learners refused to volunteer answers in case they were wrong. They preferred to remain silent than be seen to make a mistake.

To encourage her learners to share their mistakes she created a 'hazard board'. She explained that the board was a place to share the mistakes they'd made so that others wouldn't make them too. Over the course of a module of learning, she hoped this would become populated by all of the common misunderstandings that occurred.

Initially, the class were reluctant to display their mistakes, so the teacher took matters into her own hands. She deliberately started to include errors in her explanations and challenged her learners to spot them. These mistakes were then added to the board. She skilfully turned mistake-making into an interactive and engaging game.

After each mistake was added, the learners would discuss why the error had been made. What thinking led to the confusion and how could it be avoided in the future? This greater openness led to learner discussions about methods and strategies that deepened their understanding, diminished their confusion, and gave the teacher much richer feedback. This teacher now uses the hazard board as a tool to remind her learners to check their own work for mistakes before they hand it in to be assessed.

Photo: Rachel Sullivan.

One teacher we observed invited in learners from previous classes to talk about the importance of learning from their mistakes. The past learners showed how their work had improved by listening to the feedback from the teacher and from each other. For the new class it was a really important lesson. They started to realise that listening to and acting on feedback would be a key ingredient in helping them to achieve their full potential.

If you're not able to get access to your previous learners, why not make a video montage of past learners explaining how their progress has improved immeasurably as a result of listening to and acting on feedback? Likewise, it can also be a great idea to find examples of top sports personalities or musicians talking about how they owe their success to excellent feedback they were given in the past.

LEARNING FROM THE FAILINGS OF EXPERTS

Learners often think that people who are 'experts', such as famous sports people, musicians, or rich entrepreneurs, were born brilliant. They think it's all about innate talent and ability. Some learners even think that we teachers are the same! They don't see the many hours of practice, the importance of listening to and acting on feedback, and the dedication and effort that goes into achieving high levels of performance.

In his book, *Outliers*, Malcolm Gladwell estimates that it takes 10,000 hours to develop world-class performance.[13] How many of your learners give up on learning too soon? Making them aware of the importance of persistence, practice, and acting on feedback is crucial to developing a growth mindset. Showing your learners how people they perceive as experts in different fields have dealt with 'failure' along the way, and how they've overcome setbacks and learned from them, can be a very effective strategy in nurturing an openness to feedback.

13   Malcolm Gladwell, *Outliers: The Story of Success* (New York: Little, Brown and Co., 2008).

LEIGHTON BAINES

A primary school teacher in Liverpool showed her class a picture of Everton and England footballer Leighton Baines and then read out this quote by him: 'I wasn't even the best player in my youth team.' She then challenged the class to identify what Baines had done to help him move from this point to playing football for England. The class then reflected on how becoming an international footballer was like learning in school. The exercise reinforced the importance of listening to and acting on feedback, and of hard work and persistence if learners wanted to close their own gaps.

J. K. ROWLING

Many children have spent hours in flow reading the gripping tales of *Harry Potter*. In fact, these books have led many children to discover the wonderful world of reading – a world of reading for pleasure rather than because they have to. Many of these young readers will claim that Rowling is a gifted and born writer. However, the truth is very different. As Rowling told her audience at Harvard University in 2008, 'I was jobless, a lone parent, and as poor as it is possible to be in modern Britain, without being homeless.'[14] Her first *Harry Potter* book was rejected repeatedly. Success came through her persistence, her unwillingness to accept failure, and her belief that she was capable of achieving something. She concluded by saying: 'It is impossible to live without failing at something, unless you live so cautiously that you might as well not have lived at all – in which case, you fail by default.' Fortunately, for the many millions of children around the world whose love of reading has been ignited by the *Harry Potter* series, she persisted.

---

14   J. K. Rowling, 'The Fringe Benefits of Failure, and the Importance of Imagination', Commencement Address at the Annual Meeting of the Harvard Alumni Association, June 2008. Available at: http://harvard-magazine.com/2008/06/the-fringe-benefits-failure-the-importance-imagination.

> Most teachers will have some great stories to tell about how they overcame rejection, failure, and adversity at different stages in their lives. Most people do. It may be that you learned some very useful things from these experiences that might be well worth sharing with your learners.

ALONG THE JOURNEY

One of the key strategies for building Level 1a attitudes in learners is teacher persistence. Never, ever give up! Indeed, the minute we lose this focus, we stand the risk of learners' attitudes regressing. Black belt teachers then reinforce Level 1a attitudes in their learners by what they say and do. Below are three effective methods that we've seen teachers use to build and maintain Level 1a attitudes in their classrooms.

1. PRAISE THE ACTIONS NOT THE IDENTITY

Praising children for their ability is damaging! That is the startling conclusion to be drawn from Carol Dweck's work on mindsets. Let's be clear. She argues that simply praising children for being 'clever' or 'intelligent' does not signpost the specific reasons for why they succeed in a task or give them useful information about how they could improve. Instead, her research proposes that teachers should use 'descriptive' praise. She argues that teachers should praise the learners' behaviours and actions, not their identity. 'You're a very good writer' is a nice stroke but the learner may never find out what skilful behaviours have led the teacher to reach that assessment.

When learners are crystal clear about what they have done well and why, they can develop a powerful understanding of what they need to do more of, or less of, to make further progress. It's also important for teachers to check that they are giving feedback on the most pertinent aspects of learning. One English teacher we worked with noted in horror that she had got into the habit of relentlessly praising her learners for the quantity rather than the quality of their writing. 'My goodness,' she said, 'I might as well have brought in a pair of scales to weigh their work. I've fallen into the trap of giving the highest marks to the heaviest work!'

Using descriptive praise can be an excellent way of encouraging learners to act on feedback. We've outlined some praise dos and don'ts in this table.

Do praise …	Don't praise …
Effort. Learners won't maximise their potential if they don't try. Therefore, praising learners for working hard is crucial (e.g. working through a challenging problem they have encountered).	Intelligence, cleverness, or talent alone. Add descriptive praise.
Strategies that lead towards success (e.g. use of dictionaries to check spellings, proofreading work, methodical problem-solving to find mistakes).	The speed at which they complete a task. Learners need to realise that finishing first is not the primary aim. Instead, we want them to focus on completing their work to the highest quality.
Improvement through listening to and acting on feedback (e.g. praising learners who close their own gaps by using written or verbal feedback).	Ordinary or run-of-the-mill contributions. Some teachers hear themselves effusively praising learners for small things that they should expect them to do anyway. Reserve lavish praise for actions or outcomes that truly deserve it. Otherwise, there is a danger that the effect of such praise will lose its impact.
Resilience and courage (e.g. praising learners who contribute answers even when they aren't sure if they're correct).	

How do you and other adults, such as teaching assistants, praise learners?

Could you conduct a praise audit in your classroom?

Some teachers we've worked with directly incentivise their learners by changing the class rewards system they use. They introduce 'acting on feedback' as a specific action that will be rewarded. They also look for evidence of it when they are marking learners' books.

THE PB-ONLY CLASSROOM

Setting a personal best (PB) comes from the world of athletics. When athletes achieve a PB they are usually delighted as it represents a new height of achievement. A PB graph or chart is a visual way of getting learners to appreciate how their own level of performance has improved over time. The PB chart might or might not be on public display, but it works particularly well if it's linked to the school or classroom merit system to give even more incentive to each learner to do their best with every piece of work they do.

Getting learners into the habit of thinking in terms of their personal best reinforces the true spirit of assessment in learning. Focusing on setting a new PB acts to remove the comparativeness that some learners have which can lead them into the bad habit of developing a fixed mindset. PBs encourage them to stop comparing themselves with others and instead see their own performance as the only real yardstick against which to measure themselves. Am I doing better today than yesterday? How can I do better tomorrow than today?

THE HONOURS BOOK

In the rush to get each learner to make progress we sometimes forget to make time for celebration. There are various ways of rewarding learners who make progress but one really nice way is having an 'honours book'. When a learner creates an excellent piece of work, their teacher writes the name and a description of the work in the book. The book below is on display in the Early Years corridor of one school we visited. The achievements are written in gold on black paper to resonate with the gold standard that has been achieved.

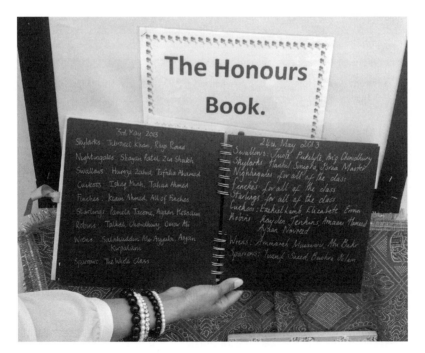

Photo: Andy Griffith.

2. TEACH LEARNERS ABOUT SELF-TALK

Nothing demotivates us more than our own negative self-talk: the inner voice that nags away at us telling us we're no good, useless, not worth it, helpless. In this way, some learners (and teachers) quickly talk themselves out of being successful. However, this kind of self-talk is something that can be influenced and changed. After all, no one but ourselves put this voice in our head in the first place, or we chose to accept what someone else told us, usually a parent or teacher.

By discussing self-talk with learners, primary teacher Catherine Smith helps them to see that they can make choices about how they influence their relationship with their inner voice. Negative self-talk can be consciously shifted to positive self-talk. Phrases such as, 'I can't do this' or 'This is impossible', can be turned into, 'I can't do this *yet*', 'This could be possible if I keep trying', or 'I didn't learn to ride a bicycle the first time I tried but now it's easy!'

The iconic Muhammad Ali always used to say to journalists and his opponents, 'I am the greatest'. His self-talk helped him to become one of the true greats in boxing history. He was certainly good at talking himself up. For older learners, we recommend that you find some footage of Ali's speech to reporters before his 1964 world title fight. At the very least, talk to learners about how toxic our negative self-talk can be and also about the power of talking ourselves up.

HYPNOTISING CHILDREN!

One way of influencing the expectation levels of learners is to hypnotise them. Not *really* hypnotising them, of course, just teaching learners about the principles of hypnosis. For this you will need a pendulum. Making one is simple: provide each learner with a small metal washer and get them to tie a piece of string or cotton to it. Then ask them all to place their elbow on the table and gently dangle the pendulum while holding it between their thumb and forefinger. The washer should be a few inches away from the table. Ask them to focus their minds and see if they can move the pendulum just by using the power of their minds. In order to do this, they are not allowed to move their fingers, hand, or arm – they must stay completely still. Insist on silence and focus. Start by asking them to allow the pendulum to move in a circular motion. A few will get their washer to move in this direction quickly, others will need to see others do it before they can make it happen, while the rest will have pendulums that won't move at all. Now ask the class to put their hands up if their pendulum moved in the stipulated direction.

Ask the learners to refocus and this time to see if they can influence their pendulum to move from side to side, again without movement of their arm. Allow some time for them to experiment and then ask again if they got their pendulum to move. Some learners are amazed by this experiment because they really believe that they've moved the pendulum with their mind – that they've become experts at telekinesis! In fact, they have made it move but perhaps not in the way that they would like to believe. What has happened is that the brain has unconsciously sent messages to tiny muscles, from the shoulder down through the arm to the fingers, which influence the pendulum to move without making it obvious.

This game can be debriefed so that, whether their pendulum moved or not, all the learners can learn about the phenomenon. For those whose pendulum moved, tell them that when they focus on a goal and really commit to it, their whole mind and body system channels and focuses energy to help them achieve it. For those whose pendulum didn't move, praise their determination and strength of purpose for not allowing it to move or for trying to prove you wrong. Tell them, 'If you can apply the same determination to whatever goals you have in life, as you just did so successfully to prove me wrong, then you will probably succeed in getting whatever you want.'

Which of the above ideas for building growth mindsets resonate most with you? Which could you try out or adapt?

How do you show your learners that you have a high quality threshold? How can you use or adapt any of the ideas above to help you raise this bar even higher?

3. CREATING HIGH EXPECTATIONS THROUGH MODELLING

According to Albert Schweitzer, the German philosopher and humanist, 'Modelling isn't the best way to teach – it is the only way to teach.' All these ideas about training learners to have high expectations of themselves will prove worthless if you don't model high expectations yourself. 'Do as I say, not as I do' never really works. Teachers who set high expectations consistently model the attitudes and behaviours they expect to see in their learners at all times.

We often call this 'good extrinsic motivation'. Whether it's good timekeeping, a well-organised and tidy classroom environment, or the use of well-thought-out instructional language, teachers can send messages about high expectations through what they say and do.

> PE teacher Tony Threlkeld sees every minute as precious. He cleverly uses language from sport in his theory lessons. He extols his classes, 'Come on lads, we know the importance of going for the full 90 minutes …', 'It only takes a second to score or concede; it only takes a second to learn something new,' and so on. He pushes his learners to make the most of every moment of their learning time.

A QUALITY CLASSROOM ENVIRONMENT

If you're fortunate enough to teach in the same classroom each day you can create an environment that is a powerful visual metaphor of what you expect of yourself and your learners. The more we can organise our classroom to show our sense of care, commitment to our learners, pleasure in what we do, and passion for learning, the more learners absorb the message that not only is this is a place of work, disciplined attention to detail, and quality, but also of shared endeavour, personal engagement, and dynamism. In other words, what happens in this space is vitally important. Even a dingy Portakabin can be transformed into a stunningly beautiful classroom environment where learners feel comfortable.

If a classroom is untidy, if wall displays are tired or out of date, if there is any sense of neglect or apathy, this gives a powerfully negative message to learners. If we want our learners to take pride in their work and to work hard, then the learning environment must show our own commitment to, and our pride in, what we do. Such a classroom environment will encourage learner traits that will help them to progress: precision, care, patience, reflection, and maybe, given time, fun, pleasure, and deep satisfaction. And the best person to model all of this for them is you.

REFUSING TO ACCEPT SHODDY WORK

When it comes to modelling, actions speak louder than words. So, when learners have put little or no thought or effort into an assignment, simply refuse to accept it. For example, have they proofread written work before handing it in? It's very frustrating for teachers to look over work that appears to have been done in front of the television. Create an expectation that learners read through their work before handing it in for marking. Have they checked facts and spellings? Does it read fluently? Expecting learners to proofread their work helps to teach them an important study/life skill and reduces teacher workload.

English teacher Sandra Jones insists that every learner proofreads their work by reading it out loud before they hand it in. She gives learners a checklist and asks them to tick off that they've done this, and that they've made all necessary corrections in terms of spelling, punctuation, grammar, and flow. This routine has proved useful for Sandra over many years. It teaches learners the importance of producing a first draft and then correcting subsequent drafts. As a result, she spends less time correcting sloppy writing and more time giving feedback on important issues, such as structure and analysis, for which learners attain higher marks and gain greater satisfaction. It's also, she points out, the way that professional writers work.

EXERCISE BOOKS AND FOLDERS

When visitors or learners enter a learning area, first impressions count. Even before they meet the teacher, they'll have formed opinions from the information and evidence before them. We've met teachers who exhort learners to take pride in their work, while there are others whose work is, to put it quite frankly, sloppy. We'll often take a look at learners' books when we're working with teachers. What we see tells us a lot. Some books are pristine, others have graffiti on the front cover! If you've got examples of exercise books from your previous learners that set a benchmark for quality you'll find it can make your life a whole lot easier. They provide a clear model for your current learners to emulate.

RESITS AND RETESTS

When teachers set a minimum pass mark for a test, and insist on tests being redone if the minimum is not met, a powerful message is transmitted to learners. Why not set the bar high in *all* the tests you set? When a learner doesn't meet the standard you've stipulated, *always* get them to redo the test after school or at lunchtime. This, in itself, encourages learners to take study and revision more seriously.

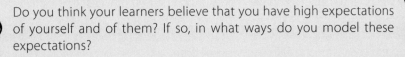

Do you think your learners believe that you have high expectations of yourself and of them? If so, in what ways do you model these expectations?

What aspects of high expectation do you believe you already model well? Which others could you most improve on? How might you do that?

The best teachers work hard to develop the knowledge, attitudes, skills, and habits of their learners over the course of the entire school year. They mould their new classes over time into classes that can perform consistently at Level 1a. They aim to make sure that by the end of the academic year, their learners are ready to progress to the next level of challenge. That might be the next school year or it could be college, university, or life in the world outside school. Whatever the context, the best teachers develop their classes as if they were going to continue with the same learners the following year. They're committed to helping them on to the next part of their journey. And what's interesting is that when they do this, they not only make their own lives much easier – for many of the reasons we've discussed in this chapter – but they also make life easier for the teachers who will inherit them next and for the school as a whole. That's a real gift to the world.

FAQS

Where do low expectations come from?

Low expectations come from all sorts of places: from authority figures like parents and teachers, from a culture of low expectation that exists in some schools, and from negative self-talk that children internalise from their experiences. The list is long. However, as teachers, we simply don't need to analyse all this. Instead, it is a better use of our time and energy to be more solution-focused. Using the tools and ideas in this chapter, we can support learners in the process of changing their limiting beliefs into more empowering convictions about themselves and their potential. We can actively support them to develop higher expectations of themselves and others.

Are high expectations about creating success? If so, are there different types of success?

The word 'success' can mean different things to different people. Our own view has been influenced by Stefan Einhorn in his book, *The Art of Being Kind*.[15] He describes two kinds of success: external success and internal success. Internal success happens when a person achieves a personal or professional outcome that makes him or her feel successful. External success occurs when what we do is evaluated positively according to criteria applied by others, such as teachers, other learners, or society at large. We think that real success has to incorporate elements of both.

Isn't there a danger of demotivating learners by setting expectations that are too high for them?

Being a teacher with high expectations is not just about being optimistic. Getting and then keeping learners motivated can be a real challenge. What we've learned from our work is that you are more likely to have demotivated learners if you don't hold high expectations of them. Having high expectations underpins all the other things in this book. We will go on to demonstrate the importance of combining these expectations with clarity about where learners are going and the steps needed to get there, and creating enjoyable and doable challenges for them to participate in.

How do you know if you are a high expectations teacher or not?

We think you're either high or you're not, sorry! The idea of a moderate expectations teacher simply doesn't fly for us. There are various ways to tell whether you have high expectations. One thing to note is your own internal dialogue. It's bad enough to think, 'These sort of kids will never make anything of their lives,' but it's even worse to externalise this dialogue in the staffroom or elsewhere. We also recommend spending time with high expectations teachers. Talk to them and observe them in action. Soon enough you'll realise whether your own expectations are as high as you'd like to believe.

---

15   Stefan Einhorn, *The Art of Being Kind* (London: Piatkus, 2010).

IN A NUTSHELL

The best teachers create high expectations for their learners. It's fundamental to the teaching backwards process. This is impossible to achieve unless the teacher (a) holds those high expectations and (b) becomes expert in moving each learner's expectations upwards. They achieve this through a combination of training and modelling. They model the knowledge, attitudes, skills, and habits that they want their learners to adopt, especially around striving to create the highest quality work possible. They train learners to become more resilient, more open to feedback, and to hold growth mindsets about their own improvement as learners. Only when a teacher can transform learners' expectations of themselves from low or average to high is great progress possible.

TEACHING BACKWARDS CHECKLIST

Setting high expectations (macro – course/academic year)	This is always part of my practice	I sometimes do this	I never do this
I demonstrate my high expectations for my learners by regarding target grades as a minimum expectation.			
I back myself to significantly raise the progress levels of my learners.			

Setting high expectations (macro – course/academic year)	This is always part of my practice	I sometimes do this	I never do this
I expect learners to give their best for every topic.			
I train learners how to become more resilient (e.g. how to behave when they are stuck or confused).			
I train learners to care about the quality of their work.			
I train learners to have growth mindsets about their potential.			
I model high expectations around quality of work in various ways for learners.			
I induct my classes and share my expectations from the outset.			
I seek feedback from many sources to check whether my expectations are as high as I think they are.			

Download this checklist from:

http://osiriseducational.co.uk/TB/resources/

TEACHING BACKWARDS ACTION PLAN: POINTS FROM THIS CHAPTER

How can you convert a 'never' to a 'sometimes' or a 'sometimes' to an 'always' in relation to this checklist? Remember, you are more likely to get your class to Level 1a if you do all these things routinely.

I need to stop/do less …

I need to start/do more …

FOR MORE INFORMATION ...

Tom Bennett's blog offers some useful tips to new teachers about getting good behaviour in the classroom:

http://behaviourguru.blogspot.co.uk/2011/05/some-general-behaviour-advice-for.html?q=tips/

Carol Dweck's website has lots of information for teachers about growth mindsets:

http://mindsetonline.com/

STARTING POINTS

Chapter 2

STARTING POINTS

'I didn't know they could already do this'

WHAT'S IN THIS CHAPTER FOR ME?

Have you ever felt time pressure to get through large amounts of content with your classes? Have your lessons sometimes been unproductive because learners didn't have the skills or knowledge you expected? After a lesson observation, have you ever been surprised to be told that some learners had made no progress? Have your learners ever been bored or puzzled because you were teaching them something they'd already covered?

If you answered yes to any of these questions, this chapter will help you to identify some solutions. The first step for teaching backwards, lesson by lesson, is to have a thorough understanding of where your learners are starting from. If a teacher doesn't really know his learners' starting points, it's going to be a whole lot more difficult for him to teach to close their gaps. Without this crucial knowledge, how can any teacher plan for progression, not just in the subject-specific knowledge and the learners' current skills and understanding of it, but also in the more general development of each learner's knowledge, attitudes, skills, and habits?

This chapter will examine the benefits of pre-assessing our learners before we start teaching them. In other words, finding out their starting points. We'll explore tools that enable this to be done quickly and accurately, and we'll look at how the principles of pre-assessment apply not just to individual learning modules but also to the learners' longer term progress over the entire school year.

WHAT'S THE THINKING BEHIND THIS CHAPTER?

Suppose you woke up one morning with a terrible headache and a rash all over your body. You ring the health centre and make an appointment. You enter the surgery and the doctor, without consulting her notes, asking you any questions, or examining you in any way, hands you a bottle of medicine. If this were to happen, you might not have too much confidence in the effectiveness of the medication. You might even wonder about the possibility of dangerous side effects. Given this scenario, you'd probably be well advised to change your doctor too!

Yet some teachers, even with the best of intentions, behave in exactly the same way with their learners. A new class begins the school year and the teacher, without any real understanding of the learners' starting points, begins to 'deliver'.

An alarming number of lessons that we've observed over the years have fallen at the first hurdle because the teacher hasn't done any accurate pre-assessment. Often, this isn't because the teachers are neglectful or uncommitted. Indeed, these teachers may have put hours of thought and planning into what and how they were going to teach. The problem is that they've made too many assumptions – assumptions about their learners' subject knowledge, their skills, attitudes and motivation levels, their literacy and numeracy. And, subsequently, many of these assumptions have turned out to be wrong.

And it's not only at the beginning of the new school year that accurate pre-assessment is essential. Knowing the starting points of learners also applies to individual lessons, new topics, and other units of learning. In fact, excellent teachers are mindful of the vital importance of pre-assessment throughout the entire school year.

One teacher we worked with neatly summed up his role in this way: 'Teaching isn't that complicated. Your class have simply got to leave the lesson cleverer than they were at the start. However, if you're guessing what they know and what they can do, chances are it's just not going to happen.'

WHAT DO WE MEAN BY KNOWING THEIR STARTING POINTS?

It was a wet and windy Thursday afternoon when Liz sat down with us, over a cup of tea, to talk about what she'd learned from watching the video recording of her maths lesson. We expected her to be downhearted – the lesson hadn't gone that well. However, within a couple of minutes of listening to her, we realised that watching herself on video had led her to a profound learning experience, one that would change her planning habits for good. 'That lesson was doomed to fail,' she boldly declared. 'There was no way it could work from the minute I walked into the lesson with my plan. I just assumed, because they all had at least level 5 on their SAT scores, that they would know how to do the basics.' She then went on to critique some of her other lessons that had been unsuccessful in the past. The common cause was an over-reliance on data 'to guess', as she put it, the starting points of her learners. 'I'm never going to guess again,' she said with a determined gleam in her eyes.

For Liz, the transformational learning was that if she was to fully embrace the practice of teaching backwards, then she would have to give more attention to discovering what her learners' starting points really were. She realised that data alone could never give her sufficient information about her learners' level of proficiency across the wide range of mathematical topics that she teaches them. Does Sarah, for example, have the same level of competence in percentages as she does in algebra or statistics? If not, then Liz would need to find out what her starting points truly were before planning the next steps.

Liz's experience is not uncommon. Far too many teachers, in our experience, make assumptions about their learners' starting points and rely far too much on the learners' scores from the previous year. The point we want to stress here is that neither guesswork nor data are sufficient for effective planning and preparation.

To get a sense of what we need instead, let's look no further than the Level 1a descriptor we set out in the Introduction. The descriptor emphasises the importance of knowing the starting points of learners from the very outset. Two particular items from the list stand out:

1   *Teachers use feedback to adapt learning within lessons and planning for future lessons.* So, in addition to gathering data from the previous year's assessments, the teacher also needs to collect up-to-date information by getting feedback on where the learners currently are at the beginning of the school year and during each lesson. Last year's data, for example, is already two or three months out of date. A lot could have happened in that time – for example, some learners will have built on the knowledge they had in June and July, while others will have forgotten or muddled it.

2   *All learners have clarity on their current position and the quality of KASH they need to develop further in order to achieve their goal.* In other words, it's not only the teacher who needs to know the starting points of the learners. It's also essential that the learners themselves understand what their starting points are, what learning gaps they have, and have some sense of what they're going to do about it. And, of course, it will be the teacher's job to support and guide them in this endeavour.

This chapter is all about exploring starting points in much greater detail. Having said a little bit about *what* they are and some of the problems that occur when we pay insufficient attention to them, we'll now turn our attention to *why* starting points are so essential and why it's worth investing time and energy into getting them right. We'll take a brief look at some of the underpinning research and some practical examples of what happens when teachers get it right or wrong. In the last part of the chapter, we'll offer some tried-and-tested 'how to' strategies to get you up and running, and we'll consider some of the contexts in which they can be used.

THE ADVANTAGES OF KNOWING THE STARTING POINTS OF LEARNERS

There are five powerful reasons why teachers and learners need to know and act on their starting points.

1. TIME

The first advantage of pre-assessment is that it saves time. Primary and secondary teachers alike talk about the shortage of teaching time. 'There's so much to get through' and 'There's never enough time to … ' are common and heartfelt complaints. But perhaps a more useful question that teachers could sometimes ask themselves is: does everything need to be taught? As we shall see later in the 'how to' section of this chapter, pre-assessment can often take as little as 10 minutes of lesson time. Yet the time saved in the long run can be many times more than that.

Smart pre-assessment allows teachers to identify existing levels of knowledge, understanding, and skills that learners already possess or lack. Through this process, teachers can quickly identify what needs to be taught and to whom, and what doesn't. This enables the teacher to reallocate time to those individuals who need more support, or to the class as a whole if the new learning is beyond their existing skills levels. On the other hand, if it turns out that the learners already have a good grasp of the necessary skills and concepts, they don't need to waste time going over old ground. The teacher can then move quickly on to the next step.

> Debbie, the head of a maths department, pre-assessed her Year 10 class by giving them the end-of-unit test for the module they were just about to begin. The results surprised her. Most of the class were already able to do 80% of the work required. This saved her three hours of teaching time, enabling her to focus more time on the remaining 20% of content and to give individual attention to those learners who needed extra support. She was delighted. She saw that pre-assessment really could help her to tailor her teaching much more accurately and enable her to more effectively close the gaps of her learners, thereby saving her a lot of time and unnecessary effort.

In the same way, teachers can also identify which of their learners' attitudes, skills, and habits (the ASH of KASH) need to be developed if they are to achieve the standards required at 'outstanding' Level 1a. For example, if a teacher is unaware that there are learners in her class who give up easily whenever the level of challenge is raised, she could easily become demotivated or frustrated. Had she pre-assessed this attitude, she would expect some resistance or apathy and not let it faze her. She would apply various strategies to support her learners to overcome the issue, such as raising the level of challenge for them in smaller steps.

2. IDENTIFYING OUR OWN AND OUR LEARNERS' MISCONCEPTIONS

Just because your current class seem much like the class you had last year, don't assume that they have identical levels of knowledge and understanding. It might be attractive to believe that education is like a conveyor belt, but think how boring teaching would be if each class were the same. We'd end up delivering the same curriculum in the same way year after year. Surely, our aim is to be like a teacher with 20 years' experience, not a teacher with one year's experience 20 times over!

Another misconception is that learners won't know 'stuff' that hasn't yet been covered on this year's curriculum. But it's quite possible that some of your learners will have come across the content before, either in a previous class or outside school.

As for the learners, some of them may have formed misunderstandings that will seriously inhibit their ability to progress. The best teachers we've worked with use accurate pre-assessment strategies to quickly identify these misconceptions. And having done so, they correct them as soon as possible, opening up greater potential in their learners to get on with learning far beyond their previous expectations.

Mary, a Year 7 science teacher, discovered through pre-assessment that some of her learners held some strange notions about global warming (the K of KASH). She therefore structured a lesson to debunk the myth that global warming only occurred during summer months. She had the additional challenge of doing so on a winter's day when it was snowing heavily!

Excellent teachers use pre-assessment to gain feedback on areas of new learning that learners are likely to find most difficult. They recognise that each class is different and will almost certainly have different starting points than any previous class they might have taught.

3. BUILDING A SENSE OF COMPETENCE

A felt sense of competence is a key motivational trigger for learners. The more competent learners feel, the more motivated they're likely to be when engaging in new learning and taking on new challenges. Pre-assessment does something really important here. It can help learners to realise that they already have some knowledge on the topic. They see they have a foundation of existing learning to build on.

Important as it is for teachers to hold high expectations of their learners, by itself this is not enough. We need our learners to have high expectations of themselves and what they think they are capable of achieving. A key element in this process is to help them to develop a core sense of competence that will give them a platform of confidence and self-belief from which they can take on new challenges. Pre-assessment enables this realisation. For example, one German teacher we've worked with always provides his class with a vocabulary list at the start of any new module of learning. He asks his class to read through the list and highlight words they think they know the meaning of. The class are usually able to recognise plenty of them, as many are quite similar to English. This builds the confidence of the class, as the teacher can point out that they already start with a huge cache of known vocabulary.

Another way teachers can enhance learner competence is by inviting learners to revisit their initial pre-assessment document as they near the end of a learning module. The teacher can ask them to update the document with the new knowledge and understanding that they've gained. This is a very concrete way for learners to build their sense of achievement from work in progress, and to recognise just how far, and often how quickly, they've travelled on their journey. As a result, it can play a significant role in raising learners' expectations and beliefs about their potential, an important theme that we developed in Chapter 1.

As learners start to compare their new levels of knowledge, attitudes, skills, and habits with their previous levels, something very important happens psychologically. They stop comparing themselves with other learners and start measuring their development against themselves. This is exactly the same technique that top athletes and performers use because they realise the only person over whom they have any direct influence is themselves. They have no control whatsoever over what their competitors are up to! They ask themselves: how can I run/swim/dance better today than I did yesterday? How can I run/swim/dance better tomorrow than I'm doing today? Great athletes and performers realise that development tends to happen when small but significant steps are taken every day. And so it is with learning.

4. GETTING LEARNERS ENGAGED: SETTING CHALLENGING GOALS

Our previous book was all about ways to get our learners fully engaged in their learning. The concept of flow was at the heart of this. Flow is a profound sense of being fully absorbed in whatever it is we're doing. But learners won't get into this state unless the level of challenge their teacher sets them is appropriate.

Pre-assessment enables teachers to accurately identify the appropriate levels at which to set challenge for their learners and avoid the pitfalls of making erroneous assumptions. The danger of underestimating the skills and knowledge of learners is that lessons will very likely lack sufficient complexity. This is a sure-fire recipe for bored and disengaged learners who make little or no progress. On the other hand, overestimating the knowledge and skills of learners is equally dangerous. If the teacher lacks accurate information about the learners' starting points, and sets the level of challenge too high, the result will likely be confused and demotivated learners who will lack confidence in their ability.

5. MEASURING THE REAL IMPACT OF YOUR TEACHING

We hold the firm view that one of the most important reasons for pre-assessment is that it enables teachers to more accurately measure the impact of their teaching. Reliable assessment of where learners started, and how far they've come by the end of the topic, module, or school year, allows teachers to measure the effectiveness of their teaching – what works well and what could be improved. If teachers don't do this, how can they know how much of the learning is the direct result of the quality of their teaching?

Classes may hit their end-of-module targets, but is this due to the teacher's expertise or did the learners manage it in spite of their teacher? Perhaps these learners could have exceeded these targets if their teacher had done a thorough pre-assessment to take into account their true starting points. Our job as teachers is to help learners close gaps. But first we need to know where the gap starts and what criteria have to be met for the gap to be closed.

One final point: when teachers make this process transparent from the outset, it allows learners to see their teacher as a model. Not only do they realise that their teacher is engaged in the process and discipline of learning, but they can also begin to intuit that learning is a lifetime endeavour.

> Have you ever had a job interview where you've been asked to teach a lesson? Here is a salutary tale from one of the outstanding primary schools that we work with. The school deliberately doesn't include the starting points of the class in the information they send out to prospective candidates. This is a deliberate test. The school is expecting them to realise the importance of getting this information to help them plan their lesson. The head teacher takes a dim view of any applicant who doesn't phone in for more details.

HOW TO PRE-ASSESS: STRATEGIES AND ACTIVITIES

There are two types of pre-assessment. The one we'll deal with first establishes the starting points of learners before each new module of learning. The second seeks to establish the starting points of learners when you first start teaching them. Usually this will be over several days at the beginning of September when you're still trying to remember, after a glorious six-week break, how to teach!

1. PRE-ASSESSMENT – MODULE BY MODULE

Pre-assessment needs to take place before the start of any new module of learning. By this, we don't mean at the start of the first lesson of the new module! Finding out learners' starting points at this stage is too late. We've not met a teacher yet who can plan a lesson and prepare the resources in 10 seconds while standing in front of their class.

Pre-assessment should take place towards the end of the previous module, so that teachers have sufficient time to adapt their planning according to the feedback they gather. The pre-assessment enables teachers to establish their learners' starting points on the relevant subject-specific skills and knowledge that have been covered during this and previous school years. The teacher will need to establish whether the learners have retained the relevant knowledge and skills or not.

Unless you're starting to teach a topic from scratch, what are you assuming that learners will know and be able to do? What key words or concepts are you expecting them to be familiar with? What thinking processes are you assuming they've internalised? You'll be well advised to devise pre-assessment activities to discover whether the assumptions you're making have any credibility.

Take a moment to consider a module that you'll be starting to teach in the near future. What are the pre-existing knowledge, attitudes, skills, and habits you're expecting or assuming your learners to already have?

Take a look through the following practical pre-assessment tools and activities and explore how one or more of them might enable you to get some quality feedback about whether your assumptions are accurate or not.

CONCEPT MAPS

Concept maps are a visual way of organising information. They are particularly useful at showing the interrelationships that exist between different aspects of that information. When we ask learners to create a concept map we're challenging them not only to demonstrate their understanding of the concept as a whole but also its underlying complexity. The quality of the learners' maps will enable the teacher to quickly gauge what learners know, how well developed their grasp of the underlying complexity is, and how mature their thinking processes are for the topic in question.

Below is an example of a similarities and differences visual organiser. A primary school teacher asked her class to complete it before beginning a module on the properties of liquids and gases. She was keen to find out what her learners already knew about the topic and also what gaps they had. She particularly wanted to assess how well developed their understanding was of the similarities and differences between materials in these two states.

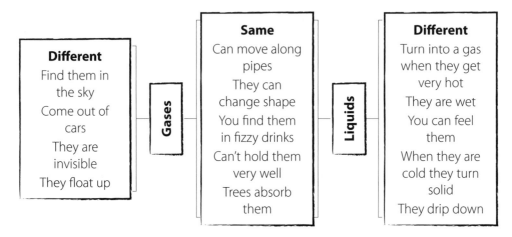

Different

Find them in the sky

Come out of cars

They are invisible

They float up

Gases

Same

Can move along pipes

They can change shape

You find them in fizzy drinks

Can't hold them very well

Trees absorb them

Liquids

Different

Turn into a gas when they get very hot

They are wet

You can feel them

When they are cold they turn solid

They drip down

Different visual organisers exist for different purposes. Try using some to pre-assess your learners. You can download a set of templates from:

http://osiriseducational.co.uk/TB/resources/

Once learners have completed their concept maps, the teacher can collate the results in order to decide on the best starting point for the module. Concept maps swiftly and clearly expose learners' misconceptions and gaps. Towards the end of the module, learners can revisit their concept maps to correct and add to the original. As we mentioned previously, this revisiting of earlier work shows learners how far they have progressed, thus building their self-esteem and sense of competence.

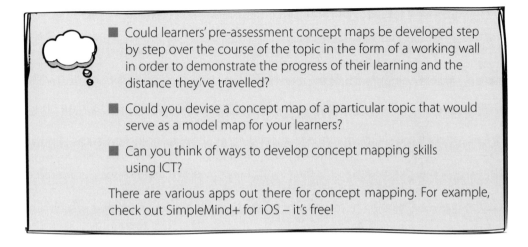

- Could learners' pre-assessment concept maps be developed step by step over the course of the topic in the form of a working wall in order to demonstrate the progress of their learning and the distance they've travelled?

- Could you devise a concept map of a particular topic that would serve as a model map for your learners?

- Can you think of ways to develop concept mapping skills using ICT?

There are various apps out there for concept mapping. For example, check out SimpleMind+ for iOS – it's free!

KNOWLEDGE GRIDS

Another really useful way to pre-assess what learners already know is to use a knowledge grid. In the example below, a Year 7 science teacher wants to find out, before she starts teaching the module, how much learners already know about global warming. She gives each learner a copy of the grid and asks them to spend five minutes completing it in silence. She does this towards the end of a lesson about a week or so before she starts the new module. This gives her time to assess the results and decide on the best starting points for each learner.

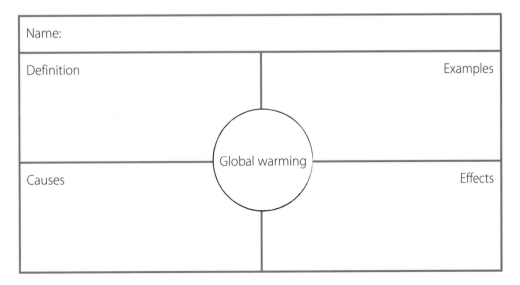

You can download this template from:

http://osiriseducational.co.uk/TB/resources/

Analysing the grids enables the teacher to build up an accurate understanding of every learner's starting point in each of the four areas.

There are two important reasons why it's more effective to get learners to write about what they know in this way than using a tick list, such as the example below. First, a tick list is likely to tell you more about the learners' over- or under-inflated view of their knowledge and understanding than anything else. Second, a list like this does nothing more than ask a non-expert to self-assess their level of expertise. Not a great idea! Furthermore, the task is very vague: there are no criteria against which the learners can accurately measure themselves. A proper pre-assessment activity gives concrete feedback, measurement against clear criteria, and leaves the final starting points under the jurisdiction of the expert: the teacher.

	Don't know	Have some understanding	Confidently understand
Causes of global warming	✘		
Understand the advantages and disadvantages of alternative sources of energy		✘	
Understand how building design can impact on global warming			✘
Understand the different gases that contribute to global warming			✘
Ways governments seek to reduce the impact of global warming			✘

ASSESSING CONTEXTUAL AWARENESS

It's often important for teachers of literature, history, social studies, and other humanities subjects to make sure their learners have a good grounding in the cultural, social, economic, and historical events of the time. For example, an appreciation of the social, political, and economic trends that created the conditions for the Russian Revolution is essential. Similarly, an understanding of 1920s America is necessary to fully appreciate and evaluate F. Scott Fitzgerald's novel, *The Great Gatsby*. Pre-assessment of such issues gives teachers critically useful insights into what the necessary starting points for their learners are before embarking on the work.

English teacher Laura McQueen used the grid below to assess her class before starting a module on Shakespeare's *Macbeth*. The feedback she obtained clearly showed that she needed to devote more lesson time than she'd expected on demystifying Shakespearean language. The feedback made it abundantly obvious that this was the key area in which her class lacked confidence and it would slow down their learning if it were not addressed at the outset.

Name:	
What do you know already about *Macbeth*?	What do you know about the period of history?
What other Shakespeare plays have you learned about, read, or seen?	What has been your experience of Shakespearean language?

STRUCTURED OBSERVATIONS

This pre-assessment strategy is really helpful where future learning requires the proficient use of a particular skill. Such skills might include essay writing, using a tool in a technology lesson, setting up a fair test for a science experiment, reading for gist in modern foreign languages, summarising a piece of text after skimming and scanning, breaking down a maths problem into parts, or applying a technique in a performance context, such as sport, physical education, or drama.

Setting learners a concrete challenge, so that they can demonstrate their level of competence in the skill in question, gives the teacher immediate feedback about where the learners need to start from. Where learners already have high competence in the skill, the level of difficulty can be raised. Where competence is lacking, the feedback shows what gaps need to be closed and what scaffolding for learning needs to be provided. Above all, it challenges any false assumptions the teacher might be holding.

Stuart, a PE teacher, told us how he'd used a structured observation to help his class to get to grips with their own starting points. He'd found that they were reluctant to work on drills to improve different aspects of their footballing skills. Instead, they just wanted to go straight into matches during his PE classes. They were suffering from what he described as 'Messi syndrome'. They thought they were fantastic but, having watched them play, Stuart knew differently. So he set up a challenge where he had the class pass the ball between two cones placed close together. None of the students could do it. As a consequence, they saw that there was a point to working on skill development. After all, with passing skills at such a low level, they wouldn't be requiring an agent for a while!

KWL

For teachers who follow a thematic curriculum, KWL is an excellent tool for pre-assessing learners. KWL is a set of questions that learners answer before they start a new module of learning:

■ What do you *know* about?

■ What do you *want* to know about?

■ What did you *learn* about?

The teacher provides a KWL hand-out (like the one on page 71) for each learner to fill out the first two columns at the beginning of the module. The teacher can then use the results to adjust their teaching to cover aspects of the topic that their class express curiosity about.

Name:		
What do I know already?	What do I want to know about (questions I have)?	What did I learn about?

To download this template visit:

http://osiriseducational.co.uk/TB/resources/

The *know* part of KWL enables the teacher to pre-assess what learners already know about a topic or theme. It also enables them to gather any misconceptions that learners may have about the forthcoming topic. The *want* part helps the teacher to draw up a list of questions the class would like to investigate as part of their learning. The *learn* part is used for learners to complete when they reflect at the end of the module of learning about what they have learned.

When outstanding primary teacher Alison Martin conducted a KWL activity she discovered she had an expert on ancient Egypt in her class. From the feedback the KWL gave her, she realised that this student probably knew more than she did and would likely be bored rigid over the next few weeks if she set him the same tasks as the others. So she set this learner an individual challenge of comparing the ancient Egyptians with the Mayans.

Source: Worcesters Primary School, Enfield.
Photo: Alison Martin.

Try using a KWL just before a weekend or school holiday – you never know what learners might come back with. A KWL activity can act as a spur for them to start investigating on their own initiative. One primary teacher returned on Monday morning to find her Year 1 class had spent the entire weekend collecting information on the life cycle of butter-flies. One boy had even brought in a plant covered in caterpillars in his school bag!

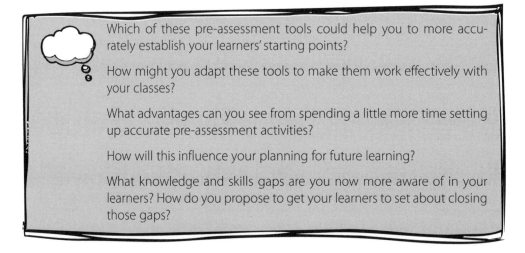

Which of these pre-assessment tools could help you to more accu-rately establish your learners' starting points?

How might you adapt these tools to make them work effectively with your classes?

What advantages can you see from spending a little more time setting up accurate pre-assessment activities?

How will this influence your planning for future learning?

What knowledge and skills gaps are you now more aware of in your learners? How do you propose to get your learners to set about closing those gaps?

What additional *resources* could you produce to help learners with the starting points you've identified?

How might you use *assistance* to support particular groups of learners with similar starting points?

2. PRE-ASSESSMENT –
RIGHT FROM THE BEGINNING OF THE SCHOOL YEAR

The class shuffle nervously into your classroom. They look around at their new environment, the place they're going to be learning with you for the next ten months or so. You might recognise some of them, but most faces are not yet connected to a name. Some of the learners stand out due to their introverted nature, others for the opposite reason.

This is the exactly the moment to start the second type of pre-assessment that needs to take place when a teacher meets his or her new class for the first time. Our experience has shown that those teachers who spend time pre-assessing not just the subject knowledge of the learners but also their attitudes, skills, and habits in the classroom, gain a much deeper understanding of whatever barriers might prevent the class from working at Level 1a. As a result of quality pre-assessment, these teachers will have a much keener awareness of what needs to be done to move their learners towards the excellence required of a Level 1a classroom. With these desirable traits in mind, they can now start teaching backwards from the starting points their pre-assessment work has revealed.

In a way, it's just like the sat nav in your car. Unless the microchip knows *exactly* where you want to go *and* where you're starting from, it won't be able to calculate the quickest and most effective route. On the other hand, teaching without pre-assessment is a bit like navigating by starlight when there's 75% cloud cover, as the following anecdote illustrates.

After working with us on one of our Outstanding Teaching Interventions, a Year 4 primary teacher fessed up about a brief conversation that had taken place at the end of one of her lessons. She'd spent the lesson teaching the children peer assessment skills. She'd devoted half an hour to slowly moving step by step through the process until she was happy that the whole class could do it. As the children dutifully filed out of the room after the bell, one of them stopped to say to her, 'Miss, that's just how we peer assessed last year with Mrs X.' The teacher was mortified: 'I've just spent half an hour teaching them to suck eggs!' Had she done a proper pre-assessment, she'd have known that these learners didn't have a gap in their KASH on this particular topic. And she'd have saved herself half an hour plus her preparation time into the bargain.

One sunny, late September afternoon, we observed a Year 12 biology lesson taught by Louise. It stood out for its quality – the learners were performing brilliantly at Level 1a. And this was only three weeks into the school year. The lesson had all the hallmarks of a teacher who knew how to teach backwards. We congratulated Louise on her remarkable achievement of developing a class so quickly to work at such high levels. She smiled and replied, 'Actually, I cheated. I taught them in Years 10 and 11 too.' Her pre-assessments hadn't taken long because she knew the learners so well.

Of course, it might not have been Louise who inherited that Year 12 class. Yet those learners would still have had KASH Level 1a. Just imagine the amazing learning experience you could have had with that class if it was you who'd inherited them! The more that teachers work to hand over their classes at the end of the school year with the highest level of knowledge, attitudes, habits, and skills possible, the more those learners, their teachers, and the whole ethos of the school as a thriving learning community will benefit.

It's not often that your learners will have KASH Level 1a at the beginning of the school year, but miracles do happen!

PRE-ASSESSING KASH: TOOLS AND STRATEGIES

The most obvious time and place to assess your learners' KASH will be the induction process at the start of a new school year. In Chapter 1, we made the point that an effective induction process is key to establishing and demystifying Level 1a expectations with any new class. It's also the first face-to-face opportunity a teacher has to accurately assess the learners' starting points.

The more skilfully an induction programme is designed, the better the quality of information the teacher will get. And the better the quality of the feedback, the quicker that teacher will be able to start teaching backwards.

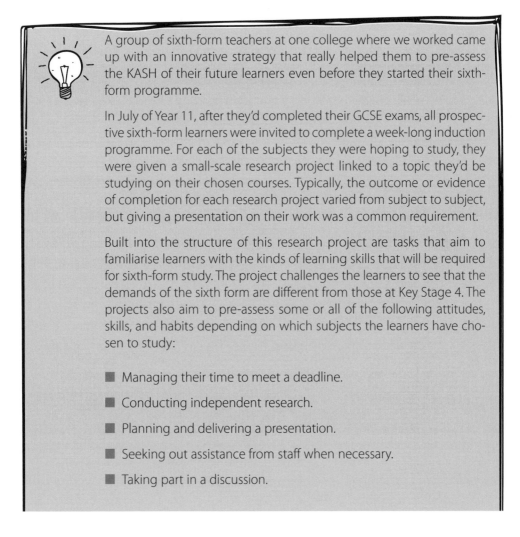

A group of sixth-form teachers at one college where we worked came up with an innovative strategy that really helped them to pre-assess the KASH of their future learners even before they started their sixth-form programme.

In July of Year 11, after they'd completed their GCSE exams, all prospective sixth-form learners were invited to complete a week-long induction programme. For each of the subjects they were hoping to study, they were given a small-scale research project linked to a topic they'd be studying on their chosen courses. Typically, the outcome or evidence of completion for each research project varied from subject to subject, but giving a presentation on their work was a common requirement.

Built into the structure of this research project are tasks that aim to familiarise learners with the kinds of learning skills that will be required for sixth-form study. The project challenges the learners to see that the demands of the sixth form are different from those at Key Stage 4. The projects also aim to pre-assess some or all of the following attitudes, skills, and habits depending on which subjects the learners have chosen to study:

- Managing their time to meet a deadline.

- Conducting independent research.

- Planning and delivering a presentation.

- Seeking out assistance from staff when necessary.

- Taking part in a discussion.

- Reflecting, enquiring, and asking questions.
- Developing a coherent argument in writing and presenting judgements with supporting evidence.

The teachers, including the head of the sixth form, collate all the information from the projects and presentations and assess how well each learner has done against the criteria. From this feedback, the starting points of each learner can be established and appropriate interventions planned over the summer. In addition to this pre-assessment work, the learners themselves acquire valuable feedback about whether or not the courses they have chosen to study are suitable for them.

The extra work this requires of teachers in July is more than made up for when the new intake arrives in September. Much of the pre-assessment work has already been done, starting points are clear, teachers and learners already have a sense of familiarity, and work can begin in earnest after a short but effective induction.

Head of sixth form Frank Lawell created his own 'sixth-form driving licence' for his learners. This was used to pre-assess learners' KASH across a range of areas, including:

- Meeting deadlines.
- Effort.
- Ability to present confidently.
- Contribution to discussions.
- Taking responsibility for one's own learning.

Frank was able to use the feedback from his pre-assessment to develop a range of bespoke study skills sessions to help learners to develop any areas in which they had gaps.

To download this editable sixth-form driving licence go to:

http://osiriseducational.co.uk/TB/resources/

SIXTH-FORM DRIVING LICENCE

BROUGHTON HALL HIGH SCHOOL

Surname

Forename

Form Class

Ability to be organised and arrive on time for lessons

Excellent ☐

Good ☐

Area for development ☐

Unsatisfactory ☐

Ability to meet deadlines

Excellent ☐

Good ☐

Area for development ☐

Unsatisfactory ☐

Willingness to participate during lessons

Excellent ☐

Good ☐

Area for development ☐

Unsatisfactory ☐

Able to work effectively as part of a team

Excellent ☐

Good ☐

Area for development ☐

Unsatisfactory ☐

Level of confidence in delivering a presentation

Excellent ☐

Good ☐

Area for development ☐

Unsatisfactory ☐

Ability to present work professionally, reference sources and avoid plagiarism

Excellent ☐

Good ☐

Area for development ☐

Unsatisfactory ☐

Willingness to take responsibility for learning, and development of exam skills, indicates that the student will achieve their target grade

Likely ☐

Possible if effort maintained ☐

Possible with increased effort ☐

Unlikely ☐

For office use only

FULL LICENCE: Student is consistently demonstrating that they have the potential to become a successful sixth-form student ☐

PROVISIONAL LICENCE: Areas for development have been identified. Student needs to improve on these areas if they are to become a successful sixth-form student ☐

NO LICENCE ISSUED: Student' skills and behaviours need to be significantly developed if they are to become successful sixth-form student ☐

BH6F

Source: Frank Lawell.

PRE-ASSESSING LEARNERS' MINDSETS

Pre-assessing mindsets needs to be a key ingredient of any effective induction pro-gramme. As we explained in Chapter 1, the quality of each learner's mindset, its relative openness or closedness, significantly affects the learner's ability to overcome challenge and to develop greater complexity in their capacity for thinking and social interaction. If learners believe that their ability is a fixed trait, and label their competence in negative or limited ways, teachers are likely to face real problems in raising their learners' game, unless these limiting beliefs can be addressed and changed.

Learners with a fixed mindset tend to give up easily when faced with challenge, become quickly demotivated, don't see the value of effort and perseverance, and perceive feedback as criticism to the extent that, instead of acting on it, they'll tend to reject or ignore it.

For these reasons, pre-assessing mindset gives us important feedback on our learners' cur-rent attitudes and habits. If we know in advance that certain learners may lack resilience when the going gets tough, we can develop classroom norms and resources that support them when they get stuck.

We strongly recommend building into your induction programme an assessment of learners' mindsets. Carol Dweck's website (www.mindset online.com) contains more information on her research as well as a mindset questionnaire to download. The wording of the questions can be adapted to make it age appropriate. Share the results openly with the whole class. Knowing we have a problem, in this case a fixed mind-set, is the first step to overcoming it! This applies just as much to teachers as to learners.

PRE-ASSESSING FOR RESILIENCE AND AUTONOMY

One primary teacher we worked with sets his class a pre-assessment task during one of his carefully designed induction lessons. The challenge is related to literacy and involves learners working in small groups. Each group has a range of resources, including a laptop, a dictionary, and a thesaurus. Their task is to produce a five-minute presentation based on a particular writer. While the learners are working on the task, which takes around 40 minutes, the teacher and his teaching assistant circulate around the class. They observe each group in turn, making notes on how effectively each group is collaborating, which learners are not contributing, and which ones are dominating. They also note how successfully the learners are using the resources to support their learning. This activity, together with the subsequent presentations, provides the teacher with valuable feedback on the gaps that currently exist within the class; gaps which, if left unaddressed, will prevent the class from working consistently towards Level 1a. Based on the feedback from this activity, the teacher then tailors the remaining induction lessons to start the process of closing these gaps.

A science teacher we worked with was trying to understand why his class were so needy. 'Why are they always asking me for definitions or for page numbers to find the examples they need?' It was only when, one October morning, he pressed his own pause button and talked to his class about this problem that he discovered they didn't have a clue about how to use a textbook's index to find information. This effectively meant that he had over £500 worth of expensive resource books lying redundant on his learners' desks while they repeatedly quizzed him for information which, with a little training, they could find perfectly easily for themselves. Had this teacher undertaken effective pre-assessment at the start of September, he would have identified this gap earlier and saved himself a lot of grief.

What skills and habits do your learners need if they are to work effectively at Level 1a?

What pre-assessment activities could you design to discover whether or not your learners have these skills and habits already?

PRE-ASSESSING WHAT ENGAGES LEARNERS: ASK THEM!

Teaching backwards involves learners being challenged to work at ever higher levels of competence. And to reach higher levels of competence requires hours of practice. Think how many hours are required for a learner to build his writing skills from the time he first starts to form letters in a reception class to being able to write an A-grade essay at A level.

In order to encourage learners to embrace challenge, and the many hours of practice needed to achieve mastery, engagement is key. Teachers who design learning that engages and motivates learners find that their learners are more willing to tackle complexity and put in the necessary effort.

How can we motivate our learners if we haven't taken the time to find out what it is that really engages them? After observing a French lesson in which the learners were utterly disengaged, we challenged the teacher to think about what had happened. As she reflected on her work, we asked why had her learners been so unresponsive, so utterly bored? Had the content and design of her lesson connected to their lives? She was forced to admit that she had no idea what her learners were interested in outside school, she didn't know what their hopes and aspirations were, and she knew nothing about their families. She said, 'I haven't got the foggiest about what their interests and hobbies are, or what gets them excited.' Our advice to her was the same punchy one-liner as the old Ask Jeeves search engine: 'Just ask!' Even better, design a pre-assessment activity and get your learners to complete it.

Steve Willshaw, creator of the Rooted in Reading project, knows a thing or two about getting his learners engaged and motivated to read. He pre-assesses his learners so he can connect them to the types of books that will excite and engage them. He knows very well that getting learners of all ages to develop a love for, and proficiency in, reading is essential for their social and intellectual development. And he knows this will occur more quickly when readers get deeply immersed in a good book that aligns with their interests and values – in other words, when they are in flow.

Steve brought to our attention a research paper by Jeff McQuillan and Gisela Conde written in 1996 which argued that four key factors need to be met for a reader to get into flow:[1]

1   The reader needs to have some prior knowledge of the subject area covered in the book.

2   The reader wants to find out more about the subject area that the book relates to.

3   The reader is interested in the subject area that the book relates to.

4   The book provides information about something the reader would like to achieve.

With these factors in mind, Steve created an excellent pre-assessment tool that can be adapted for different age groups so that the teacher can connect the right books to the right learners and get them into 'flowful' reading.[2]

THE ROOTED IN READING GUIDE TO CHOOSING A BOOK YOU WILL ENJOY		
Name:	Teacher:	Date:
Step 1		
What are you interested in? In the box on the right, list all your hobbies, interests and issues that you find engaging. This could include authors you enjoy reading.		
Step 2		
What do you know about? In the box on the right, list all subjects that you know something about. This could include authors you have read before.		

1   Jeff McQuillan and Gisela Conde, 'The Conditions of Flow in Reading: Two Studies of Optimal Experience', *Reading Psychology: An International Quarterly* 17 (1996): 109–135.

2   Steve Willshaw, 'Flow and Reading for Pleasure', *Steve Willshaw* (31 May 2013). Available at: https://stevewillshaw.wordpress.com/tag/rooted-in-reading/.

Step 3	
What would you like to know about? In the box on the right, list all your subjects that you are interested in knowing more about.	
Step 4	
What would you like to achieve? In the box on the right, list all the things you would like to do, know more about or think would be useful to you.	
Recommendations: Read the answers above very carefully and suggest below any books that you think the person might enjoy reading.	

Malcolm Gladwell's *Outliers* emphasises the importance that deliberate practice plays in achieving success. Indeed, it is the hours of deliberate practice that a person puts in that are more important to their eventual success than any innate talent they might have. We believe this is crucial learning for teachers. Knowing what engages their learners will enable teachers to plan lessons that make deliberate practice more engaging for them.

Gladwell's book came to mind as we sat in on a highly engaging maths lesson where the class were learning about the mean, mode, median, and range. The teacher had used her pre-assessment of their interests to plan the lesson. She had found out that many of the class, all boys, were obsessed by fast cars. Therefore, she used data about the relative performance of different cars for the class to work with. The teacher reflected afterwards that since she'd started pre-assessing what engaged her learners their progress had accelerated. Why? Because they were much more engaged in lessons.

As well as inductions, there are other sources of information that can significantly help us to pre-assess learners' starting points.

PARENTS

Parents are a great resource. Take whatever opportunities you can to get parents onside. Not only can they be a pillar of support but, particularly with younger learners, they can be a rich source of information on their child's background and interests, as well as on what motivates them. Inductions, parents' evenings, and home visits all allow you to build better relationships with parents.

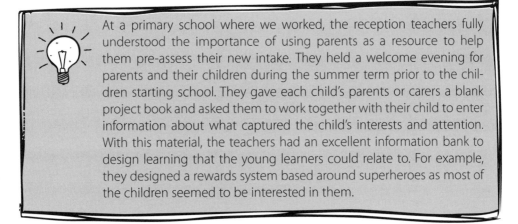

At a primary school where we worked, the reception teachers fully understood the importance of using parents as a resource to help them pre-assess their new intake. They held a welcome evening for parents and their children during the summer term prior to the children starting school. They gave each child's parents or carers a blank project book and asked them to work together with their child to enter information about what captured the child's interests and attention. With this material, the teachers had an excellent information bank to design learning that the young learners could relate to. For example, they designed a rewards system based around superheroes as most of the children seemed to be interested in them.

PREVIOUS TEACHER(S)

Any teacher that is worth her salt who has spent a whole year with a class of learners should have a pretty good idea of how each one is performing. She should have a good awareness of their preferred ways of learning, their strengths and current limitations, and what gaps need to be closed if the class are to move to Level 1a.

These previous teachers are a great resource, so it makes sense to spend some time talking to them before you take over their old class. There's likely to be a lot of questions you could usefully ask them, such as:

■ How mature are they in giving and receiving feedback?

■ How good are their group working skills?

■ Do they all take an active role in class discussions?

- How good are their listening skills? Do they listen to their peers as readily as to the teacher?

- What is the quality of their presentations like?

- How willing are they to offer answers in lessons, even when they are unsure if they are correct?

- Which of the learners gives up easily when faced with a challenge?

TAKING A LOOK AT THE PREVIOUS YEAR'S EXERCISE BOOKS

The focus of inspections has evolved so that the quality of teaching in schools is now judged over time rather than in 30-minute classroom observations. For this reason, it's important that teachers maximise whatever resources are available to monitor learner progress. These may include conversations with the learners, evidence from their books past and present, and other forms of data on their progress over time.

A great deal can be learned about learners' knowledge, attitudes, skills, and habits by looking over their books. When pre-assessing a new class, taking time to seek out their previous teacher and look at their past work can be really informative.

Even a quick five-minute skim through each learner's books can help a teacher to access vitally important information, such as:

- How much pride do they take in their work, and what is the level of quality in their presentation of it?

- How open or not are they to feedback? Do they respond to feedback from their peers and teacher in their next piece of work, or do they ignore it?

- What is their usual effort level, their norm for 'hard work'?

- How effective are they at communicating and putting across clear ideas and arguments? In other words, which elements of Level 1a KASH are already there and which need to be levelled up?

Skimming through previous work provides information about each learner's ability to describe, explain, and build a logical argument, as well as his or her ability to use subject-specific terminology appropriately. This kind of detailed and specific information tends to be much more useful than an overarching level or test score.

A little time taken with books will provide a valuable list of the learners' existing gaps. It will also challenge any assumptions a teacher might have about the starting points of their new learners.

Why not ask learners to give you their exercise books from their previous class? One secondary school did this with their new intake. It really helped the Year 7 teachers to build up a better picture about the starting points of their new arrivals.

How do you induct new classes?

Does your induction programme provide sufficient information to accurately pre-assess the KASH of the learners?

How could it be adapted to provide you with better feedback?

FAQS

Won't pre-assessment take too much time?

Many hard-pressed teachers have had eureka moments once they've understood or experienced the impact of quality pre-assessment. They see that the time and effort saved significantly outweighs the time and effort expended.

Does this mean I have to change what I teach?

As with most answers to complex questions the answer is, it depends. Surely our role as teachers is to teach what learners don't yet know or understand, not just to deliver information to them indiscriminately. If we fail to pre-assess accurately, we may well end up wasting time and losing the engagement and motivation of our classes.

Wouldn't this be easier if we developed a whole-school or departmental approach to pre-assessment?

Yes, it would, but why wait for this to happen? Revolutions start one person at a time. And what better way to convince your colleagues that collaboration and the sharing of teacher techniques, skills, and resources is a great idea than to let them see for themselves how your effective pre-assessment pays dividends through the motivation and progress of your learners and the results you and they get? Having discovered the merits and advantages of pre-assessment, and collated clear evidence of its impact, one teacher we know persuaded the rest of his team to change to a pre-assessment approach too. They now derive significant value from pre-assessment and also find that this more collaborative approach has given new energy and identity to the department.

IN A NUTSHELL

Pre-assessment is one of the most valuable tools in the outstanding teacher's toolkit. It saves you time and energy by helping you to discover where your learners currently are and what has to be done to get them to the desired destination. Ideally, this will be the KASH criteria of Level 1a. Accurate pre-assessment shows you that you don't need to train your learners in all aspects of the criteria. It gives you quality feedback on what they currently can and can't do. This is the beauty of teaching backwards: if you've accurately pre-assessed their starting points and developed a plan to close the gaps, you won't need to waste time developing elements of KASH they already have.

Knowing the starting points of your class is one of the first steps in teaching backwards. Only when the starting points are accurately known can you map out a course to close whatever gaps exist between them and the final destination for which you and they are aiming. Defining and demystifying that destination is the topic of our next chapter.

TEACHING BACKWARDS CHECKLIST

Starting points (micro – module of learning)	This is always part of my practice	I sometimes do this	I never do this
I design pre-assessment activities that 'test' all knowledge and skills that learners will need for the forthcoming module of learning.			
I understand and use all available data about learners to help me understand their starting points.			
My pre-assessment does not solely rely on assessment data.			
I pre-assess learners' starting points before every new module of learning.			
The pre-assessment activity is designed to identify any misconceptions the learners may have.			
I pre-assess learners so that I have sufficient time (e.g. a week) to use the information to adapt my planning.			

Starting points (micro – module of learning)	This is always part of my practice	I sometimes do this	I never do this
My planning is informed by the results of the pre-assessment.			
The results of the pre-assessment activity are revisited later in the module to enable reflection on progress.			

Starting points (macro – course/academic year)	This is always part of my practice	I sometimes do this	I never do this
I design pre-assessment activities that 'test' all aspects of the KASH that learners will need to work consistently at or towards Level 1a.			
I use, where possible, the following to pre-assess learners' KASH: ■ Feedback from previous teacher. ■ Feedback from parents. ■ Feedback from learners' books. ■ Feedback from learners themselves.			
I use an induction programme to help me to pre-assess the KASH of my learners.			

Starting points (macro – course/academic year)	This is always part of my practice	I sometimes do this	I never do this
My long-term plan to build Level 1a KASH with my class(es) is informed by the results of the pre-assessment.			
The results of the pre-assessment at the start of the school year are revisited later in the module to enable reflection on progress.			

Download this checklist from:

http://osiriseducational.co.uk/TB/resources/

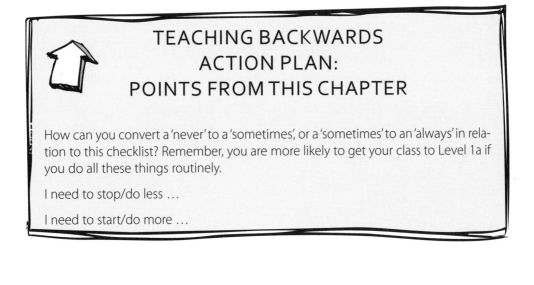

TEACHING BACKWARDS ACTION PLAN: POINTS FROM THIS CHAPTER

How can you convert a 'never' to a 'sometimes', or a 'sometimes' to an 'always' in relation to this checklist? Remember, you are more likely to get your class to Level 1a if you do all these things routinely.

I need to stop/do less …

I need to start/do more …

FOR MORE INFORMATION ...

The importance of pre-assessment and formative assessment:

http://totallytremendousteachers.wikispaces.com/The+Importance+of+Pre-Assessment+and+Formative+Assessment/

Rooted in Reading:

http://www.nate.org.uk/index.php?page=11&cat=30/

Reading for pleasure:

https://stevewillshaw.wordpress.com/tag/rooted-in-reading/

Defining
and
Demystifying
the
Destination

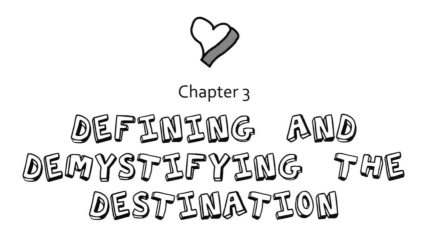

Chapter 3

DEFINING AND DEMYSTIFYING THE DESTINATION

'I need to be more *Blue Peter* and less *Scooby-Doo*!'

Media studies teacher Emma Cairns describes a game-changing shift in her thinking about the way she should teach. It occurred as a result of watching a video of herself during one of our Outstanding Teaching Interventions. 'I need to be more *Blue Peter* and less *Scooby-Doo*!,' she joked.

Let us explain. *Blue Peter* was a children's television programme which included a weekly feature where one of the presenters made something and encouraged the young viewers at home to make it too. Just as the children started to make an Easter hat, a jewellery box, or Tracy Island from *Thunderbirds*, the presenter would without fail bring out an example of the finished article with the words, 'Here's one I prepared earlier!' The viewers got to see what the finished article should look like. This gave them both a standard to aspire to and a clearer sense of direction. *Scooby-Doo* was another children's programme of the time. Each episode usually concluded with the 'big reveal'. This almost always involved a monster or ghost being unmasked. The crook would then bring the show to a close with a line like, 'Drat! I'd have got away with it if it hadn't been for you meddling kids!'

Teachers who follow the *Blue Peter* model show learners excellent examples of what they are looking for from the very beginning of the learning process. They then help learners to break down the process into small and manageable steps. On the other hand, *Scooby-Doo* teachers leave their learners floundering, trying to solve the mystery of how great work is constructed and wondering by what criteria their work will be assessed.

Having transformed from a *Scooby-Doo* teacher into a *Blue Peter* teacher, Emma now behaves very differently and so do her learners. In the past, she would deliver lots of information to her learners in what she thought was a clear way. She would gradually give them what she judged was the right amount of information for each topic before introducing them to questions.

These days it's different. Whenever Emma introduces a new topic, she gets the learners to take a careful look at different examples of work right from the outset. She makes sure that they're all very clear about the qualities required to achieve different standards of work and what they need to do to produce work of that standard. Up front, she spends a lot more time demystifying each learner's destination, and the journey they'll need to take to get there. As a result her classes are transformed. Learners are much clearer and much more confident than they used to be. They are more certain about the gaps that they have in their knowledge or skills. They now have more focused conversations with others about how they can close these gaps. Emma recognises that it was her shift towards being a *Blue Peter* teacher that really improved her own clarity, enabling her, in turn, to develop the clarity of her learners.

WHAT'S IN THIS CHAPTER FOR ME?

■ How much thought do you generally give to the relationship between lack of learner motivation and their lack of clarity and direction?

■ Have you ever wanted your learners to be more effective in managing their own learning and clearer about what they need to do to close their gaps?

■ Has your teaching ever been criticised for lacking differentiation? Would it be useful to gain some powerful techniques to address this?

■ Have you ever wondered how you could get your learners to be more focused on their learning journey and on their learning destination?

WHAT'S THE THINKING BEHIND THIS CHAPTER?

Blue Peter teachers truly teach backwards because they start from an excellent model of what is to be achieved and have analysed the key steps, behaviours, and qualities that the learners will need to get there. They start with the end in mind. On the other hand, *Scooby-Doo* teachers leave their learners in the dark, with little or no idea about what is expected of them or what they are trying to achieve. This is a common feature of teachers who teach forwards from content or activities. Now don't get us wrong. We're big fans of the importance of mystery and curiosity in the learning process. But when it comes to helping learners to assess themselves and understand how to move themselves forward, it's essential that they know what success looks like. How to achieve success should be clear from the outset. It shouldn't be like trying to solve a *Scooby-Doo* mystery.

Whether we realise it or not, we all have blind spots when it comes to teaching. Some of these blind spots we've already covered, such as wrongly assuming that our own expectations are the same as those of our learners or making false assumptions about the starting points of our learners. In this chapter we want to pay attention to the blind spots some teachers have around the issue of clarity. Are they really as clear as they think they are? Are they more *Scooby-Doo* or more *Blue Peter*? How can they avoid *Scooby-Doo* habits and behaviours? As for the learners, do they really know what they are required to do? Are they clear about the steps needed to get there?

We'll consider why clarity is so vital, and how teachers can develop greater understanding about what clear and motivating destinations might look, sound, and feel like for each learner based on their personal starting points. If all learners are going to make progress through your teaching, then they'll need to be given destinations based on their starting points. Sometimes a single destination is appropriate, sometimes not. We'll show you that when teachers have real lucidity about the destination(s) both for themselves and for their learners, they're on the road to being much more effective.

To guide you, we'll share some of the most effective tools and strategies used by teachers we've worked with to ensure that learners achieve this clarity. We'll also explain how this process can help you to cater for all your learners and how it can be built into planning highly engaging modules of learning.

THE IMPORTANCE OF CLARITY

We will start by exploring why clear destinations are so critically important for teachers and learners in terms of autonomy, motivation, and progress.

BUILDING LEARNER AUTONOMY

When teachers create real clarity for their learners around what success looks like, learner autonomy improves dramatically. Emma, and many other teachers like her, now ensure that their learners know where they're going and know what they have to do to get there. As it says in the Level 1a descriptor, 'Learners have clarity on their current position and the quality of KASH the need to develop further in order to achieve their goal. As learners develop greater clarity about the journey ahead, their grades tend to improve rapidly, and they become less and less likely to keep pestering their teacher with questions for clarification. This enables the teacher to spend less time teaching the class as a whole and more time teaching individuals or groups, thereby addressing specific rather than general learning needs. Many teachers who have been through our Outstanding Teaching Intervention are finding that they now have more time for working with small groups and individuals due to the increased autonomy of their classes.

Autonomous learners can lead themselves to success. They waste less time wondering whether what they're doing is actually helping them to make progress, and invest more time in getting on with the things that really advance them to where they want and need to be, such as planning next steps, redrafting their work, and incorporating feedback. We can't get to Level 1a without clarity. In *Leaders of Their Own Learning*, authors Ron Berger, Leah Rugen, and Libby Woodfin assert that teachers need to know exactly where they and the class are headed. Unless this is the case, they 'cannot effectively involve learners in the assessment process or coherently track learner progress themselves if they haven't established clear learning targets before instruction begins'.[1] When learners are certain about what they have to do, and the steps that are necessary to get there, the quality of classroom conversation tends to increase markedly. Questions such as, 'What do I need to do now?' and 'Is this right? I'm not sure …' get replaced with, 'I'm pretty sure I've got that bit right, but do I need to …?' When learners have clarity they can plan better, ask themselves and others better questions, and give more accurate feedback to themselves and others too.

MOTIVATING LEARNERS

Many teachers face learners who lack motivation and this can be a major source of pain for both parties. There are all sorts of reasons for motivational deficits in learners. We touched on many of these in our book, *Engaging Learners*, and offered various strategies to address them. Time and again, the research shows that motivation plummets when learners are in the dark about what they need to do. The feeling of incompetency can really affect their motivation. On the other hand, when this situation is reversed and learners are shown how to develop and build a felt sense of skill and achievement by working step by step towards clear and relevant goals, they can become very focused indeed. In his book, *Flow*, Mihaly Csikszentmihalyi describes flow as an activity that completely absorbs a person. However, if the challenge seems too high, learners will often feel threatened and withdraw from the task. Sometimes this task is well within the learner's ability to achieve. The important point is that the learner doesn't think it is.

---

1   Ron Berger, Leah Rugen and Libby Woodfin, *Leaders of Their Own Learning: Transforming Schools Through Student-Engaged Assessment* (San Francisco, CA: Jossey-Bass, 2014), p. 334.

In his book, *Visible Learning for Teachers*, John Hattie shows that the biggest determinant of learner success at school is their own expectation of success.[2] Most learners naturally feel insecure about their current levels of knowledge or skill, and this is significantly compounded when they are unsure about what they have to do. Feelings of incompetence can soon swamp them and lower their expectations. However, when learners are clear about the journey, and clear about the key steps they need to take, and get constructive feedback from their teacher and peers throughout that journey, they will be much less likely to give up. They will remain resilient and stay in flow.

We chose the *Blue Peter* versus *Scooby-Doo* anecdote because it helped Emma to realise that she was making too many assumptions about her learners' mind-reading skills (Surely they think the same as me? Surely this is obvious?) and she was unaware of this blind spot in her own teaching. She discovered it was not at all obvious to her learners. As a result, they were getting increasingly demotivated and she was finding it harder and harder to teach them.

Poor motivation is a serious issue in schools and one that we're passionate about addressing. Our experience of working with black belt teachers around the country has shown us that they use great strategies to support their learners to achieve clarity. We've seen teachers rapidly become successful at showing each learner their destination, getting them to turn that into a personal goal, and then helping them to feel competent. The learners achieve this sense of competence because they see the value of the destination and feel confident that they can successfully manage the doable steps needed to get them there. Flow once again becomes possible. Poor motivation is replaced by high motivation as learners begin to connect with a growing sense of mastery.

CLARITY MEANS PROGRESS!

It's no accident that teachers who provide the greatest clarity about destinations get better results. The clarity that they hold about learners' destinations, and ways of getting them there, allows these teachers to instruct learners better and provide them with appropriate examples to aspire to and model. It also enables them to quickly adjust their teaching to get learners back on track if challenges arise. We've worked with many teachers, in both primary and secondary settings, who have an excellent track record of getting great results year after year.

One of the key features of their success is the clarity that they have built up over their teaching career. They know what they're looking for from their learners, not just at the end of a topic but throughout. They've become black belts at demystifying success.

---

2   Hattie, *Visible Learning for Teachers*, pp. 53–54.

First, they've learned this for themselves, and then they're able to transfer this clarity to their learners.

In his book, *Embedded Formative Assessment,* Dylan Wiliam quotes a number of research studies which demonstrate that learners make more progress when they have a clear 'understanding [of] what they are meant to be doing'.[3] These studies show how important it is for teachers to be consciously deliberate about where they want their learners to go. The findings also suggest that teachers would do well to develop greater empathy towards their learners as they struggle to make sense of the journey ahead – a point we'll take up later in the chapter.

THE CLARITY GRAPH

There is no question that clarity of destination, and the steps to get to that destination, are essential for achieving great results. But let's now consider where each of us might be clarity-wise. Consider the graph below.

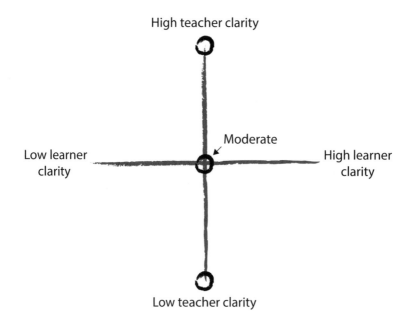

3   Dylan Wiliam, *Embedded Formative Assessment* (Bloomington, IN: Solution Tree Press, 2011), p. 52.

On the vertical axis we have teacher clarity and on the horizontal is learner clarity. Each axis goes from low to high. We'll consider learner clarity later on, but let's start by addressing the issue of teacher clarity.

WHERE ARE YOU ON THE TEACHER CLARITY AXIS?

The three circles on the teacher axis distinguish between different levels of teacher clarity: low, moderate, and high. Where do you think you are? How do you know? To help you to consider these questions let's start at the bottom of the axis and work up.

LOW TEACHER CLARITY

Let's face it, we've all been here as teachers at one time or another. For example, we might have found ourselves here when we were trainee teachers. We were both given A level classes right at the beginning of our careers; sure, we had degrees in the subject but we were complete novices about how we would go about assessing our learners. Our clarity about the *content* of the subject was strong but our clarity about the *process* of training and nurturing our learners was weak. At that time, we were both aware of a little voice in our heads saying: 'I'm low and I know.' When starting out in the profession, when teaching a topic you've never encountered before, or experimenting with any new strategy or technique, a teacher is likely to be at this point. If you are unaware of this, it's a problem. If you are aware, you're ready to take the first steps to learn and change.

MODERATE TEACHER CLARITY

Let's define moderate as less than perfect. Most teachers move up the teacher clarity axis as they progress through their career. However, some teachers never get all the way to the top of the axis. They never become expert at establishing clear destinations and mapping out manageable steps to help their learners get there. Even worse, many teachers are blissfully unaware of this. They think they're a lot clearer than they really are! There are many reasons why this might be. We simply call them blind spots. The severity and number of our blind spots determine how low we might be on the teacher clarity axis. Here are three of the main ones that we frequently encounter.

1. THE CURSE OF THE EXPERT

Nobody sets out to be a *Scooby-Doo* teacher, but sometimes our expertise blinds us to the barriers that learners might face when trying to learn something new. Some teachers know their stuff like they know the back of their hand. They've taught it so often that they think it's simple. They've forgotten that once, many years ago, even for them, it was difficult. The danger for these teachers is that their expertise in delivering content leads them to teach forwards. Teaching backwards requires more empathy with the learners. Ian Macleod was Andy's first head of department and a major influence on him. Ian's mantra was, 'If the teacher finds it easy, imagine that the learner finds it hard; if the teacher finds it difficult, imagine that the learner finds it impossible.' We continue to see this as good advice. Teachers who consistently get their classes to Level 1a don't just know their subject well; they find out their learners' starting points and lay out clear pathways for them. What is sometimes referred to as 'the curse of the expert' happens to many teachers. They've forgotten what it was like to struggle to understand and they fail to see the myriad ways that learners might find learning something difficult.

2. NOT FULLY UNDERSTANDING ASSESSMENT LEVELS

Some teachers are not clear about assessing the level or the quality of learners' work. They might not fully appreciate exactly what is required for a piece of work to be measured or judged at a particular level, or understand the critical differences between one level and another. Such lack of clarity makes it hard to give learners useful feedback.

This example highlights how a teacher discovered a blind spot that had spread through the whole of her department. A head of English we worked with told us that she'd had a startling realisation. She had discovered that not all the teachers in her department really understood what an A* grade essay looked like. This wake-up moment had prompted her to arrange some extra moderation meetings. She paired up those teachers who had strong models of A and A* quality work with those of her staff who were less confident. This collaboration and sharing of expertise and insights enabled the whole department to move forward and to become more confident as a team.

It also helped them to create consistent guidelines for their learners to more easily understand exactly what was required for them to progress through the different grade boundaries. Learners rely on their teachers to give them clarity about their destinations and the steps each of them needs to take to get there. When she realised that some of her department had blind spots around assessment levels she was able to do something about it.

This example of lack of clarity around assessment criteria showed that some of the teachers in the department weren't as effective as others. By helping them all to achieve real discrimination in assessment clarity, the head of department was able to close her teachers' gaps. But she also realised that by itself this wasn't enough. She realised that they also had to develop greater awareness about the different destinations of each learner, and have different strategies to help them get there. She saw that unless teacher clarity was high, they wouldn't be able to transfer this clarity to all of their learners. By discovering and then addressing this, her teachers are now able to offer their learners higher quality teaching. Each teacher in the department is furnished with appropriate models for the different levels, they have a shared understanding of the ingredients necessary to achieve each level, and they have more confidence about how to help their learners master each level.

We've also worked with some phase leaders in primary schools who realise that time needs to be spent ensuring that all teachers have strong clarity on assessment levels. Many schools have started to realise that showing learners examples of great work is an essential precursor to success.

3. LACK OF AWARENESS OF ONE'S OWN LACK OF CLARITY

Another potential blind spot is the assumption that learners understand what you want from them. Do they really get everything about where you want them to go and how you want them to get there? Some teachers don't realise that their clarity can be improved. In our one hundred miles an hour education system it can be hard to find opportunities to observe other colleagues teaching, let alone plan lessons with them or critique each other on a regular basis. But it is something that we have both made time for throughout our careers.

We've had the privilege of working directly with hundreds of teachers. This has enabled us to build up a lot of understanding around the KASH of different teachers. Often, we find that within the same school, even along the same corridor, there will be huge differences in the levels of teacher clarity. In one classroom, we'll find a teacher who has created a classroom full of learners who know where they're going, understand the steps they need to get there, and have the motivation to take those steps. Next door, however, the situation is markedly different. The learners are making some progress but, due to the teacher's lack of clarity, they're getting there more slowly, with less sense of direction, and far less motivation.

There are two main reasons why some teachers fail to realise the link between clarity and progress. The first is because they've never had the chance to observe the work of more effective teachers – teachers who create clearly signposted pathways and compelling destinations. The second reason is more alarming. These are teachers who tend to blame the learners for their lack of progress, which is a tendency that effectively prevents them from taking a long hard look at themselves.

If some teachers can make faster progress with similar learners then much of this is due to the way they set out the destinations and pathways for their learners. If you're one of these teachers already, you'll know how important it is not to get complacent. It's crucial that we continue to work on our clarity throughout our career. As we'll see later in this chapter, one of the best ways of getting feedback about our clarity can take some courage: asking our learners directly. Seeking evidence from our students about how clear we are is much more effective than simply assuming that we're good enough.

Achieving the high clarity associated with outstanding Level 1a is what this chapter is all about. A variety of tools, techniques, and strategies that will help you to work towards this level follow the next short section on learner clarity.

WHERE ARE YOUR LEARNERS ON THE CLARITY AXIS?

Just as with the teacher's clarity axis, there are also three circles on the learner's axis: low, moderate, and high. Where do you think your learners are? How do you know? This time we'll start at the top of the axis and work down.

On rare occasions, a learner's clarity may be higher than that of the teacher. We've certainly come across learners who would have done well despite having us as teachers! Learners might already be pretty accomplished at a certain task or challenge because they have encountered it before or have a particular talent or obsession. For example, a teacher of French may have a learner who has a French parent. A science teacher may be teaching a learner whose parent works on the Large Hadron Collider and regales them every weekend with the science behind it rather than telling them bedtime stories. A sports teacher might have an Olympic level gymnast in his or her class who is currently being coached by an Olympic gold medallist. It may also be that a learner has a specific passion for a subject or has made an early choice about a particular pathway that they want to take in life.

These examples aside, the only other way that learners are going to achieve high clarity in terms of their destination, and the pathways that will get them there, is going to come from their teacher. The most effective teachers build this lucidity into everything they do. They recognise that it is their responsibility.

By this same logic, the reasons for moderate and low learner clarity are down to the teacher too. Awareness and self-honesty are essential here. If we see that learner clarity is low, we can take steps to address this by changing how we plan and teach. The biggest problem is when teachers either don't know or wrongly assume that their learners' clarity is better than it really is.

In the following section, we'll explore how we can develop both teacher and learner clarity. Before we set out some strategies to improve teacher clarity, here's an analogy. When travelling by air, parents are always advised to put their own oxygen mask on first should there be a problem with cabin pressure. In the same way, teachers need to sort out their own clarity before they can improve that of their learners.

DEVELOPING GREATER TEACHER CLARITY

Here you will find five tried and trusted techniques that have helped teachers to level up their clarity. These strategies are particularly useful when identifying destinations and in anticipating any obstacles that might prevent learners from achieving them. They are:

1   Being a model collector

2   Becoming a curator of models

3   Conducting pre-mortems

4   Becoming a black belt assessor

5   Searching out your blind spots

Let's explore these ideas one by one.

1. BEING A MODEL COLLECTOR

When teachers build up an extensive collection of exemplars, it helps them to better understand the ingredients required for achieving different levels of work. Not all the models have to show what is excellent – they can show work of differing quality. You can even have bad models in your portfolio. They key is that the teacher understands whether this particular piece of work is great, good, mediocre, or awful.

The models may be created by you or by other teachers. You can collect models from the professional world, from exam boards, from experts in the field, from current learners, past learners, or learners from other schools or colleges, some of whom could be on the other side of the world. The models can be in many different formats ranging from physical examples, such as written work or pieces of art, *YouTube* clips of presentations, or podcast demonstrations (e.g. for a PE class). Having models at your disposal can help other teachers, as well as your learners, to appreciate the criteria required to achieve a specific standard of work.

When we use the word 'model' in this context, what we're talking about is an example (what you want to see) or a non-example (what you don't want to see). These models might be of a final product or of a particular process of learning, or they might incorporate both.

We'll see later in the chapter how teachers can teach backwards from models by deconstructing them with their learners. Having done this, it's relatively straightforward to develop clarity of destination and the steps required to get there. This is impossible if the teacher doesn't have any models to show! We recommend that you find or create many different models of work throughout your teaching career.

> What models do you have already?
>
> Where can you gather models for an upcoming topic?

2. BECOMING A CURATOR OF MODELS

Collecting models is one thing, but teachers need to be able to accurately articulate the quality of each piece of work based on clear criteria. When teachers understand these models they get much better at understanding the ingredients needed to achieve different standards of work, and they can learn to judge quality quicker and communicate what is required for improvement to a higher standard.

So, it's not just about having a collection of models. It's about using them to deepen clarity about quality components within them and quality differences between them. Like a good museum curator, when a teacher can eloquently and accurately explain to others the innate qualities or faults of a piece of work, it's a sure sign that they have clarity.

Teachers often develop a deeper understanding of quality through discussion with colleagues. These discussions tend to be much richer if (a) some of the colleagues present have recognised skills in judging the quality of specific pieces of work (so it's not a case of the blind leading the blind), and (b) you are looking at actual models of work as you are holding these conversations. What's especially instructive here is to take an observer stance and watch the way that colleagues with greater clarity quickly highlight or annotate those models. This process is sometimes referred to as moderation, and it can be an enlightening experience.

If you're in a position to lead or train other teachers we suggest that you set aside time to explore different models of work. This will help the groups you work with to acquire a deeper collective understanding of what makes some pieces of work excellent and what deficiencies keep other examples at lower levels. If you are not in such a position, ask your head of department if you can spend some time with colleagues who have built up good techniques for demystifying success criteria and communicating these to their learners.

Are you confident about the ingredients required to attain the different standards, grades, or levels of achievement? Are you clear about the differences between them?

How could discussing these models with colleagues enable you to develop a better understanding about these differences?

3. CONDUCTING PRE-MORTEMS

There are occasions when it's prudent for the teacher to do in advance the work that their learners are going to be expected to do. By doing this, teachers can better appreciate the aspects of learning that the learners might find particularly troublesome. It also helps the teacher to carry out a 'pre-mortem'.

Whereas a post-mortem is conducted on a person after they die, a pre-mortem is conducted before a death takes place. In fact, pre-mortems are very useful in helping us to avoid a death. In this case, we're trying to avoid the death of learning – or the death of a teacher's self-esteem and enthusiasm! Pre-mortems help us to anticipate the things that might go wrong.

By doing a piece of work yourself, you might start to anticipate how some learners will fail. For example, by doing the mid-topic test before giving it to learners may enable you to appreciate the potential pitfalls of certain questions. This knowledge will help you to recognise where more clarity is needed.

Pre-mortems involve some DIY on the part of the teacher. A good pre-mortem entails speculating on what could possibly go wrong before it does! Here are some suggested pre-mortem questions to ask yourself:

- What will learners find the most difficult aspects of this topic?

- What might some learners find impossible?

- Which learners lack aspects of KASH that could hold them back?

- How can I address KASH gaps before and throughout the teaching of the topic?

- Has the pre-mortem, or any other pre-assessment, thrown up any issues where I might need to create extra resources to stretch learners or strategies to support them (e.g. step-by-step guides, writing frames, or additional one-to-one support)?

What pre-mortems do well is help teachers to teach backwards from a deeper understanding of the concepts that underpin the content of the upcoming topics or modules of learning. Taking the time to carry out pre-mortems, either on your own or even better with colleagues, can get you to stop and think about where you need more clarity and where your learners might need most help and support. When combined with sound pre-assessment strategies, pre-mortems will give you real insights into where your learners are likely to struggle.

When pre-mortems are done well, we guarantee that you will have fewer frustrating experiences, less confused work to mark, and fewer repeated lessons or revision sessions to run. If you're teaching an exam class, which would you prefer: a bit of extra work on pre-mortems, which will mean your learners are more likely to get it first time round, or an embarrassing post-mortem with your head teacher or line manager when the results of some of your learners fall below their targets?

How might conducting a pre-mortem enable you to better anticipate which learners might require more *assistance*? What do you anticipate they will find particularly hard to do?

How might a pre-mortem help you to create different *resources* to support learners in the upcoming topic?

How might the learning from a pre-mortem affect the tasks you set different learners?

4. BECOMING A BLACK BELT ASSESSOR

When teachers invest some time and energy into finding out how their learners will be assessed in the exam room, it usually pays off. There are various ways to do this. One approach is to think about teaching backwards from the 'exam-ready class'.

A history teacher we worked with told us: 'I used to be a 90:10 teacher; 90% content, 10% assessment technique. Now I'm a 70:30 teacher. My class go into the exam with greater confidence because I've taught them the KASH required to get high grades in the paper. I know and they know what the assessors are looking for.'

He came to this conclusion after doing some marking for the same examination board that his learners sat papers for. It wasn't just that he became more familiar with the way marks were allocated. As a result of marking scripts from other schools and colleges, he came to the realisation that he needed to change his focus more towards teaching backwards from exam success criteria.

There is only so much time that a teacher can spend with a class, and how we spend that time is crucial. It's also true that our time is limited when we want to develop our teaching skills outside the classroom. But when teachers do invest some of this time talking to those in the know about assessment it can really pay dividends. Why not find an opportunity to talk to experienced teachers with excellent track records and pick their brains? Some teachers we've worked with have qualified as markers for examination boards or have researched assessment documents and discussed them with colleagues. When teachers do one or more of these, they tend to move rapidly up the teacher clarity axis.

We observed a head of maths teaching in a school that has been recognised as outstanding by Ofsted on three separate occasions. She completely exemplified our point about understanding assessment criteria. She certainly knew what she was looking for from the learners and was very precise in her instructions. And as it happens, she is also a senior examiner for an exam board and uses this to help her department to have absolute clarity about what is necessary to get high grades. As a result, her department's grades are in the top 1% in the country. No one is overly concerned about her teaching style because the results that she and her colleagues get from their learners are so stunning.

> How close or how far away are you from being a black belt assessor?
>
> Who in your school/college, or in your wider network, could help you to get more clarity on how to assess particular topics or how topics are assessed?
>
> If you teach an exam class, could you become a marker for the exam board or connect with someone who is?

5. SEARCHING OUT YOUR BLIND SPOTS

The curse of the expert and a less than complete grasp of the necessary assessment criteria for each of the levels are just two areas where blind spots can occur. Having blind spots is nothing to be ashamed of – we've all got them! The important thing is to realise what our blind spots are, own them, and then work to remove them. That's a much healthier position than living in the illusion that we don't have any.

The first question we need to ask ourselves is, are our existing blind spots preventing us from effectively teaching all our learners? The next question is, what are we going to do about it? Through our Outstanding Teaching Intervention programmes, many teachers have realised that their teaching was not as clear or efficient as it could be. Other common blind spots that teachers have become aware of on our programmes, particularly through video analysis and book scrutiny, include:

- I thought I was good at giving explanations and instructions.

- I thought I was teaching all levels of learners equally well.

- I thought I understood what was required to get an A*.

- I thought I had better empathy with learners who struggle.

- I thought I was better at stretching the most able learners.

- I thought I was getting accurate feedback from the class.

Try videoing a few of your lessons. Many people resist change when they don't understand the need for it. When a person sees something that bothers them it can often spark questions which lead them to change their own KASH.

One teacher we worked with realised that he was doing everything far too fast. His instructions and explanations were delivered at machine gun speed, and his transitions between activities often meant that learners hadn't finished the task they were on before they were hurtled into the next one. Not surprisingly, his learners experienced significant amounts of frustration and even resentment at this lack of empathy for their learning needs. Once he became aware of his blind spot he started to deliberately slow down everything he did. He undertook some research and experimented with ideas such as Slow Writing and read the work of Robert Bjork[4] who, like us, advocates slowing down the learning process to enhance the transfer and retention of learning.

How can you become more aware of your own blind spots? Have you tried video analysis or comparing your learners' work with that of the students of your colleagues?

As you become more aware of your own KASH, how could you start to develop it? Can you create a development plan for yourself?

Put yourself in the shoes of (a) your head of department/phase leader and (b) your learners. From each of these two perspectives, identify five blind spots they might think you have.

4   Robert Bjork, 'Desirable Difficulties Perspective on Learning', in Harold Pashler (ed.), *Encyclopedia of the Mind* (Thousand Oaks, CA: Sage Reference, 2013). Available at: http://bjorklab.psych.ucla.edu/pubs/RBjork_inpress.pdf.

DEVELOPING LEARNER CLARITY

As important as it is to develop your clarity as a teacher, this won't be enough to guarantee that your class perform at Level 1a. The next step is to transfer your clarity to your learners. We've both worked with colleagues who have excellent subject knowledge, PhD level in some cases, but that's no guarantee that they can successfully demystify destinations and journeys for learners. Highly effective teaching is not just about having strong subject knowledge. It's also about how the teacher uses this knowledge to build their learners' clarity. Let's see how it's done and how you might improve your own ability to do this.

In this section we're going to share some of the best methods we've observed that outstanding teachers use to get real lucidity about journey and destination into the minds of their learners. Each of these techniques, used separately or together, will enable learners to move up the clarity axis. They fall into three categories:

1   Using models to demystify destinations and journeys.

2   Using models to co-create success criteria with learners.

3   Mastering the art of explanation.

Let's look at each of them in turn.

1. USING MODELS TO DEMYSTIFY DESTINATIONS AND JOURNEYS

In the previous section, we made the point that collecting models of differing quality aids teacher clarity. These same models can also help learners to understand and appreciate nuances of quality. With the right strategies we can help learners to realise why particular models are so good, so cool, so efficient, so effective, or so beautiful. After that, we'll want to get them to aspire to raising their own work to a similar standard. What follows are some of the most successful ways that we have found for doing this.

THE BLUE PETER TEACHER

When asking learners to do something well or to a high standard, it would clearly be a complete nonsense to show them bad examples to aspire to! When 'good' or 'quality' models of work are examined they can inspire learners. This is what educator Ron Berger calls 'tribute work'.[5] We want to pay tribute to the excellence or beauty of the model by imitating its qualities. Just as a picture of the finished dish in a recipe book can help us to see

---

5   Berger, *An Ethic of Excellence*, p. 85.

how our dinner should look, good models, good templates, good checklists, and good steps to success can really help learners to see which features of their work are on a par with the model and to recognise the current gaps in their work.

Remember, not all learners have the same destination. How can you provide different models for different learners?

How can you use these models as live *resources* throughout a topic?

IT'S GOOD TO IMITATE

Many teachers shy away from using models up front in the mistaken belief that this is encouraging learners to copy. We say that imitation or modelling is the first step towards mastery. In the arts, in science, in the world of sport, in business, and in many other areas of achievement, top performers frequently express their gratitude to others for the examples they've set and the pathways they've trodden. Musicians learn from the work other musicians, writers find their literary voice by first replicating the voice and style of other writers, business leaders emulate the insights of successful entrepreneurs, scientists build their ideas on those who have gone before them. As Isaac Newton wrote in a letter to Robert Hooke, 'If I have seen further it is by standing on the shoulders of giants' (a quote, incidentally, which he modelled from someone else, Bernard of Chartres!). We all imitate others and have done so from birth. It's a life skill. The easiest way to learn anything is to do it the way a 'master' does it. Once you've mastered the technique, you can find your own ways to improve on it and make it your own. Otherwise, you're trying to reinvent the wheel each time.

Modelling is often an unconscious process. We recommend that teachers encourage their learners to imitate and model consciously and more explicitly. The first step is for teachers to get their learners to learn more efficiently by being really clear themselves about what process(es) their learners should follow.

In a busy curriculum, it can save a lot of time if we get learners to copy established protocols for doing something in a particular way. The teacher demonstrates a process which he expects learners to imitate. The process that the teacher uses could be the safest, the most efficient, or simply the best. Sometimes referred to as 'steps to success', these processes save time and energy and encourage learners to imitate a model of mastery.

STEPS TO SUCCESS

Design technology teacher Paul Quinn knows it will save him time, and the class their fingers, if he clearly models how to work with dangerous tools before they get their chance. By watching him demonstrate, learners can see how it's done. Paul demonstrates first in real time and then shows the process again in slow motion, talking the learners through each step as he does so. As he models the process, the learners observe, listen carefully, and make notes. He then acts as a robot, inviting the learners to tell him what to do, step by step, so that he can successfully complete the work. However, as Paul responds *literally* to the instructions they give him, the learners usually have to improve the clarity of their instructions for the job to get done properly.

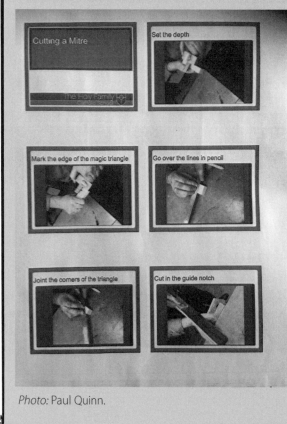

This stage of the lesson usually provokes a lot of laughter as they master the precision of the work. Once Paul is confident that his learners have got the stages and instructions clear in their minds, he gets them to use their mini-whiteboards to guide each other through the steps and safety tips. These will be on permanent display throughout the lesson. Only now does he get them started on the real work. As he walks around the room, closely observing their practice, he challenges any learner who seems to be in danger of straying from the prescribed process to explain what he is doing against the (by now) very well established success criteria.

Photo: Paul Quinn.

Daniella Sacco is a Year 1 teacher. When she teaches her class how to write she puts her steps to success on permanent display. As you can see from the image, the steps are: speak, listen, write on the line, use a capital letter, use a finger space, use a full stop, ask questions, and evaluate.

Since she started using these steps to success, and making them visible and transparent, she has found that her learners make much faster progress. They know exactly where they're going and what they need to do to get there.

Photo: Michelle Carter.

Tania Ackernley is also a primary teacher who teaches writing proficiency. She has her own versions of 'steps to success' on permanent display for whatever she is teaching. Since she started using them, and making them visible, she too has found that her learners are progressing much faster.

Photo: Tania Ackernley.

'I wish we'd had this before we started the work!' We overheard this muttered comment from a Year 6 boy to his pal while we were doing a teacher observation. It was prompted by their teacher explaining his assessment criteria for marking their work – work that he'd just handed back to them. After some conversations with, and feedback from, his class, this teacher now routinely shows his learners examples of quality work and clear assessment rubrics *before* he asks them to have their first go at it.

Art teacher Juliana Charltonova wants all of her learners to get A grades. She knows that if they are to achieve this then they need to demonstrate to the examiner that they are independent artists. Part of this process involves examining the work of some of her former learners. To help them find their independence, they first appraise examples of work from her most successful learners from previous years. She makes sure that students spend time unpicking why these portfolios of work received such high grades. She regularly uses them in her one-to-one discussions with learners so that they understand how their own portfolios rate, both in relation to the models and to the marking scheme. Then she gets learners to write down their targets so that they can close the gaps between their work and the models.

Why is this good? Top grade? Compare to yours and make notes.

Photo: Andy Griffith.

WAGOLLS

WAGOLL stands for What A Good One Looks Like. Teachers can explain the qualities of a particular WAGOLL and leave it on display. Learners can then refer to it whenever they wish while they create their own versions of the work in progress. The great thing about WAGOLLs is that they powerfully demonstrate the positive features of a piece of work. If that exemplar also happens to be the work of a classmate, it can also help learners to learn from each other. When a teacher carefully talks through the features of a WAGOLL, learners can better understand what level of work they should be aspiring to. WAGOLLs can help learners to visualise what needs to be done.

For example, a WAGOLL can be put into one circle of a Venn diagram. Learners then put their current attempt inside the other circle. In the space where the circles overlap each other they can enter any similarities between their own work and that of the model. Outside the circles they can write a list of things that their work is currently lacking.

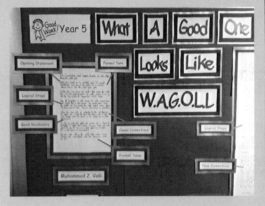

Source: Valley School, Bolton. *Photo:* Natalie Packer.

Starting a topic with a model of the end product gives learners the big picture right from the outset. It's not impossible to complete a 1,000 piece jigsaw puzzle without looking at the picture on the box, but it's a lot easier when you can see it. Knowing what the finished article should look like can make learning a whole lot easier and quicker. Often learners can't create work of a high standard because they can't visualise what excellence might look like. So, before you start teaching a topic, develop a clear idea about what you want to see at the end of it. What will the final product look like? And, during the journey, what will the intermediate stages look like? If you've never taught a topic before then, at the very least, try to find an excellent model or even create one yourself. Then teach backwards from it.

ANNOTATING A MODEL

Anne Riley is an English teacher of some renown – her results have been stunning for over 30 years. She routinely shows a high quality piece of work to her learners and says something along the lines of, 'The reason this piece of writing is beautiful is because … ', thus enabling her learners to appreciate the components, facets, qualities, and characteristics of the model before they undertake a first draft themselves. She also likes to get her learners to elicit these qualities for themselves. For example, Anne might use an example of excellent writing for learners to unpick. She hands out the model on A4 paper to learners working in pairs, and then gives them a piece of A3 or A2 paper to place underneath it. Their job is to annotate around the work and see if they can pick out the features of excellence. Once the learners start to run out of steam the teacher can add her own comments. Now the learners are ready to emulate the qualities identified in the writing with a real grasp of what is expected.

WORKING WALLS AND DISPLAYS

Walls and displays can help learners to demystify work of varying quality. In the example below, art teacher Rachael Eymond has identified

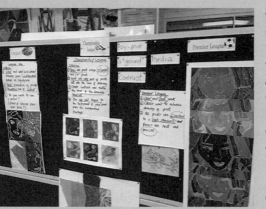

three different levels of work which she labels Premier League (the best), Championship, and League One. Her descriptions of the qualities of each piece of work enable learners to identify where the standard of their own work is in relation to the examples. In this way, learners can more easily see what they need to do to improve.

Photo: Mark Burns.

Not all learners can attain the highest grade. Nevertheless, you could provide *resources*, such as displays or WAGOLLs, which can help them to see the standard they are aiming at, its ingredients, and how it might differ from other pieces of work.

In another example, geography teacher Hannah Ahmet encourages learners to aspire towards quality by placing excellent work on display. The feedback and annotation she adds to the display explains clearly why each particular piece of work has been judged at this level.

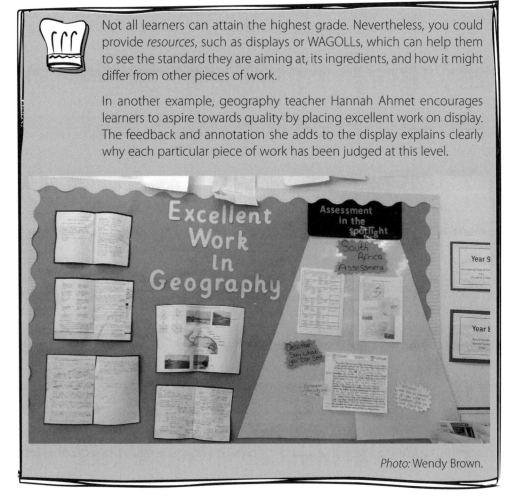

Photo: Wendy Brown.

How could you/do you show models of work to learners?

How do you draw out the best features of these models so that learners emulate them?

How could you be a more effective *Blue Peter* teacher?

How could you be more up front about what you are looking for in a piece of work?

2. USING MODELS TO CO-CREATE SUCCESS CRITERIA WITH LEARNERS

This section looks at ways the teacher can collaborate with learners to ensure that they better understand and appreciate success criteria, and the ingredients necessary to achieve them. This way of working requires the teacher to support and facilitate learners as they struggle to make sense of different levels and standards of work on their own, so that they can develop greater expertise at understanding quality around topics, products, and processes. Rather than the teacher immediately imposing his or her own standards, giving the learners a chance to work out quality and success criteria for themselves gives them a sense of ownership and opens their curiosity to listen to their teacher's perspective later on.

When working in this way, it's important to get the balance of the teaching style right. Your classroom should not be a dictatorship, but it's not a democracy either! It's good practice to encourage learners to struggle with notions of quality. Which is best? Why is it the best? What might make it even better? However, they should not get the final say as to what constitutes high quality until they become as expert as the teacher. Although we recommend that the teacher is the final arbiter of excellence, it's always a good idea for learners to openly discuss and wrestle with what they consider to be the positive or negative features of a piece of work. Working with models of different levels of quality is a particularly helpful method.

Here is a suggested structure for working in this way:

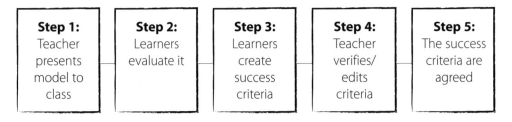

| **Step 1:** Teacher presents model to class | **Step 2:** Learners evaluate it | **Step 3:** Learners create success criteria | **Step 4:** Teacher verifies/ edits criteria | **Step 5:** The success criteria are agreed |

Let's look at some strategies you can use with your learners so that you can collaborate with them and get them to be more discriminating.

VISUAL ORGANISERS

We're great fans of using visual organisers to get learners to appreciate quality. Take a simple Venn diagram as an example. Learners can start to compare what aspects of their work is as good as the exemplar work and what it lacks. What we like about this technique is that it enables learners to realise that they have already made some progress in their learning journey. At the same time, by studying a piece of work that is of greater quality than their own, they can get a real feel for what they need to do to improve further.

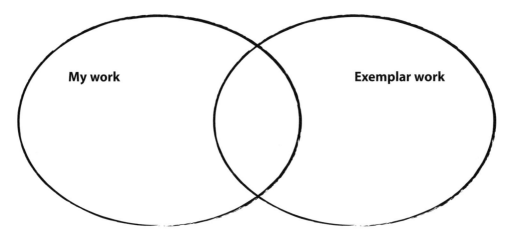

You can download a variety of visual organisers from:

http://osiriseducational.co.uk/TB/resources/

VIDEOS AND PODCASTS

The model that a teacher presents to the class has to link with what learners are expected to do. One teacher wanted to assess his class on their oral presenting skills. So, before they were asked to go away and prepare their speeches, they watched some models of excellent and not-so-excellent presentations. Here are links to two very different quality presentations. The first one is a brilliant speech from Barack Obama in 2004 when he was still a senator in Illinois, and the second is from a US high school student:

- http://www.youtube.com/watch?v=OFPwDe22CoY/
- http://www.youtube.com/watch?v=1ZiYMrjFFc4/

By watching them both, the class were able to list the features of what a good speech looks, sounds, and feels like, as well as things to avoid from the less accomplished example.

From these presentations, the learners created a checklist of desirable qualities:

- Clear enunciation
- Open gestures

- Positive expression

- Eye contact

- Use of story

- Logical and clear development of story/argument

- Repetition of key phrases

- Stillness and pausing

Learners found that generating a list from the examples helped them to think about a higher standard of presentation from the outset. The checklist also enabled better quality peer assessment as all the learners knew, shared, and agreed on the same assessment criteria. 'How do we make our presentations more Obama-ish?' became the mantra for the class.

CONVERTING A MODEL INTO SCORING RUBRICS

Neil Belshaw set his BTEC PE class quite a challenging assignment. In pairs, they had to create a 'professional' podcast which thoroughly explained the body's physiological systems: respiratory, skeletal, muscular, and so on. He found a few exemplar podcasts and played them to his learners. He then asked them to decide on and rank the five key elements that make for a great podcast. Meanwhile, he had come up with five of his own. He was curious to discover whether his learners had the same sense of quality as himself. The final podcast rubric was co-created between himself and the learners over two one-hour lessons.

They decided that there were five criteria: format, subject knowledge, organisation, engagement, and looking professional. Below is an extract from the full rubric of what they decided makes for a professional looking podcast. It shows what is required of learners to get the full four marks in this particular section, the technical and professional aspects of the podcast.

	4 points	3 points	2 points	1 point
Professional look	The podcast is the very best quality using the equipment provided. It is suitable to act as a model for other learners. Audio is clear and the volume is perfectly consistent. Images are varied and interesting, combining still and moving pictures. Transitions are perfectly smooth. Captions help the audience to learn from the podcast.	The podcast is of high quality. Audio is clear and the volume is consistent and audible. Images combine still and moving pictures. Transitions are smooth. Captions help the audience to learn from the podcast.	The podcast has some aspects of quality. Audio is clear and consistent throughout. There is a combination of still and moving pictures. Transitions are not perfectly smooth.	The podcast has some aspects of quality. Audio is clear in some places. The images within the podcast are mostly those of moving pictures.

Because the learners fully understood the success criteria, all of them were able to quickly improve the quality of their podcasts. They looked to level up each version by exploring what gaps existed between the mark they'd attained and the next level on that section of the rubric. The gap enabled them to create an action plan for attempt 2, attempt 3, and so on. As they were aware that the final podcast might be as far as two weeks away, they could create a timeline of what they needed to do, step by step, to get the full 20 points. In the end, the podcasts the students created were even better than the models that Neil had found on the internet. In fact, they were so good that when he teaches this topic to next year's learners, he's going to use the models that this year's group produced!

The advantages of scoring rubrics are that learners can see specifically what the next level requires and can plan what to do to close that gap. It is likely that some learners will be more advanced in certain aspects of the rubric than others. The whole class can level up by using the more advanced learners' work as a shared resource. This sort of approach to co-creating assessment criteria particularly lends itself to project work or work that may take some weeks to complete. Learners can be challenged to assess and reset targets for themselves on a regular basis. This type of rubric also encourages learners to look back in order to look forwards, thereby recognising the journey they have made which, in turn, can motivate them to tackle the next part of the challenge.

Download the full podcast rubric at:

http://osiriseducational.co.uk/TB/resources/

How can you get learners to understand the differences in quality between different examples of work?

Remembering that your classroom isn't a democracy, but it's not a dictatorship either, what strategies can you use to verify, challenge, and, if necessary, amend their ideas?

3. MASTERING THE ART OF EXPLANATION

When the quality of a teacher's explanations and instructions gives learners real clarity about what is expected of them, they must be doing something right. In the next chapter, we'll look at how excellent explanation can really help learners to close gaps. Here, we'll look at how it can help learners to understand where they are going.

In their book, *Explaining,* Ted Wragg and George Brown use a simple definition: 'Explaining is giving understanding to another.'[6] A teacher might need to explain a journey, a concept, a set of relationships, the steps of a process, the features of a product, or the reason for doing a piece of work in a particular way. The more clearly a teacher can do this, the more likely it is that learners will understand what is required of them first time around. But teachers can only explain something well if they are clear about it themselves, and if they've taken some time to think about exactly what they're going to say and do. The sug-

---

6   Edward Wragg and George Brown, *Explaining (Classroom Skills)* (London: Routledge, 1993), p. 3.

gestions in the teacher clarity section of this chapter (pages 95–109) can help you to improve your conceptual confidence, but you'll also need to make the time to work on and practise your explanations. This section gives you some ideas on how to do this, so all your learners can achieve clarity.

So, what is it that makes for a good explanation, and how can teachers become better at it? First, we should recognise that no one method will work for all learners. Our explanations have to meet individual needs as well as whole-class needs. We are loathe to use the term 'learning styles' here, as they have been so rubbished in some educational research – for example, in John Hattie's *Visible Learning for Teachers*. But the fact remains that people *do* learn in different ways! Appreciating that one mode of explanation will not suit all learners is essential for becoming a better explainer.

We've set out a number of ways that teachers can more effectively explain the steps to a desired destination or goal by working with their learners' learning preferences. There are many ways to talk about preferences, but here we'll just consider the vital role our senses play in this, because it is through our senses that our brain receives 'messages'. It's useful, too, to bear in mind that while we use all our senses, each of us tends to have more skill and more acuity with some senses than others. For example, some of us are very good at noticing visual information, others at hearing shades of meaning in words and tone, others at doing things physically or sensing things emotionally. The main point is that if we can include *all* these sensory aspects in our explanations, more of our learners are likely to get it first time around.

THE IMPORTANCE OF EXPLAINING IN A MULTI-SENSORY WAY

We need multi-sensory stimulation and input to understand and learn effectively. Imagine the scenario of a magic trick for teaching a particular skill. The trick in question is a nine-step sequence that involves knotting a loop of string around the fingers of one hand and then 'magically' untying it. If we were to show you how it's done as a demonstration without words you would be amazed by the magic and see that it's possible. However, you would need us to repeat this visual demonstration many times and slow us down quite a lot to understand how it's done. Some learners would find this much more difficult than others. Many of you would be saying, 'Give us some clear verbal instruction.'

Alternatively, we could describe the steps to you in words, without showing you the process. For you to succeed, we would need to be incredibly precise in our instructional language. Most of you would probably be begging us to show you the process at the same time as describing it verbally.

If we were to show you and describe the process to you in words, but not give you a piece of string to practise with, you might have a conceptual understanding of the trick, but you'd have no practical way to know if you'd really got it.

Or, if we showed you once and described the steps once, and then said, 'Here's a piece of string. You've seen it works. You've got an idea about how to do it. Now experiment till you get it right,' the chances are that most of you would find it hopelessly difficult and lose motivation very quickly.

But, if we explained the trick using visual *and* verbal input and physical practice in a systematic way, everyone will find a way to master the challenge, even if it takes some a little longer than others. The great thing is you can use the learners who've just learned it to do one-to-one teaching with those who are still working at it.

Now, this may seem obvious, but the fact is that most of us teach in the same way that we prefer to learn. So, if you particularly prefer to learn by seeing maps, charts, graphs, photos, pictures, and so on, the chances are you'll tend to teach in the same way. And the same applies if you prefer to learn by listening or by doing. Your preference can skew your approach to the techniques and strategies you use.

All we're saying is be aware of this if it's a blind spot of yours. Make sure you 'translate' across all these areas so that all your learners get explanations through the sensory channels with which they feel most comfortable. The best way to do this is to consciously make sure that you use powerful visuals, clear verbal explanations, and include plenty of opportunities for your learners to touch, feel, connect with, and walk through the steps of their learning. In some classes, such as chemistry, biology, and food technology, smells and tastes will be important too.

All the following examples contain elements of the three main senses – seeing, hearing, and touch – which cover both doing (external) and feeling (internal). However, we've sorted them into categories where one of the senses 'leads' and the others are used in support.

LEADING LEARNERS VISUALLY

Your TV is on mute and you see the UK weather forecast for a British summer's day. Would you understand what clothes to wear this afternoon? If yes then it's because you understand the symbols associated with weather and the numbers associated with temperature.

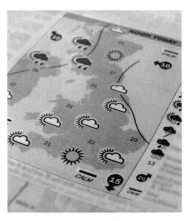

If you understand these symbols you might not need any additional explanation. Sometimes just seeing something helps you to understand. Words might add some extra useful detail, but actually a good image can convey a lot of powerful information very economically. Notice how this visual with its sun symbols might start to make you feel a little warm.

EXPLAINING JOURNEYS VISUALLY

When it comes to thinking about our future, most of us visualise it rather than hear it or feel it. For this reason, when we talk about destinations and journeys with our learners, visual explanations tend to be the most effective. Making the learning journey graphic is particularly useful for things like projects and thematic learning topics. The example below, created by Claire Hodgson for an art class, uses the familiar map of the London Underground to create a clear understanding of the route and the destination. We love the simplicity of this visual. Learners can refer to it throughout their journey through the topic, understanding what 'stop' they are currently at, what they need to do to get to the next one, and where they'll finally end up. Visual journeys like this enable confident, purposeful conversations between teacher and learners, learners and learners, and even learners and inspectors!

Notice that while this example is primarily visual, there is a significant verbal contribution and a powerful emotional pull: 'We hope you enjoy your learning journey with Garforth Academy Art Department.'

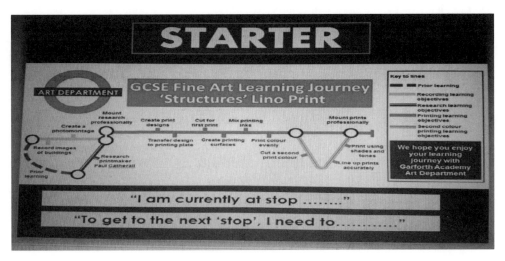

Photo: Claire Hodgson.

USING VISUALS TO REFLECT ON THE JOURNEY AHEAD

Most people, learners included, find it helpful to think about the journey ahead, and consider what challenges or difficulties may arise, instead of just rushing into it. When learners get into the habit of looking before they leap it can save time and energy and greatly enhance the quality of their work. As we've already mentioned, we're great fans of visual organisers. They're a wonderfully useful and versatile tool for planning, sequencing, and structuring thinking and can be applied to a wide range of subjects. Visual organisers, such as flow diagrams for breaking a process into a series of manageable steps, can really help learners to achieve clarity and structure in their thinking.

Another way visual organisers can be used is in modelling pre-writing strategies. A spider-gram or mind map, for instance, can assist learners to think about what features need to be included in their written work and in what sequence. This visual way of organising material will benefit many learners compared with producing a written plan.

As we've seen, the most successful teachers are up front about what they want their learn-ers to do. They usually start their lessons or topics of learning with a good explanation before learners embark on their journey. And where journeys are concerned, most of us find it helpful to have a clear visual map of the road ahead.

Try making your own Underground Map for an upcoming topic. This link will help:

http://beno.org.uk/metromapcreator/

USING MNEMONICS

A mnemonic is a pattern of letters or ideas that aids the memory. The Greek word from which it originates, *mnēmōn*, means 'mindful'. In other words, it's a mindful or conscious way of getting information to stick in the memory. Traditionally, mnemonics are mainly verbal techniques – acronyms like VIBGYOR or pithy sentences like 'Richard Of York Gave Battle In Vain' for remembering the sequence of colours in a rainbow. But the power of verbal mnemonics can be greatly enhanced when we add visual, physical, and emotional qualities to them. By making our mnemonics more multi-sensory they're even more likely to be memorable.

The mnemonic below, from a religious education class, is a great example of this. There are quite of lot of words but they are visually organised into brief but attractive chunks of information. The acronyms that are used are supported by visual symbols or pictures. The use of colour makes the mnemonic more engaging. The information is displayed on a laminated table mat which means it can be touched, poked, and prodded. Some learners need this sense of physical connection to their learning, just as many people remember better when they engage in the physical process of writing things down.

Photo: Kerry Burns.

Finally, there is a strong emotional pull. This mnemonic was created in a school in Liverpool where most of the class were die-hard Everton supporters. If they were to be asked in an exam to write on the topic of religious expression, they would just need to remember a champagne glass (SIP) and the Everton badge (EFC) to retrieve the key points of the information required. The technique worked really well for this class of learners because they know that Everton is the best football team in the city! And they sip champagne when they go out!

WORKING WITH A VISUALISER

Visualisers can be found in many classrooms. They enable you to visually project whatever is placed under the
lamp onto a screen or wall. The beauty of this simple
tool is that teachers can use it to show information visually and then add the dimension of movement to it. For
example, the teacher could project a piece of written
work or a diagram onto the screen. Then, in real time,
she could draw her learners' attention to certain parts of
it and add annotations. In an art class, a writing class, or
a biology class on dissection techniques, the teacher
can demonstrate a technique in real time and the learners can then model it.

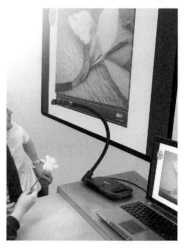

Photo: courtesy of Aver Information Europe B.V.
www.AVer.com/UK.

We think that using a visualiser and training learners to use them has
many advantages. For one thing, you (or your learners) are able to face
the class rather than have your back to them, as when using a whiteboard. If you've never used a visualiser before, try borrowing one from
a colleague and see the difference.

We include more on using visualisers to level up feedback in Chapter 6.

THE PHYSICAL DIMENSION OF LEARNING

There's a proverb in Papua New Guinea which runs, 'Learning is only a rumour until it's in
the muscle.' Some learners really do need to learn by doing, usually with several repeti-
tions, to be really confident that they've learned something and will be able to remember
it. The act of doing can also be an emotional and memorable experience, and it is particularly useful when we want to give learners a deeper awareness of a notion or concept. For
instance, a science teacher might want his learners to get a more visceral understanding
of how viruses attack healthy cells, so she might demonstrate this by ripping away pieces
from a lump of modelling clay or a sponge. A history teacher might want his learners to
experience the horrors and alienation of trench warfare, so he transforms the classroom

into two distinct 'trenches' with upturned tables in the middle of the room behind which each 'side' sits.

If you're interested in reading more about the importance of multi-sensory learning for deepening engagement and memory, we recommend Chip and Dan Heath's book, *Made to Stick*.[7] Physical and emotional engagement are particularly important if we want learning to stick. Yet as learners go further through their school careers, teachers often drop physical and emotional input in favour of the conceptual and intellectual. We think this is a mistake; both are necessary. The physical and emotional can make learning much more concrete, engaging, and memorable for many learners.

USING PROPS TO HELP EXPLAIN DESTINATION AND JOURNEY

Another way to help learners to get clarity is by using well-chosen props. A good prop is like the right kind of bait on a fishing line. It will attract attention and curiosity. Different props can evoke different sensory responses. They can be seen, heard, touched, smelled, or tasted. Many props achieve several of these. They can also arouse powerful emotions such as curiosity, puzzlement, amusement, sympathy, and even disgust, also known as the yuk factor!

A history teacher we've worked with brings in two personal items before he starts teaching his learners about the First World War. The first item is a German sniper's brass bullet that wounded his grandfather in the neck. He explains how he can still remember the scar on one side of his grandpa's neck where the bullet went in, and the scar on the other where the surgeons took it out. He tells the learners that the bullet missed the carotid artery by millimetres – they were that close to having a different history teacher! The second item is a 16-page letter written by his grandfather from the front line. Not only does the letter tell a gripping story about some of his experiences but there isn't a single spelling or grammatical mistake in it. This from a working-class lad who'd left school at the age of 14. He uses both props to help learners to be clear about what he's looking for from them. He wants each

---

7   Chip Heath and Dan Heath, *Made to Stick: Why Some Ideas Take Hold and Others Come Unstuck* (London: Arrow, 2008).

of them to create a series of letters written from 'the front' which captivate the reader and are grammatically correct.

It's amazing how props can get learners' attention and help us to level up the quality of our explanations. And the better our explanations, the more clarity our learners will have. In the next chapter, we'll show how teachers can develop the explanation skills of their learners. When learners can explain clearly what they've just learned, it further consolidates their learning. When they can explain and demonstrate their new learning, the teacher has tangible feedback that shows they really have got it.

VERBAL EXPLANATIONS AND WORDSMITH-ERY

Using words alone to explain things is one of the hardest of skills, although one well worth working on. Language is inherently vague and open to misinterpretation. To explain things using precise language, so there is no room for misunderstanding, takes careful thought and practice. The example of the string 'trick' earlier in this chapter suggested that it would take real linguistic skills to explain the steps to others, simply and precisely, without visual support.

This is why we strongly suggest that you make your explanations multi-sensory, as there are more hooks for learners to grab that enable their understanding. Having said that, many learners do like listening to words that are well chosen and well used. Stories and anecdotes are a great way to explain things and introduce topics, as in the example of the history teacher and his grandfather.

TELLING STORIES

Stories can be personal, humorous, shocking, or instructive; they can be messages of hope and insight; they may contain values and perspectives. They are brilliant at generating emotional responses that get learners engaged. Research suggests that story-telling and story-listening capacities are hardwired into the brain. They are the basic way in which all human beings learn about the world, about themselves, and about each other. We've been using stories to convey messages for thousands of years. Above all, the best stories are multi-sensory and highly memorable. All that's really necessary is to make sure that any anecdote, analogy, parable, tale, case history, or story that you use with your learners is relevant to the key elements or themes of whatever it is you want to explain. For more on this read Nick Owen's brilliant book, *The Magic of Metaphor*.[8]

One of the easiest ways to weave stories into your explanations is to consider the main points that you want to get across. Now ask yourself whether any of these points can be followed by a 'for instance', or whether they remind you of a story from your own experience, such as something that happened in last year's class when they learned the topic. Stories are everywhere. Your own life is a huge resource bank of stories, and you'll also find them in newspapers and books and on television and radio. If you think about it, all life is an unfolding story; we cannot live without them. The only thing to add is that stories work much better if your learners can make strong associations with them. So choose your stories with your learners in mind.

One teacher we know has often used the following story when he thinks his learners need to take more responsibility for themselves and their learning:

When I was your age, about 12 or 13, I used to live in a house near a girls' school. Sometimes I'd get home from my school before the girls walked down my street. I'd stand in the window watching them and say to myself, 'If only that cute one with the black hair and turned-up nose would turn left up my pathway, ring the bell, and ask me out, life would be wonderful.' And do you know what? She never did. And I soon realised that if I was going to have the life I wanted, I'd have to change my strategies and get a bit more proactive.

USING METAPHORS, ANALOGIES, AND STORIES

The word metaphor comes from the Greek *metapherein* meaning 'to transfer'. Thus, a metaphor explains or describes something in terms of something else. It makes a point of comparison between two otherwise unrelated objects. This could be a word, a phrase, an idea, or a story.

At its simplest we could talk about a *new-born day*, which links the dawn and the beginning of a human journey. Such comparisons can offer unexpected and engaging perspectives about the nature of early morning – or babies!

---

8   Nick Owen, *The Magic of Metaphor: 77 Stories for Teachers, Trainers and Thinkers* (Carmarthen: Crown House Publishing, 2001).

A more complex metaphor would be:

All the world's a stage,

And all the men and women merely players.

They have their exits and their entrances,

And one man in his life plays many parts.

As You Like It, Act 2, Scene 7

The world is not a stage, but Shakespeare draws a comparison between the two to suggest a relationship between the mechanics of the world and the lives of the people who inhabit it. Similarly, in the teacher's story of waiting for the girl he fancied to knock on his door, the courage he requires to ask her out is not the same as taking greater responsibility for learning, but the mechanisms are the same. The link is made: it speaks to the listeners in their world and it stays in the mind.

Using metaphors, similes, analogies, and stories can help learners to get a firmer grasp on what the teacher is trying to get across. A teacher of English we've worked with explores the relationship between Romeo and Juliet in terms of weather metaphors. Learners map out the transitions in the lovers' relationship with ideas such as sunny, bright, dark, spring-like, cloudy, and storm-tossed. Such techniques can really help learners to understand how the quality and energy of the relationship between the lovers changes over the short time that they're together.

It's often helpful to choose metaphors, analogies, and stories that learners already have an association with. This means getting into their world, perhaps utilising popular culture such as pop music, television programmes, teen magazines, and sports teams. This is something we encouraged you to do in Chapter 2 on pre-assessment. If you took the time to establish what your learners are interested in when you first met them back at the start of the school year, it will pay dividends when you come to use these methods.

One teacher we know works with a football obsessed class. He uses this knowledge to link whatever he teaches them to the world of football. This gives him a way into talking about managing information (tactics); structural processes (player formations such as 4-4-2 or 5-3-2); how you build up a piece of work step by step to achieve/score your goal (passing); when one way isn't working you use a different technique or strategy, or when a piece of work doesn't meet the criteria you do another draft (substitution); and pointing out the poor use of KASH skills (yellow card). One of the beauties of working with metaphors is that they not only enable clarity and engagement, but they can really open up new creativity and perspective in the way you and your learners see and appreciate what they are required to do for a topic.

Other examples to consider include:

- How is writing an A* essay like great dancing?
- How are the steps to completing this excellent piece of work like going on a first date?
- How are the ingredients for excellence in this topic like a recipe?
- How are the different levels of work in this topic like a computer game?
- How is the journey through this topic like Formula 1 racing?

Two points. First, the more unlikely the comparison, the more creative, fun, and memorable the exploration can be. Second, although the comparisons can invite generalisation, the work that results can often show teacher and learners alike where they find value in the topic and what they would like to pursue more deeply.

REHEARSING WITH COLLEAGUES

The best way to develop your skill at explaining is to practise it. Why not get together with some colleagues to do this and give each other feedback? You might watch each other explain the finer points of a quality piece of work by annotating it or highlighting the sections that you want your learners to particularly take note of. You might help each other to devise stories or analogies that bring clarity to individual learners or to a whole class. Practising your explanation techniques with colleagues can be a great way to hone your skills, especially when everyone has a go and offers each other constructive feedback. Even better, why not collaborate to agree on the relevant success criteria and use it to rate your performances. This is a great way to level up your own skills and to support each other's development.

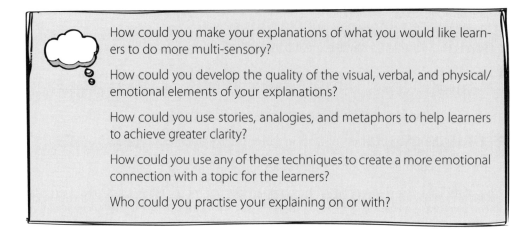

How could you make your explanations of what you would like learners to do more multi-sensory?

How could you develop the quality of the visual, verbal, and physical/emotional elements of your explanations?

How could you use stories, analogies, and metaphors to help learners to achieve greater clarity?

How could you use any of these techniques to create a more emotional connection with a topic for the learners?

Who could you practise your explaining on or with?

FAQS

There isn't much in this chapter about written learning objectives. Why?

We tend not to talk overmuch about written learning objectives or intentions. For us, the insistence on the part of some educators that every lesson should start with learning objectives can run the danger of creating low engagement in the early part of the lesson. Our concern is shared by Mick Waters who reckons that learners write about a mile-and-a-half's worth of learning objectives throughout their primary school careers!

If your school insists on learning objectives then at least make sure that they are very clear, and find engaging ways to check this out with your learners. Too often, learning objectives are thrown up on a board for learners to write down without the students, and sometimes even the teacher, understanding what they mean or how they can best be achieved. What we encourage is that an excellent model of work is shown and then deconstructed to pinpoint the success criteria. But which type of success criteria will best help learners? When designing any rubrics, success criteria, recipes, or checklists, one should keep in mind that the purpose is to help the learner to achieve quality work over a set period of time and over that time they will be required to practise.

Supposing I want to show models but I don't have any excellent models of work to show?

In the first instance you may have to create your own. It's sometimes a good idea to try to do a piece of work yourself before you give it to learners. This also helps you to appreciate what aspects the learners might find the hardest. Creating a model or exemplar piece of work helps us to pre-empt the most common errors that might arise. Some schools are now so convinced about the merits of having models available for learners that it is becoming a standard operating procedure for them. We very much endorse this policy.

Won't these ideas over-structure learning?

Original thought is always to be encouraged. However, original thought doesn't come out of nowhere. Mastery usually comes from a process which begins with the modelling of exemplars. Structure and discipline need to be acquired, along with an understanding of what the 'rules' are. Once this has been achieved, original thought can occur by deliberately breaking the rules for a higher purpose. Music is a good example. There are just five lines on a stave and there are only 12 musical notes. But that doesn't stop inventiveness and the constant creation of new forms. The structure in no way inhibits creativity; in fact, it enables it. Structure is essential for coherence.

IN A NUTSHELL

Teachers who are clear about the destinations of their learners, and the steps they need to take to get there, are more successful than other teachers. First, they need to acquire clarity for themselves. In doing so, these teachers develop a deeper awareness about what passes as high quality work and high quality explanation. Once they achieve this, they can transfer this clarity to their learners as they 'unpick' and deconstruct the learning with them. A model we suggested was the *Blue Peter* presenter, one who shows learners what they are aiming for up front. We also said that the classroom is not a democracy and it's not for learners to determine what does and doesn't constitute high quality work. But your classroom shouldn't be a dictatorship either. Getting learners to wrestle with different notions of quality in different ways, both before and during the learning process, helps them to become clearer about how they can move towards making their work the best it can be.

TEACHING BACKWARDS CHECKLIST

Defining and demystifying the destination (micro – module of learning)	This is always part of my practice	I sometimes do this	I never do this
I collect models and examples to help me improve my clarity around quality.			
I collaborate with colleagues to develop a better shared understanding of quality.			
I seek feedback from learners about how clear I am in demystifying the destination.			
I ensure that success criteria are clear and understandable to learners.			
I use models of excellence or WAGOLLs to help learners understand their destination.			
I make the thinking steps explicit to learners.			

Defining and demystifying the destination (micro – module of learning)	This is always part of my practice	I sometimes do this	I never do this
I make models of excellence available for learners to use throughout the topic.			
I use models of excellence to co-create success criteria with learners.			
I challenge learners to compare and contrast examples of different quality work.			
I explain new learning using a range of different strategies.			
I help learners to visualise the journey they'll take through the module of learning.			

Defining and demystifying the destination (macro – course/ academic year)	This is always part of my practice	I sometimes do this	I never do this
My classes take more of a role in judging quality as the year progresses.			

Defining and demystifying the destination (macro – course/ academic year)	This is always part of my practice	I sometimes do this	I never do this
I help learners to become ready for their exam or next key stage by developing the KASH they will need to succeed.			
My learners become more confident in being able to articulate their destinations and their gaps.			

Download this checklist from:

http://osiriseducational.co.uk/TB/resources/

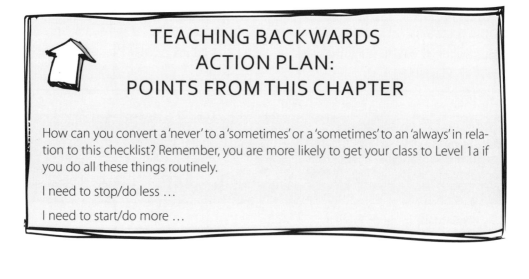

TEACHING BACKWARDS ACTION PLAN: POINTS FROM THIS CHAPTER

How can you convert a 'never' to a 'sometimes' or a 'sometimes' to an 'always' in relation to this checklist? Remember, you are more likely to get your class to Level 1a if you do all these things routinely.

I need to stop/do less …

I need to start/do more …

FOR MORE INFORMATION ...

The excellent Ron Berger and Austin's butterfly:

https://www.youtube.com/watch?v=hqh1MRWZjms/

Some useful ideas from Alex Quigley on how to improve your explaining skills:

http://www.huntingenglish.com/2014/06/05/infectious-explanations/

http://www.huntingenglish.com/2014/05/10/magic-metaphor/

A good video clip of Robert Bjork talking about the need to slow down learning:

http://gocognitive.net/interviews/desirable-difficulties-slowing-down-learning

Information about the Slow Writing technique:

http://www.triptico.co.uk/media/temp/slowWriting.html

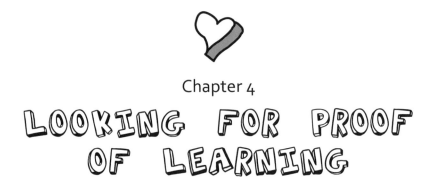

Chapter 4

LOOKING FOR PROOF OF LEARNING

'I don't just think they've all made progress, I know they have!'

WHAT SANK THE *TITANIC*?

This was the first question that a teacher gave his class in a history test. The *Titanic*, of course, sank after colliding with a massive iceberg. This is what the class had been taught. But the teacher had used an analogy to explain the mechanics of the tragedy. He'd said that the damage caused by the ship's impact was 'as if it had been ripped open by a giant tin-opener'. It was a powerful and memorable image likely to stick in the mind and aid recall. However, when the teacher set the test a few lessons later and sat down to mark it, there was one answer that really surprised him. 'The *Titanic* was sunk by a giant tin-opener.' For whatever reason, perhaps learner inattention or lack of teacher clarity, the boy hadn't grasped the nub of the lesson. These things happen. The real problem was that the boy had continued in this delusion for two further lessons. It wasn't until the teacher marked the test that he realised there was a problem. For two whole lessons, thinking that everyone had understood the facts of the sinking, the teacher was just as deluded as the boy.

This situation might be described as a 'triple disaster'. The first disaster was the sinking of the ship and the appalling loss of life. The other two disasters were these: the learner didn't know what sank the *Titanic* and the teacher didn't know that the boy didn't know for over three hours of teaching time. This was an utter revelation to the teacher because the boy seemed to be working diligently and without confusion throughout these lessons.

The teacher learned three things from this triple disaster. First, his teaching was not as clear as he thought it was. Second, his methods of detecting whether learners had understood were flaky in the extreme. Third, he had assumed too much from the boy's busy-ness and demeanour of competence. He realised he had some learning to do.

We've no idea whether you've ever been in a similar situation or not, but we can confess that the teacher in question was one of the authors of this book!

WHAT'S IN THIS CHAPTER FOR ME?

■ How do the best teachers avoid the kind of situation described above?

■ What techniques and strategies are available to help you monitor learner progress?

■ How can you make sure your learners really are up to speed with what they're supposed to be doing?

■ How can you support learners to become more confident at articulating the progress they're making on their learning journey?

WHAT'S THE THINKING BEHIND THIS CHAPTER?

This chapter is all about finding proof and avoiding assumptions. You'll have noticed that we've been waging a war against assumptions all the way through this book. In Chapter 1, we looked at the importance of setting and then embedding high expectations. High expectations need to be clearly defined. We can't presume that learners have the same understanding of them as their teacher. In Chapter 2, we stressed the importance of getting to know our learners' true starting points rather than guessing them. In Chapter 3, we showed the importance of being clear about what success might look like from the outset rather than assuming that learners know what's expected of them. This chapter is about helping teachers and learners to see more accurately where they are in relation to the destination they're heading for. Rather than presuming learners are making progress, we need to have concrete proof – real hard evidence that they're headed in the right direction.

So, we're going to put a metaphor to work in this chapter, that of the teacher as detective. We'll put our minds to addressing how we can find evidence and proof that learning is taking place, and we'll explore which techniques and strategies offer us better quality feedback on learner progress. We'll also show how becoming a better learning detective can help a teacher to be judged as outstanding. Finally, we'll share some effective and engaging ways to seek proof of learning: within lessons, over the course of a topic, and during the whole academic year. We'll explore the many ways that great detectives and excellent teachers have a whole lot in common.

THINKING LIKE A GREAT DETECTIVE

Detectives, like teachers, are busy people. They have a number of puzzles to solve at any one time. Some of these puzzles are straightforward: the culprit is found at or near the scene and admits their involvement immediately. In other cases, there can be a scarcity of information or too many contradictory pieces of evidence. In others, there appear to be no clues at all.

We've all probably got a favourite TV detective. Ours is Lieutenant Columbo played throughout his career by the brilliant Peter Falk. If you've never watched an episode then put this right as soon as you can! Take it from us: every episode of *Columbo* is a lesson in teacher training and development. Every episode is structurally the same and, how fitting for this book, every episode is planned backwards.

We watch a murder committed at the start of each instalment and we actually get to see who the murderer is. The murder is usually premeditated and meticulously planned, and the murderer always takes great care to hide the evidence. Some 10 minutes or so into the episode, in walks Columbo, dressed in a scruffy coat, looking tired, disorganised, and forgetful. His job, of course, is to solve the case. To do this he needs clues from which he can piece together sufficient proof to find and convict the perpetrator.

Detectives, whether fictional or real, need evidence, but they come to realise that some types of evidence will prove more robust and rigorous than others if their case is going to stand up in the hothouse of the courtroom. In exactly the same way, teachers need to gather evidence that learning is taking place. And evidence of learning also has different types and levels. Let's examine this further.

ALL EVIDENCE IS NOT AT THE SAME LEVEL: ELEMENTARY, MY DEAR WATSON!

If you've read *Engaging Learners* or been on any of our outstanding teaching training courses, you'll be used to the phrase 'level up'. This simply means that the level above is better than the current level. In the same way, we need to acknowledge that there are 'levels' of proof. Detectives are faced with this on a daily basis. Take the following clues or types of evidence. Some of them are clearly more robust and revealing than others. Imagine there are five suspects in a murder investigation. Which items of evidence do you think a detective would pay most attention to?

Suspect 1 – Has same size feet as a footprint found at the crime scene.

Suspect 2 – Lacks an alibi for the time of the murder.

Suspect 3 – Her DNA has been found at the murder scene.

Suspect 4 – Acts suspiciously under interrogation.

Suspect 5 – Is a known enemy of the victim.[1]

And so it is with teaching. When it comes to finding out whether learning has really taken place, some types of evidence will be more useful and informative than other types.

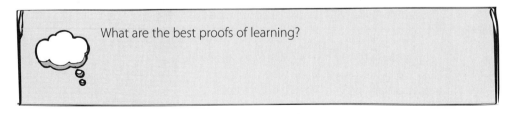

What are the best proofs of learning?

Below is a list of possible proofs of learning from five different learners. Each one *could* be a potential proof of learning, but some are clearly more grounded and revealing than others. When asked, 'Do you understand?' which of the five learners have proved that they really do?

Learner A – Has a positive facial expression.

Learner B – Can express understanding convincingly in their own words.

Learner C – Gives the thumbs-up sign.

Learner D – Is part of a group that shows they understand by holding up a green traffic light symbol.

Learner E – Has significantly added to their pre-assessment knowledge grid (see page 67).

These 'proofs' are not all at the same level – some of them are more illuminating, more robust, and more accurate than others. The weaker proofs might mask the fact that a learner is pretending to have got it or believes he's understood when that is not the case at all.

Here are the answers from strongest to weakest: Learner B, Learner E, Learner A, Learner C, and Learner D. Why? Learners B and E are able to show their progress in a tangible way – Learner B through speaking and Learner E through writing. Learners A and C could be pretending they have learned. Learner D may not understand what the rest of the group have understood.

Later in the chapter we'll show you some practical and proven techniques to explore how you can elicit *real* proof that learning has taken place. And we'll suggest ways to eliminate any tendency you might have to accept weak evidence of learning. But first, let's explain why gathering high quality evidence is so important.

WHY BECOME A BETTER TEACHER DETECTIVE?

1. IT SHARPLY FOCUSES YOUR PLANNING

Everything starts at the planning stage! In the previous chapter, we discussed destinations and how you can make these clear to your learners. We also described the importance of considering the steps your learners will need to take to get to these destinations. Now it's time to think about how you'll know if your learners are on the right track.

Let's imagine we're teaching a topic to which we've allocated 16 hours of teaching time. At the end of the topic the learners will be assessed with a written test, and your aim is for all the class to ace this. To achieve this they'll need to fully understand all the concepts and relationships within the topic. The summative test will prove whether or not the desired level of understanding has been reached. But what about intermediate proofs that can be gathered during the 16 hours leading up to the test? Will you simply wait until the end of the 16 hours to test for learning and risk a *Titanic*-style disaster? Or could you instead gather some evidence during the first hour? Or during the fourth hour? Or the tenth? Between lessons? This sort of strategy could help you to avoid any icebergs that may be lurking along the way.

To achieve this, it clearly makes sense to teach backwards from the questions and tasks that you know will appear in the summative test. When teaching backwards, a teacher will lay out the journey for her learners, signpost by signpost. How will she do this? With 16 hours of PowerPoint presentations? Definitely not! As she negotiates this 16-hour trip with her class, she'll need to gather proof of how each learner is doing at each stage of the journey. By knowing the destination in advance, and the steps required to get there, she can start thinking about how to gather evidence that will definitely let her know whether or not her learners are on the right track. And this isn't just during lessons, it's between lessons as well. How can she also use homework assignments to gather evidence of progress? And what kind of evidence will she look for? Just as it is with detectives, different types of evidence or proofs of learning carry different weight.

To put it bluntly, teachers who teach forwards just don't plan like this. They often lead with activities that they think the class might enjoy or find stimulating. While this is not a bad intention, the measure of an excellent teacher is how they choose activities best suited to the needs of the learning journey – the journey that will take learners by the most effective route towards their destination(s). As we'll explore further in Chapter 5, creating the right level of challenge for each learner that both engages them and helps them towards their destination is what proper, robust planning is all about.

2. YOU'LL BE MORE FLEXIBLE

There's an old saying, 'The more right you are, the more inflexible you become.' The best detectives are flexible: they have curious minds. They have a particular mindset which is open to feedback and which values listening more than telling. They value receiving feedback and welcome it from as many different sources as possible. They know that feedback can only add to what they know. They may learn nothing from it sometimes, but it can never diminish their existing knowledge or awareness. Finally, they also know that it's the quality of the feedback they get that in the end will provide the proof they're looking for to conclude their investigation.

Yet sometimes even the best detectives get stuck. They find that their investigation isn't making progress. So, what do they do? They change their approach. Even great detectives like Columbo make mistakes and go down blind alleys. But when this happens he takes it in his stride. His ego never gets in the way of him admitting he got it wrong. The success of the investigation is more important than him being right or looking good. He's not only a great detective, he possesses humility too. And perhaps that's one of the key reasons why he's such an excellent detective.

Some teachers we've worked with have got into a bad habit – it's called 'Keeping to ze plan'. They've created a lesson plan and you know they're going to see it through to the end come hell or high water. However, other teachers have changed this unhelpful habit through their experience of the Outstanding Teaching Intervention programme. Video analysis has given these teachers a powerful flash of insight into their lack of flexibility. Some have watched themselves skilfully seeking out and finding proof of learning during a lesson, but then have hung their heads in shame as they see themselves ignoring or failing to take action on it. Others have watched themselves wait and wait and wait for the results of a test or homework to see whether or not their learners have got it. It's a revelation for these teachers to realise how much time they've wasted. Mark remembers a conversation with one such teacher. The dialogue went like this:

Mark: *How do you know they understand this?*

Teacher: *I'll find out next Tuesday.*

Mark: *Why, what happens next Tuesday?*

Teacher: *I collect their books in.*

The problem is the approach that some teachers bring to their planning and teaching. In some cases they stick to the plan even when it's not working. Either through habit, or lack of empathy with learners, they find change difficult. Some of this, it must be said, is down to an age-old problem: the sensitive ego.

In his book, *Super Teaching*, Eric Jensen shows how teachers with different levels of ego have different attitudes and responses to feedback and change.[2] Whereas 'high ego' teachers are very concerned with being right, 'low ego' teachers are looking to do whatever it takes to help and support learners. Pride does not get in their way. They admit mistakes and want to create a learning environment where learners can own their mistakes too. Unlike high ego teachers, those with a lower level of ego are ready and willing to change tack. These teachers have a positive attitude to feedback and they act on it as soon as they can. Even if a lesson plan has worked brilliantly with other classes before, they don't want to keep to this plan if it's not working now. They want to respond flexibly and effectively to those learners who they are teaching right here, right now. Unless they build the right ways of getting the right evidence in a timely way, by teaching and planning backwards, they will not be able to make these necessary adjustments.

3. YOU'LL SAVE YOURSELF TIME AND ENERGY

For detectives and teachers time is of the essence. For detectives, the quicker they can find quality evidence, the quicker they can wrap up the case. For many crimes it's said that the first 48 hours are the most crucial because the evidence is freshest. When investigators arrive at a crime scene they hope to find quality clues that can secure a quick arrest. The best detectives develop a methodology which is efficient in these situations. A crime has been committed and they work to solve it as quickly as possible. They work as a team, allocating roles to different officers – forensics, witness statements, database searches, and so on – and they expect to have results in as short a time as possible.

Most teachers don't have the luxury of a team, beyond perhaps a teaching assistant. They have to do it themselves. But like good detectives, the best teachers develop efficient and effective ways to gather quality evidence about learning to get an accurate reading of what's really happening in their classroom. They use their own versions of forensics, witness statements, and database research to find out who's learning and who isn't. As a result, they're able to adjust their teaching from lesson to lesson and even during lessons.

When teachers develop a sound methodology for gathering evidence of learning, a huge amount of time and energy can be saved. When the teacher is up to speed with what is really going on in a learner's head a number of key things can happen. For example, teachers will know which learners can carry on working by themselves and which need more support and assistance. Consequently, there'll be less need to reteach the topic later on, class revision will be more effective, and the quality of written work and homework will improve so marking will be less onerous.

---

2   Eric Jensen, *Super Teaching: Over 1000 Practical Strategies* (Thousand Oaks, CA: Sage, 2008).

We're not just talking about time spent in lessons but also time spent between them. Planning lessons and marking can take up lots of time. When you develop the skills of an excellent teacher detective you become a better marker and a better lesson planner. You'll find that marking can become a highly effective tool for proving that learners really are making progress. Effective marking gathers evidence that teachers can use to inform their planning. Armed with sound evidence about whether learners are advancing or not, planning becomes quicker and easier, and teachers can avoid wasting hours marking incorrect work. As Dylan Wiliam has memorably said, 'Marking can be seen as the punishment given to teachers for failing to find out that they did not achieve the intended learning when the learners were in front of them.'[3]

4. YOU'LL GATHER MORE ACCURATE FEEDBACK ON LEARNER PROGRESS

Experienced detectives develop a methodology for solving crimes. They may also call on their instinct, developing a professional 'nose' for facts that don't fit and for incongruent behaviours. But they know that hunches alone are not enough. They're only a guide that spurs them on to unearth the real hard evidence that lies beneath the surface of things. The kind of hard evidence that will stand up in court. The kind of evidence that's robust enough to convict someone beyond reasonable doubt. The history of policing is littered with cases in which lack of rigour or due diligence allowed guilty people to go free or innocent people to be wrongly convicted. Without diligent sleuthing, good planning, and solid evidence the truth cannot come out.

In our experience, the best teachers don't go into a classroom *hoping* for proof. They go in with a clear idea of how they are going to get it. In other words, they plan for it before they start teaching. It's vitally important for teachers to know how much progress their class is making because it's increasingly how they are judged. The teacher that derives the best data from a class is deemed, often justifiably, to be a more effective practitioner.

Time and again in our classroom observations, we've seen that the most successful teachers teach backwards from the knowledge of what robust proof will look, sound, and feel like. And they ensure that those proofs provide evidence beyond reasonable doubt that the targeted learning is indeed taking place. By thinking, 'What should learners be able to say or do at this point of the topic to prove their progress?' they are designing a learning environment based on rigour and clarity.

By thinking and planning in this way, teachers demand that learners clearly demonstrate their learning step by step as they progress through a topic and over an academic year. Outstanding teachers create multiple opportunities to gather quality proofs of progress

---

3   Wiliam, *Embedded Formative Assessment*, p. 78.

which enable them to have richer conversations with their learners, and also with colleagues with whom they might happen to share a class. As a result, they are not only able to offer high quality feedback to their learners (for more on feedback see Chapter 6), but also articulate confidently to parents, colleagues, and inspectors exactly where learners currently are in their learning journey, how far they've come, and how far there remains for them to go.

In our experience, the best teachers share similar qualities with the finest real and fictional detectives. Using sound strategies, they develop excellent habits for noticing clues and gathering proof. As a result, they are able to find out how well learners are doing as they progress through each lesson, each topic, and over the whole academic year. Their success is based on the fact that they plan which proof-discovering strategies they will use before the teaching starts. These may have to be adjusted based on the feedback that emerges, but they know that pre-planning and flexibility are the essence of teaching backwards.

COLUMBO OR CLOUSEAU: THE CHOICE IS YOURS

To illustrate the point about ego levels, we invite you to compare two famous TV detectives: our hero, Lieutenant Columbo, and the fictional French detective Chief Inspector Jacques Clouseau played by another brilliant actor, Peter Sellers. We're big fans of Peter Sellers too but only because he makes us laugh. We're certainly not fans of Clouseau's detection skills.

Columbo	Clouseau
Great questioner	Poor questioner
Great listener	Poor listener
Hard to fool	Easy to fool
Low ego	High ego

We've put some YouTube links showing both of these detectives in action at the end of this chapter.

How effective are you at detecting learning? What sort of proofs do you seek?

How easy do you find it to articulate accurately to yourself and others the progress that your learners are making?

On a scale of 1–10, how good do you honestly think you are at discovering real proof of your students' learning? How good would you like to be? If there's a difference in the scores, how do you plan to close the gap?

BECOMING A BETTER TEACHER DETECTIVE

We suggest that if you want to become more Columbo-esque in your pursuit of proof, you'd do well to imitate some of his characteristics. We've summarised these into four key areas:

1 Questioning for proof.

2 Listening for proof.

3 Being hard to fool.

4 Small or big ego.

The four areas are not mutually exclusive. In fact, there's quite a lot of overlap between them. For instance, it's no good creating great proof-seeking questions if you don't listen to the answers that learners give you. Equally, there's little merit in setting your ego aside so you can better understand the needs of your learners if you aren't going to use this knowledge to change your teaching approach. So, let's look at how you can become progressively better at seeking proof of progress through developing your skills as a teacher detective. We'll examine Columbo's four behaviours of excellence one at a time to see how we can translate them into the classroom 'crime' scene.

1. QUESTIONING FOR PROOF

The main reason that detectives ask questions is to gather information so that the investigation can progress. They ask questions of themselves, their colleagues, witnesses, victims, and suspects. By processing the answers to these questions they gather the information required to establish the proof that they need to get a conviction. But they will not get this proof if their questions aren't sharp enough.

Teachers also ask questions to get proof. In this case it's the confirmation that learning is or isn't happening. Some teachers use superb questioning techniques to acquire this evidence. Like detectives, they employ a variety of strategies to achieve different things. These include questions that:

- Check for misconceptions and weak understanding.
- Create deliberate confusion to see how learners deal with it.
- Challenge learners to provide evidence for their answers.
- Help the teacher to understand whether the learner's thinking process is robust and on track or not.

Here are some techniques to help you question for proof.

INVITATIONAL QUESTIONS

One effective questioning technique is a series of requests. For example:

- Tell me what you're trying to achieve with this piece of work.
- Tell me what you've learned so far in this topic.
- Tell me what you can about … (magnesium, the causes of the First World War, etc.).

The responses to these open, invitational requests can give you a strong sense of how well your learners are progressing towards the goal you've set them or that they've set for themselves. By simply posing a challenging request for information, and demanding that any answer be accompanied by proof, you begin to establish a culture of greater academic rigour in your classroom which will serve you and your learners well.

QUESTIONING FOLLOW-UPS

The questions we teachers ask, and the way we respond to the answers we get, tend to focus our learners' attention on what they think we expect of them. If we expect justification and proof as a matter of course, learners will get into this habit soon enough. But if we simply accept answers that are not backed up by justification or evidence, even if it is the right answer, we should ask ourselves, does that really count as proof of learning? The answer is no, of course. Just being able to give the correct answer doesn't prove a thing.

A memorable mantra we often hear from English and literacy teachers is 'PEE on your work'. They train learners to follow up a Point with Evidence and Example(s). Successfully embedding this habit helps learners to expand their writing skills and be better rewarded for it in tests and exams.

Similarly, the structure 'Point, Because, Therefore, However …' helps train learners to follow up any statement or answer they give with evidence, example, consequence, and counter-example. Some teachers we've worked with now have established routines where they pose a question but accept no answer unless it has at least two pieces of supporting evidence. The learners' first response is likely to be, 'What do you mean by evidence?' It will be up to you to train them so they'll know precisely what constitutes good evidence.

Primary teacher Aratin Singh expects learners to supply evidence when they respond to her questions. Using gestures, such as widening her arms or by pausing after learners have answered, she both encourages them to reflect on what they've said and allows time for them to expand on or justify their answers. This use of 'wait time' is pedagogically very sound. It's essential that learners are given time to think through their answers and deepen the quality of their responses after making an oral contribution. She uses this technique for individual, pair, group, and whole-class questioning. As the school year progresses, her learners become increasingly skilled at expanding their answers with evidence through deepening the quality of their thinking and reflection.

QUESTIONS LINKED TO ASSESSMENT RUBRICS

To show what we mean by assessment rubrics, let's revisit a checklist we showed you in Chapter 3 (see page 119–120) which set out the criteria for what makes a great speech or presentation. It was a grid that was co-created by the teacher and the learners, with the learners working to discover the criteria first before input from the teacher. The model for excellent speech-making was a presentation given by Barack Obama, and when it comes to making great speeches it would be fair to say, 'Yes, he can!'

A great way to check learner understanding is to use 'I can …' statements. Underneath each 'I can …' statement for the speech- and presentation-delivery criteria, let's put some questions that the teacher can pre-plan to check whether this proof of learning has been met or is close to being met.

I can show clear enunciation.	*I can* use open gestures.	*I can* show positive expression.	*I can* use eye contact.
What is enunciation? What makes enunciation clear? Why do some speakers not achieve this?	What is an open gesture? Can you show me some open gestures? What do open gestures convey to an audience?	What do we mean by positive expression? Can you talk me through some examples of this? How will you use positive expression in your talk?	Why is eye contact so important? Why might some speakers not use it effectively? How do you intend to remind yourself to use it?
I can show use of story.	*I can* use logical and clear development of story/argument.	*I can* use repetition of key phrases.	*I can* show stillness.
Why is story such a powerful tool for speakers? How do you intend to use story? Where are you getting your story ideas from?	What are the important features of a good story/argument? How will you begin and end your story? How does your story fit in with the rest of your talk?	What phrases will you repeat? Why is repetition so important? How will you check that these phrases have registered with the audience?	What do we mean by stillness? Why do some speakers struggle with this? How do you intend to convey stillness?

Try creating your own pre-planned questions matched to a checklist or rubric. Devise them based on how well they will provide you with evidence that learning is taking place.

The learners' responses to these pre-planned questions will give the teacher information and evidence beyond a reasonable doubt as to whether or not they have understood what the criteria really mean. Only when the criteria have been understood can we expect learners to achieve their full potential. If the learners demonstrate any confusion or lack of clarity, it's great feedback for the teacher that he or she will have to do some gap closing with the learners before letting them loose on the task.

The nice thing about putting 'I can …' statements into a grid format is that it enables the teacher to isolate each statement and generate questions that might test proof before the topic even starts. This can be done for any topic. We recommend that you devise questions in such a way that they clearly elicit the proof that you're looking for. If you've conducted a pre-mortem for this topic (see Chapter 3), then you can particularly focus on posing questions for those aspects of the topic where you anticipate learners are most likely to struggle.

HINGE POINT QUESTIONS

Hinge point questions are posed by teachers at or near the start of a lesson in order to gather proof about which learners are at the stage to confidently tackle the challenges of the lesson and which are not. These questions can be answered on mini-whiteboards, for example, and will give the teacher vital information as to whether they can move on or whether they need to do a bit of reteaching or pre-teaching first. In his book, *Embedded Formative Assessment*, Dylan Wiliam suggests that asking a hinge point question 'should take no longer than two minutes, and ideally less than one minute, for all learners to respond'.[4] They should also work individually to ensure that a stronger partner or group leader does not mask other learners' true level of understanding. Multiple-choice formats can be an effective way of asking hinge questions without taking up too much time.

---

4   Wiliam, *Embedded Formative Assessment*, p. 101.

META-COGNITIVE QUESTIONS

The type of questions that you devise to seek proof of learning should not just be about whether or not the learners have got the answers. They should also check how they got them. Here are some examples you can use *before* starting a piece of learning:

- What parts of the topic do you feel most/least confident about?
- How have you solved problems like this before?

Here are some examples you can use *during* a piece of learning:

- What parts of the learning do you find easiest/hardest to explain to someone else?
- What are the steps or stages that best explain this concept/problem?

Here are some examples you can use *after* a piece of learning:

- How will you remember this learning?
- If you did this again, how would you do it differently?

Questioning for proof is not just about checking to see if learners have got the answers right at a particular point in the learning journey. Meta-cognitive questions provide better proof to the teacher that the learner has really got it, and not just stumbled on the answer by accident or by using a process that won't help them to solve similar problems in the future or in different contexts.

Meta-cognitive questions can be asked before, during, and after learning has taken place. For example, a few skilful meta-cognitive questions asked while learners are at the planning stage of an essay can give both you and them a sense of where they might be about to go wrong. This is a great time to intervene with some tips and pointers that will shift them towards a much more successful piece of work.

Asking a high ratio of meta-cognitive questions in the normal course of your teaching is a great model for your learners. Encourage them to do the same and to ask themselves meta-cognitive questions while they are *planning* a piece of work, *doing* a piece of work, or *reflecting* back on a piece of work and considering how it can be improved.

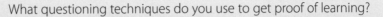

What questioning techniques do you use to get proof of learning?

What percentage of your questions do you create before the lesson or topic even starts?

What percentage of your questions are meta-cognitive in nature? When do you ask them?

2. LISTENING FOR PROOF

No detective worth his salt begins an investigation with a set of ready-formed ideas about who has committed the crime. That's the stuff of bent cops in the movies. Such a detective would be accused of folly or high-handedness at best; malice, prejudice, or corruption at worst. It's not even an excuse to say that such behaviour is expedient and would save time. When miscarriages of justice occur, as they do, the appeals process can be long, and means that everything has to be thoroughly re-examined.

The best detectives, like Columbo, are active listeners. They listen intently to colleagues, victims, and suspects. They keep their minds active, open, and curious so they can elicit high quality evidence to find proof of what has really happened.

And so it is with the most effective teachers. They listen intently to what others say, particularly their learners. They listen carefully to the answers learners give to their judiciously crafted question as they probe for evidence of learning. These teachers are attuned to the feedback they get from their learners because it helps them to meet their learning needs more effectively. These teacher detectives realise that ploughing on regardless, thinking that they know best, is counterproductive. Clouseau-like teachers might get through the module in six lessons rather than seven or eight. But it's highly likely when they see the poor quality of the end-of-module test results that they'll need another three or four lessons to reteach what many learners didn't get first time round. Columbo-like teachers, on the other hand, testing as they go for what is really happening in their classroom, rarely find that their *Titanic* has been sunk by a giant tin-opener.

Here are some proven strategies for how to listen for proof.

CLASS SURVEYS

Maths teacher Darryn Robinson has developed a survey that he asks his class to complete at the end of each term. He doesn't have to do this – it's not school policy. It's just his way of working towards becoming a better listener and a more effective teacher. By seeking out quality feedback from learners, he demonstrates a fantastic teacher detective characteristic: he wants to learn about his learners.

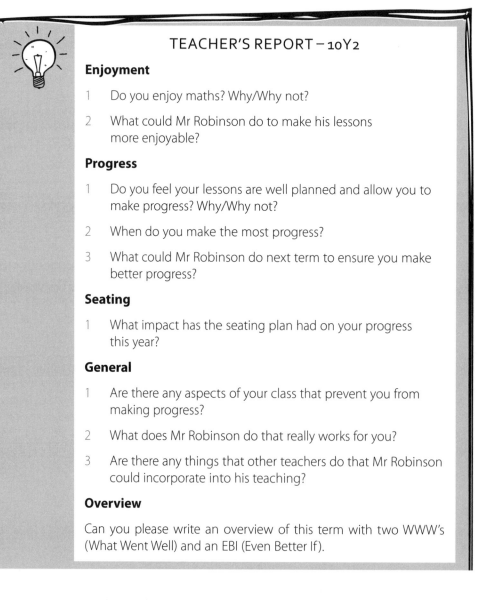

TEACHER'S REPORT – 10Y2

Enjoyment

1. Do you enjoy maths? Why/Why not?

2. What could Mr Robinson do to make his lessons more enjoyable?

Progress

1. Do you feel your lessons are well planned and allow you to make progress? Why/Why not?

2. When do you make the most progress?

3. What could Mr Robinson do next term to ensure you make better progress?

Seating

1. What impact has the seating plan had on your progress this year?

General

1. Are there any aspects of your class that prevent you from making progress?

2. What does Mr Robinson do that really works for you?

3. Are there any things that other teachers do that Mr Robinson could incorporate into his teaching?

Overview

Can you please write an overview of this term with two WWW's (What Went Well) and an EBI (Even Better If).

As you can see, lots of the questions pertain to progress. Progress is his focus and he wants that to be his learners' focus too. It takes him a while to read through their responses and to think about how he will integrate their suggestions into his teaching. But he knows that the time spent is worthwhile and, over time, his listening and reflection has paid off with increasingly better results.

LISTENING AROUND YOUR CLASSROOM

A great many teachers who have been through the Outstanding Teaching Intervention have become more proficient at getting evidence of progress through listening. Among the more effective behaviours they develop are the detective's skills of being more curious and more hands-on. In other words, they become less didactic and less likely to be stuck at their desks or lecturing from the front of the class for long periods. Good detectives can usually be found interacting with the 'crime' scene. In the case of teachers, the crime is not knowing whether their learners are getting it or not because they're too busy delivering from the front of their classroom and not engaging sufficiently with their learners.

But it's also possible to be too interactive – to go too far towards the other extreme. In his quest to get proof of progress, one Year 5 teacher we worked with must have burnt over 500 calories in the lesson buzzing around his classroom. No learner, it seemed, went more than five minutes without him commenting on their work. At the end of the lesson, we watched fascinated as he berated his class for the disappointingly small amount of writing they'd done. Twenty-four hours later, after watching the video of his lesson, he suddenly understood why so little progress had been made. He had intervened far too much. Since this epiphany he still moves around the classroom, but he's training himself to act more as an observer. He's now more reflective and he takes notes from listening in on learners' conversations rather than butting in all the time.

When teachers move around the classroom in a thoughtful and purposeful way they can interact with their learners and actually talk *and* listen to them. These conversations will often enable the teacher to gauge what has been learned and what still needs to be done. These real investigations with individuals and with groups allow the teacher to become a far better teacher detective – a listening teacher can tune into his learners' answers and be able to pick up on who seems confident, who still seems unsure, and who is completely stuck. The awareness that comes from this high quality feedback enables the detective teacher to reassess, recalibrate, reteach where necessary, and move everybody forward.

UNCONDITIONAL POSITIVE REGARD

It may seem too obvious a point to make but when people are in the presence of a really good listener they tend to feel totally at ease. Columbo was very good at this. Through attentive listening he really got to know, and often respect, those he was trying to chase down. Great teachers also put the learners at ease. They create a classroom environment that values individuals and their differences. We particularly like the technique called unconditional positive regard.

In *Engaging Learners*,[5] we describe how the term 'unconditional positive regard' was coined by the humanist writer and thinker, Carl Rogers. In his book, *On Becoming a Person*,[6] he suggested that it can be most helpful, when working with people you find tricky, to hold them in unconditional positive regard. The fact is, unconditional positive regard is a helpful belief to hold when working with any learner, tricky or not. Thus, any teacher who takes a genuine interest in their learners, does not hold grudges, regularly uses their names, believes they can do well, works hard to build their confidence, and is not afraid to engage in straight talking and honest feedback with them when necessary, is likely to be demonstrating unconditional positive regard.

Take a moment or two to reflect on the quality of your listening. Consider whether or not there might be occasions when you could be perceived by your learners (or colleagues, or friends, or family) as judgemental or as having favourites. Adopting the mindset of unconditional positive regard offers you a strategy for listening to everyone in your class for roughly equal amounts of time and without judgement.

FINDING MORE TIME FOR ONE-TO-ONE CONVERSATIONS

Many teachers we've worked with find they have more time for one-to-one reviews with their learners. This is due to the fact that they use some of the time that they used to spend delivering to the whole class to create more time for individuals. Some are able to do this on a termly basis, some even more regularly. During these one-to-ones, books can be scrutinised and evaluative questions asked which help teachers to discover just how much each learner has understood about a particular topic or learning module.

---

5   Griffith and Burns, *Engaging Learners*, p. 66.

6   Carl Rogers, *On Becoming a Person: A Therapist's View of Psychotherapy* (London: Constable & Robinson, 1961).

ICT teacher Mark Harrison likes the fact that his teaching enables more purposeful one-to-one discussions with learners. He creates appointments that he emails to learners and they email back their acceptance. He now routinely finds time to interview each of his learners on three separate occasions during the academic year. Each interview lasts about 10 minutes. In the sessions he asks learners to take him through their portfolios. These portfolios can be presented in digital form or a more traditional paper-based format, such as ring binders. At their best, portfolios can provide another way for teachers to get proof of learning. At the same time, they can also become an immense source of pride for their owners. After all, portfolios are used in many different professions, such as architecture, design, fashion, and the arts. Professional portfolios can powerfully demonstrate the owner's level of skill and range of expertise to potential customers, employers, or even examiners. They serve a similar function for Mark's learners, but the springboard for their development is when the learners first sit down in their one-to-one to talk him through their progress and their gaps. Learners know the session will be 10 minutes long and they know that they will be expected to do most of the talking. So, his routine also serves the purpose of getting learners to be more organised, more articulate, and to take greater responsibility for their progress.

No one really trains teachers in how to conduct one-to-ones or reviews, but here are a few suggestions about how you can use them to seek proof that learning is taking place:

- Create the space for them. Establish routines, appointments, and schedules and let learners know about this in advance. Advise them that they will do at least one of these per term so they don't think it's a one-off.

- Focus on progress. Have some good probing questions prepared (especially meta-cognitive ones) and expect the learner to do most of the talking. Praise appropriately learners who are working hard to achieve and even go beyond their targets, and be ready to admonish those who appear to be coasting.

- Use this kind of review as an opportunity for getting feedback through listening. Ask learners whether they're enjoying their learning. Can they speak confidently about their target and the steps they need to take to get them there? What gaps do they currently have in their learning or KASH?

How good are your listening skills? How do you know?

How much time do you dedicate in your lesson plans for listening?

How much time do you make to listen attentively to individuals?

How well do you monitor your listening and conversations for unconscious judgements or favouritism?

3. BEING HARD TO FOOL

Columbo doesn't make assumptions. He has a healthy mistrust of the surface appearance of things. He also knows that the techniques that were successful in wrapping up his last case might not work for the present one. Columbo never guesses although he may have the occasional hunch. In short, he has a healthy and enquiring scepticism. And even when he's confident that he's tracked down whoever is responsible for any wrongdoing, he doesn't rest on his laurels. He knows that when he takes the case to court, he'll need to provide proof of guilt beyond any reasonable doubt.

If you revisit the quiz at the beginning of this chapter (see page 147), you'll see that the most robust evidence for learning came from those activities where learners were required to perform in some way. By asking learners to put something into their own words, explain using a diagram, or deliver a presentation, the teacher gets hard evidence about the true depth of their learning. Simply getting them to repeat what they've been taught 'parrot fashion' doesn't give the same level of proof. Hard evidence is required that learners can not only apply what they've learned but can also recreate it in other formats.

PROOF THROUGH LEARNING PERFORMANCES

A learning performance is any challenge that requires learners to show, prove, or demonstrate in some practical way that they really do understand what they've been learning. Learning performances come in many formats and they offer innovative ways to get learners to prove their learning has achieved or exceeded the standards you demand. According to Grant Wiggins and Jay McTighe:

> In general, we can say that if learners really understand something, they can effectively apply and explain it in some performance. By 'performance' we do not mean a mechanical, scripted response or mindless plugging in of a memorized formula. Rather, we expect learners to flexibly and intelligently use what they know, in a complex situation where higher order thinking in the use of content is required.[7]

The performance formats that we suggest below are by no means exhaustive. You can find or create others of your own. Some can be used as free-standing assessments at the end of a unit, whereas others may be better employed as stepping stones during a module of learning. We've chosen ones that learners find engaging and which offer strong sources of proof of progress for the teacher.

LEARNER PRESENTATIONS

In this format, learners plan a presentation and deliver it. This can be done individually, in pairs, or small groups, as long as each learner has a discrete part to play in both the planning and delivery. The key is not to get learners simply repeating back what they've read or been taught. They need to be encouraged to find ways of making the learning their own and expressing it clearly through the presentation format they've chosen. The challenge to present and be evaluated on their learning gets them to think hard about how they summarise, put across what they've learned, and bring it to life. Various presentation formats can encourage learners to enact the role of the teacher. This is a very powerful pedagogic exercise. We have both found that, as teachers and as trainers, getting topics across clearly and memorably is a much tougher challenge than simply writing about them as we did when we were at school.

It's a good idea to insist that the presentations are interactive so that the presenters have to take questions from the audience at the end. Learners really are demonstrating understanding of a concept when they show that they can teach it to others and respond in the moment to challenging questions.

Learners' presentation skills can be improved through levelling up using a simple rubric covering areas such as preparation, delivery, visual aids, audience, and structure. Download the full rubric at:

http://osiriseducational.co.uk/TB/resources/

---

7   Wiggins and McTighe, *Understanding by Design*, pp. 22–23.

Outstanding Teaching Intervention trainer Phil Badham uses iPad apps to great effect to help learners become better presenters. Traditionally, learner presentations have often been produced outside of the classroom and delivered in class to an audience of peers. This has a rather daunting and formal quality, and it can provide a whole set of challenges for less confident learners. For schools where mobile devices are used by learners and teachers, presentations can become spontaneous, interactive, engaging, and be a truly shared experience, often taking a fraction of the time normally reserved for these activities.

Apps such as Explain Everything, Nearpod, Educreations, and cloud-based presentation applications like Prezi allow learners to assemble presentations of their work in a much more immediate and dynamic fashion by drawing on the native functions of the device (e.g. camera, video). In conjunction with creativity and productivity apps, these allow learners to assemble sophisticated responses in a multimedia presentational form quickly and easily *in situ*, rather than having to go home and spend hours on a static presentation.

- Explain Everything. The name says it all. This versatile app enables learners to pull content from their devices (e.g. text, images, video) and assemble it quickly into attractive presentations. It uses video recording and audio recording so learners can demonstrate examples of live processes (e.g. mark on a map the progressive expansion of the British Empire) and record audio over the top. These pieces of learning evidence can be shared directly with teachers or peers using cloud-storage applications like Dropbox.

- Nearpod. For true engagement and interactivity, Nearpod is a fantastic presentation tool that enables learners to include polls, web pages and searches, videos, and interactive activities in their presentations (e.g. quizzes or quick questions). Nearpod also has the great feature of letting an audience view the presentation on their own devices, but the presenter can 'lock' the slides until he or she is ready to move on. Probably best suited to more in-depth presentations, Nearpod is a powerful tool for engaging the whole class and helping the learner to become the 'teacher'.

- Prezi. This is a cloud application that can be accessed from any device with an internet connection. It differs from normal presentation tools in a number of ways, but its principal draw is its ability to be non-linear. Although the presenter can create and follow a sequence, or path of points, Prezi actually holds all the information on one massive page which can be zoomed in and out of at any point and explored in numerous different ways. It allows embeddable video and images which can be searched for and placed directly from Google. The presentations are stored online, so learners can get easy access to them without having to worry about having the right software or about the size of the file.

- Haiku Deck. A simple but attractive presentation tool, Haiku Deck uses high impact visuals and large text to quickly create slideshows. It is designed to hone learners' presentation skills by not filling up the slides with lots of text. This puts more emphasis on the learners' ability to communicate and engage through their performance without merely relying on the slide content.

- Adobe Voice. Designed as a story-telling app, Adobe Voice is perfect for the classroom as it blends audio commentary with easy-to-use templates to create short explanatory 'movies'. The app comes with an abundance of soundtracks, backgrounds, and images which are ready for use. However, users can pull their own content into the programme if they prefer. Its beauty lies in the speed at which engaging content can be produced and shared. Although the movies themselves do not require learners to present in a formal environment, in terms of capturing evidence of learning it melds speed with functionality and encourages succinctness.

In the previous chapter we offered some advice on how teachers can become better at explaining. The same techniques can be used to great advantage with your learners. Challenge them to explain to each other, or to you, what they've been learning. For example, they can be asked to describe a model of good practice. This exercise can be used in any subject from art to zoology. Explanation formats can be used with exam questions, exam answers, coursework, assignments, essays, maths calculations, scientific formulas, and so on.

One example of an explanation format requires learners to study a text or piece of practical work and find fault with it. Learners explain clearly what the faults are and then describe how they would fix them. We call these 'find and fix' challenges.

Maths teacher Steve Bodman regularly gives his learners, working in pairs or small groups, examples of work to critique. Embedded in the work are problems that need fixing. Learners may have the same or different examples to work with. As time passes, he'll expect his learners to get better at identifying what the problems are, why they are errors, and then explaining to the rest of the class how they can be fixed. In short, Steve is training his learners to skilfully 'mark' the work against agreed criteria.

Examples of work with common errors are instructive and can also be good fun. It's reasonably straightforward to devise a points system, such as 1 point for spotting an error, 2 points for fixing one, and 3 points if you can explain it clearly to others. However, you lose points if you identify an error when there isn't one there. So, challenge the learners occasionally by giving them some perfectly correct worked examples and invite them to spot the errors!

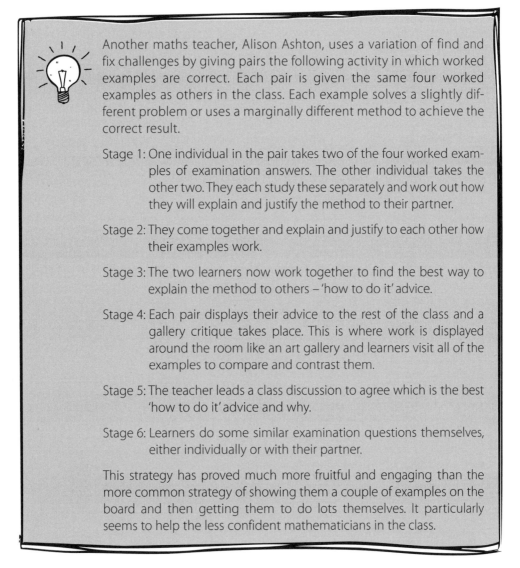

Another maths teacher, Alison Ashton, uses a variation of find and fix challenges by giving pairs the following activity in which worked examples are correct. Each pair is given the same four worked examples as others in the class. Each example solves a slightly different problem or uses a marginally different method to achieve the correct result.

Stage 1: One individual in the pair takes two of the four worked examples of examination answers. The other individual takes the other two. They each study these separately and work out how they will explain and justify the method to their partner.

Stage 2: They come together and explain and justify to each other how their examples work.

Stage 3: The two learners now work together to find the best way to explain the method to others – 'how to do it' advice.

Stage 4: Each pair displays their advice to the rest of the class and a gallery critique takes place. This is where work is displayed around the room like an art gallery and learners visit all of the examples to compare and contrast them.

Stage 5: The teacher leads a class discussion to agree which is the best 'how to do it' advice and why.

Stage 6: Learners do some similar examination questions themselves, either individually or with their partner.

This strategy has proved much more fruitful and engaging than the more common strategy of showing them a couple of examples on the board and then getting them to do lots themselves. It particularly seems to help the less confident mathematicians in the class.

EXPLAINING BY USING METAPHOR

Barry Hymer has written extensively on how using metaphor can help to deepen learning.[8] He advocates inviting learners to come up with a metaphor to explain aspects of their learning. This encourages them to 'perform' a more robust proof of their learning

---

8   Barry Hymer, *Gifted and Talented Pocketbook* (Alresford: Teachers' Pocketbooks, 2009).

– or lack of it. Metaphors are particularly good for drawing attention to the relationships between things, whether these are people, characters, or historical, scientific, or mathematical relationships.

Finding an apposite metaphor takes time. Learners will need to reflect, test, and consider. This process naturally develops learner understanding. Getting students to work on metaphors in pairs or small groups is also very productive. You can then direct the class to share their metaphors and decide on which they think is best. Of course, 'best' can mean many things – for example, the most memorable, the most accurate, or the most fitting.

USING VISUAL METAPHOR

A visual metaphor is the representation of a person, place, thing, or idea by way of a visual image that suggests a particular association or point of similarity. Try asking learners to come up with a visual metaphor by way of explanation. Learners can use mini-whiteboards or slips of paper to create an image or series of images which they feel best represents the concept or relationship being studied. For example, learners studying a character in a novel or short story who is on the point of moving home or changing jobs could be asked to look at the image of the leaping fish below and invited to suggest connections.

Alternatively, you can give learners a series of images and ask them to choose one or rank them according to a set of criteria. In each case, it's usually a good idea to ask them to verbalise their thoughts around the image(s) so that you get to hear the learners' reasoning. Make sure you leave enough thinking time whether learners are working alone, in pairs, or small groups.

The internet is a great resource for high quality visual images to use in the classroom. Try building up your own collection. There are great images that can be used with learners at:

http://www.theguardian.com/world/series/eyewitness/

http://commons.wikimedia.org/wiki/Main_Page

QUIZZING FORMATS

Establishing routines where learners are regularly tested is as old as the hills. We still remember our weekly spelling tests in primary school. The pressure of these tests certainly made some of us work harder. When these sorts of routines are well established it tends to focus both teacher and learners.

Teacher Abbie Tucker has been experimenting with routine quizzes for her learners. Her quizzes always take place on a Friday morning and have proved very useful for helping her to find out both what has been learned and what has been forgotten. They take place in silence and learners are not allowed to collaborate on answers. She calls these 'inter-leaved' assessments because the tests are not just about the topic that is currently being studied. As the year progresses, the quizzes embrace all five of the key topics that her learners have to cover during the course of the academic year.

She uses these quizzes to do two things. First, they help her learners to remember what they've been working on so that their learning really sticks in the memory. At the same time, she acquires powerful evidence about learner progress. The results of the tests give her immediate feedback about where her learners are and what she might need to reteach and to whom.

Different types of quizzes can be an enjoyable way to review topics. Contemporary quiz formats that the learners are all aware of, such as *The Chase*, *Who Wants to be a Millionaire?*, *Blockbusters*, and *Mastermind*, can be adapted for groups as well as for individuals. A sense of cooperative competition with learners vying against each other in teams can be very productive. Mini-whiteboards can come in useful for learners to record their answers.

LEARNERS AS QUIZ SETTERS

It can be very effective to invite learners working in small groups to set quizzes and tests for their classmates on a topic they've been studying. This has several advantages. First, learners tend to set tougher tests than their teacher because their natural competitiveness wants to make life for their classmates as hard as possible. Second, to set tough test questions you need to have a good command of the material, so it encourages the learners to go deeper into the topic they've been studying. (It's important to set a rule here: each group must be able to provide a model answer for each question they set.) Third, it saves the teacher time and energy. The learners set the test, not the teacher. The learners do the marking using their model answers. All the teacher needs to do is check the quality of the questions and the adequacy of the model answers.

How do you get learners to 'perform' their learning? How can you set different performance *tasks* for them? What resources could you provide to support different learners through their performances?

4. SMALL OR BIG EGO

Detectives and teachers with a low ego are nearly always more effective. Peter Falk's Columbo is a modest, self-effacing soul. We're not sure whether Columbo would have made a great teacher, though, as teaching is not just about detective work. Certainly, some head teachers or ministers of state might not have appreciated his general scruffiness and laid-back demeanour! However, we've loved every minute of watching him on TV over the years, fulfilling his detective role with excellence and giving us some great ideas about teaching and training.

We've come across many low ego teachers in our time in schools. They tend to care a great deal about their learners and take pride in doing well by them – usually much more so than those teachers who have high egos. They want to make the learners the heroes of the learning journey, and for that we often find them inspirational. In essence, low ego teachers are much more likely to teach backwards.

One area where low ego teachers particularly outshine their high ego colleagues is in the area of proof seeking. They're more likely to seek proof through establishing routines, such as pre-planning questions, investing time to get to know their learners, listening to and observing their learners, and using this feedback to find the most suitable learning activities to help them to make progress. Furthermore, they don't have to be right all the time. They can acknowledge their mistakes and see them as an opportunity to improve their teaching skills, particularly in the area of adapting their teaching to what the learners really need. As one of our own teacher trainers said to us many years ago, 'If the learner can't learn the way the teacher teaches, it's useful if the teacher can learn to teach the way the learner learns.' And you can't do that if you think you're the one who's always right.

FAQS

I use a range of methods for checking that my teaching translates into learning but I didn't realise some methods were better than others. What more can you add?

Some teachers are better than others at reading facial expressions or creating an environment where learners feel confident to openly express themselves when they're confused. As it's clearly not possible to work with all of you personally, we wanted to share our thoughts about the most robust forms of proof finding. A lot of teachers have come across the term Assessment for Learning (AfL). But not all AfL techniques have similar impact. It's wrong to think of AfL as something to tick off in a lesson – 'I've done traffic lights'. The main thing we want to invite you to do is think about the relative quality of the techniques that you use to gather proof of learner progress. We suggest you particularly think about this at the pre-planning stage. Seeking robust proof from learners enables you to better adjust your teaching when some learners go off track. Experiment using different methods. All we suggest is that you continually evaluate their effectiveness.

There seems to be a lot in this chapter about the frequency of seeking proof. How often do you recommend that we check where learners are heading?

We've recommended a variety of proof-seeking methods in this chapter. It's true to say that the quicker we get feedback from learners, the more accurate we're likely to be in judging their progress. We recommend that you seek proof as often as you need to in order to be sure that learners are clear about what it is you want them to achieve. If your habit is to wait until the end of the lesson to check understanding, then it will be too late to correct any misapprehensions and false assumptions they have until the next lesson. At the other end of the scale, use your judgement so that your checking doesn't get in the way of learner flow, as in the case of the teacher cited earlier in the chapter.

We suggest you get into the habit of seeking proof earlier in the lesson/topic and seek it regularly. And we strongly advise that you plan the ways that you are going to do this before you start teaching a topic. Some of this will be proof from outside of lessons – for example, from marking homework. Most schools now have a policy on marking frequency that forms an entitlement for learners, so that they never go more than a few weeks without being given written feedback. Certainly, a good maxim is to seek proof robustly and on a little-and-often basis.

IN A NUTSHELL

Thinking like a detective can help teachers to become better at proving that learning has taken place. Detectives know that they need to gather hard evidence to create the level of proof required to secure a conviction. Similarly, teachers need to distinguish between weak and robust forms of evidence so that they can articulate the progress of each learner in their class. When teachers improve their skills of questioning, listening, and being harder to fool, they gather better proof that learners are on track, or not. The best teachers are like the best detectives. When they're able to put aside their egos and the need to be right, they get a far quicker and more accurate picture of what's really going on. This feedback can help them to adapt their teaching accordingly, just as detectives will adapt their investigations when new evidence comes to light.

TEACHING BACKWARDS CHECKLIST

Looking for proof of learning (micro – module of learning)	This is always part of my practice	I sometimes do this	I never do this
When I design modules of learning I think about how and when I will get proof that learners are on track.			
I have clarity about what learners need to be able to do or say that proves they have reached their destination.			
My ways of seeking proof of progress are robust. I don't just assume that learners are making progress.			
I plan my questions to seek proof that learners are progressing towards their destination.			
I make time to gather evidence of progress from every learner.			
I use a variety of different learning performances to gather evidence that learners are making progress.			

Looking for proof of learning (macro – course/ academic year)	This is always part of my practice	I sometimes do this	I never do this
I use a low ego approach in my teaching – inviting feedback on my teaching from learners.			
I don't make assumptions about whether learners have made progress and consistently seek strong evidence.			

Download this checklist from:

http://osiriseducational.co.uk/TB/resources/

TEACHING BACKWARDS ACTION PLAN: POINTS FROM THIS CHAPTER

How can you convert a 'never' to a 'sometimes' or a 'sometimes' to an 'always' in relation to this checklist? Remember, you are more likely to get your class to Level 1a if you do all these things routinely.

I need to stop/do less …

I need to start/do more …

FOR MORE INFORMATION ...

For those of you not familiar with Lieutenant Columbo this short YouTube clip might help:

https://www.youtube.com/watch?v=pZiv8vkxMac/

For those of you not familiar with Inspector Clouseau this short YouTube clip might help:

https://www.youtube.com/watch?v=93ZDOcU2TL4/

Answers from p. 146: From most likely to least likely: Suspect 3, Suspect 5, Suspect 4, Suspect 1, and Suspect 2.

Chapter 5
CHALLENGE

'Now I know they've really got it'

During one of our Outstanding Teaching Interventions in a secondary school, a teacher admitted to us that he'd become addicted to a certain bad habit. It was a habit he'd not even realised was a bad habit until that very afternoon. In fact, he said he'd even been quite proud of it. What followed took the form of a pedagogical confession.

He talked of his addiction to what he described as GLAs or 'good little activities'. He spoke candidly about how he spent hours assiduously sourcing new GLAs from various education websites, blogs, courses, and colleagues. Like an ardent trainspotter, he got a kind of fix every time he discovered a new GLA. He had numerous box files stuffed with GLAs in his stockroom. He used these GLAs to pop into lesson plans whenever he felt that the plan, well, how else can it be said … needed the fix of a GLA or two. And when he was planning lessons that were going to be observed, he would add extra GLAs so that the lesson had a special buzz.

We asked him what made a GLA from his perspective. He said that to qualify an activity had to create for him the feeling that the learners would really enjoy it. But now he reflected, after our intervention, that perhaps it wasn't enough just to create a warm feeling of enjoyment in his lessons. Perhaps it was the overall process of learning that ought to take centre stage.

We observed him teach a lesson to his Year 10 class. The lesson had two distinct halves. The first half contained his usual sprinkling of GLAs, whereas the second half had a much more challenging activity that pushed his learners to generate work that was of a very high standard. The learners' work was truly inspiring. Not only were they in flow but they had all produced thoughtful responses that were well above their target grade.

We discussed the lesson with him on the following day. We focused on the impressive responses he'd elicited from so many of the learners and challenged him to reflect on his own, and the class's frustration, that they had run out of time at the end of the lesson

– time that would have been available if the GLAs had been stripped out of the plan. His conclusion was clear and unequivocal: he needed to focus on creating high levels of challenge in lessons that pushed his learners to close gaps. He realised he could only do this if he planned backwards and stripped out any GLAs that did not support the key learning goals.

You may think this confessional is an extreme case. But, in our experience, it is a trap that a substantial number of teachers fall into. While we certainly support the need for enjoyment in the learning process, there is always the danger of losing sight of the bigger picture. As a result, some teachers fail to open big enough gaps in their lessons for some or all of their learners. As a consequence, opportunities are missed for learners to make much greater progress in their lessons. And the main reason is lack of sufficient challenge to allow them to do so.

WHAT'S IN THIS CHAPTER FOR ME?

■ Have you ever fallen into the trap of using activities without considering whether they really contribute to the overall aims of the lesson and needs of the learners?

■ Have you ever wanted to create more challenging lessons but needed additional tools?

■ Have you ever wished to progressively improve the quality of your learners' learning lesson by lesson?

Among the thousands of lessons we've had the privilege of observing over the years, the best are those that attained the standards of the Level 1a descriptor set out in the Introduction (see page 7). The key to this attainment has always been twofold. First, that the learners are actively challenged (i.e. both teacher and learners demonstrate excellent questioning of themselves and others) and second, that the learners actively engage with the challenge.

In this chapter, we'll explain how teaching backwards influences the level of challenge in lessons. We'll explore how each step in the teaching backwards process informs lesson planning; in direct contrast to the process of the GLA-inspired teacher we met at the start of the chapter. We'll seek to justify the importance of creating high levels of challenge in lessons and why the spoon-feeding approach is flawed. This justification is supported by extensive educational research and cognitive science.

We'll then explore practical tools and strategies to create higher levels of challenge, drawing on the best examples from the wide range of lessons we've observed across all key stages. The tools and strategies within this toolkit of ideas have been chosen for their flexibility and effectiveness. With each example, we'll provide questioning strategies and effective techniques to introduce differentiation.

WHAT'S THE THINKING BEHIND THIS CHAPTER?

Some teachers, mostly in secondary schools, argue that in this target-focused age, surely it's quicker just to tell. They talk about many of their learners wanting their learning broken down into bite-sized chunks that are easily digested without them having to think too much. Some teachers even speak of the almost tangible sound of plastic spoons being put down on classroom tables. One teacher recalled a conversation where a learner objected to having to think. 'Why don't you just tell me the answer?' the learner complained.

However, and this is the nub of this chapter, there's a huge amount of research and practice which strongly suggests that effective learning is achieved by the diametric opposite of spoon-feeding. The key words in this approach are challenge, engagement, and flow, plus the practice of CATERing for the needs of all learners. In the rest of this chapter, we describe some strategies that create excellent practice and outline some of the research that underpins it.

CHALLENGE: IT'S WHAT THE EXPERTS DO

In his book *Visible Learning for Teachers*, John Hattie, drawing on numerous examples of research and practice, draws a distinction between 'expert' teachers and 'experienced' teachers. He concludes:

[E]xpert teachers *do* differ from experienced teachers – particularly in the degree of challenge that they present to learners, and most critically, in the depth to which learners learn to process information. Learners who are taught by expert teachers exhibit an understanding of the concepts targeted that is more integrated, more coherent, and at a higher level of abstraction than the understanding achieved by learners in classes taught by experienced, but not expert teachers.[1]

---

1   Hattie, *Visible Learning for Teachers*, p. 30.

Our own experience over the last six years of leading the OTI programme in hundreds of schools has been the same. Those teachers who consistently achieve outstanding results, the ones that you'd want to teach your own children, all share this characteristic: they delight in making their learners' brains hurt and plan their lessons accordingly.

When teachers plan lessons that are high in challenge, we've found that the feedback these lessons provide has been more effective in helping learners to close gaps. The greater level of challenge provides richer opportunities for questioning and for generating the proof, or otherwise, that learners have closed gaps. In particular, it provides the teacher with more valuable feedback on where learners are getting stuck or are struggling – feedback that can help the teacher to quickly reshape the lesson to address the problem areas.

Without these high levels of challenge, and subsequent feedback, a lesson might easily proceed without the teacher or learners even being aware that there is a problem! One teacher described a particular activity he had planned for a lesson as being, 'A great opportunity to test the class's understanding to breaking point. I want to see if they really have mastered this learning.' Without high challenge, it is difficult to establish the extent to which learners fully understand the new learning being presented and therefore the effectiveness, or lack of it, of the teaching and learning taking place.

CHALLENGE AND MEMORY

A crucial element of learning is the ability to remember things. In his thought-provoking book *Why Don't Students Like School?*, Daniel Willingham, professor of psychology at the University of Virginia, examines the reasons why learners often forget what they have been taught. His conclusion is that 'memory is the residue of thought'.[2] Therefore, if you don't spend time thinking about information and grappling with challenges, then there is less chance of you remembering it.

We observed an excellent example of this when science teacher Steve Cullen created a fantastic challenge for his Year 8 biology class. The class arrived at the lesson to be greeted by the 'bleep, bleep' of a life support machine. Steve settled the class and informed them that they were working as trainee doctors in an accident and emergency unit. They then proceeded to work on a really thought-provoking scenario that we'll explain in more depth later in this chapter.

Steve contacted us a couple of weeks after the lesson. When we met up with him he had a massive smile on his face. He explained that the end-of-unit test results for these learners

---

2   Daniel Willingham, *Why Don't Students Like School? A Cognitive Scientist Answers Questions About How the Mind Works and What It Means for the Classroom* (San Francisco, CA: Jossey-Bass, 2009), p. 54.

were much better than anything they had previously achieved. He was delighted. Why were these results so much better? Why were the learners able to remember so much more of what they had been taught? The answer lay in the experiential challenge he had set them: making them think about a true-to-life scenario and some possible applications of what they were learning about. They had applied their knowledge and understanding to a real scenario and this had not only helped them to make meaning of it, but it also supported them to remember it.

Creating challenges in lessons that encourage learners to experience and think about the meaning of what is being taught is crucial to learning and sense-making. Whatever is meaningful and real enables learners to process more deeply and remember more effectively.

CHALLENGE, ENGAGEMENT, AND FLOW

As we explored in *Engaging Learners*, learners only get into flow if there is a suitably engaging level of challenge. We've found, time and again, that it is only in lessons that are high in challenge that learners can enter this flow state. As the internationally renowned researcher and author Mihaly Csikszentmihalyi has persuasively argued, challenge pitched at the right level is a fantastic motivational trigger. When this flow state occurs, learners can become so immersed in their learning that the teacher is often left standing idly by considering for once what a great job teaching really is!

Flow emerges when learners are motivated to work on an appropriately complex challenge. The teacher sets up the task and then ensures learners have the time and support to complete it. This way of working often requires learners to work collaboratively, promoting high quality discussion and peer teaching. A group of teachers in a secondary school in Shropshire with whom we were working found that raising the level of challenge in lessons made a huge impact on the engagement of their learners. They realised that their previous approach of taking the thinking and challenge out of learning had made their lessons dull and uninteresting for the learners.

 A key phrase in the previous paragraph is 'appropriately complex challenge'. As the level of challenge is raised, all learners will require access to more support and more resources, and these will be different for each learner. This is where the importance of the CATER framework that we described in the Introduction comes into its own. The five components of skilful differentiation – community, assistance, tasks, extension, and resources – are essential if we want our learners to embrace and overcome high levels of challenge in the classroom.

There's an expert teacher we work with – we know she's expert because her learners consistently outperform their GCSE target grades – who says: 'I refuse to differentiate learning, so that I give C-grade learners C-grade work and A*-grade learners A*-grade work. Whatever my school leadership team says when they observe me, my data over time proves me right because my learners with lower target grades massively outperform their target grades. If I give C-grade learners C-grade work it becomes a self-fulfilling prophecy. I believe they can *all* achieve A*, and many of them do.'

She is a passionate advocate of the CATER framework, applying it in ways that support all her learners to achieve their full potential. She constantly sets her students outcomes that are above and beyond what they themselves think they are capable of. How does she make it happen? She sees her class as a *community*. She takes them with her as they progress together through the year. She refuses to leave anyone behind. When available, she uses her teaching assistants wisely. She sets tasks appropriate to the development of each learner and stretches them through extension activities, encouraging them to go further whenever possible. Finally, she focuses on providing resources (such as writing frames and glossaries) that support learners with lower target grades to tackle more demanding work.

To provide her students with appropriate levels of challenge, she makes frequent use of a set of strategies that we call 'challenge frameworks'. These are designed to support learners to get into flow while they close the gaps between their starting points and their destinations. Alongside these strategies, she uses the CATER framework to continually remind herself that insufficient challenge creates boredom and excessive challenge creates anxiety. We'll talk more about these challenge frameworks later in the chapter.

THE VALUE OF META-COGNITION

Before asking students to work on any demanding task, it's generally very effective to set a meta-cognitive frame around the task in hand. This focuses learner attention on the best ways to approach what is required of them. Without sufficient framing it's very easy for learners to get lost in the sheer amount of data with which they are faced.

An English teacher we were working with reflected on this, having watched himself teach on video. He was shocked that having got his class to read through a particular passage in a novel, very few were satisfactorily able to answer a series of questions on it. His realisation was that they would have done much better had he given them some advance framing about the nature of the questions they would be asked. They had read the passage generally; framing would have challenged them to read much more critically. Their reading would then have had much more focus on the nature of the challenge ahead of them.

Meta-cognition (literally, higher order thinking) can help novice learners to think more like expert learners. It is thinking about *how* to do the task. For meta-cognition skills to develop effectively in our learners, it's essential that we ensure that the *how* and *why* are as explicit to them as the *what*. If we don't do this, there's a risk that they won't be able to get to the point where they can successfully apply their learning to other situations.

Before starting to work on a challenge, learners need to have in their minds a clear and effective plan of the key steps they are going to work through to address the task. The teacher can support this process by skilfully modelling for them the critical thinking steps they will need, as in the following example.

An A level business studies teacher is about to read through a case study with her class. Her aim is to prepare them with the skills required to answer an A level exam paper, so that they can ace it. Before starting to read, she asks her class, 'What clues or prompts should we be looking for when we read this?' She is seeking confirmation that her class are thinking like 'expert' learners. As she reads through the passage, she models her thought processes, giving her class a commentary on her own thinking, including the questions she is asking herself and the reasons why she underlines certain bits of information in the text.

Another example: in a Year 5 maths lesson, the class are asked to critique several examples of answers that include a range of mistakes. The learners work in pairs to identify what the errors are and why they might have been made. This activity forced the learners to think through each step explicitly and consider how best to avoid making the same mistakes themselves. The class even created a rhyme that helped them to remember the correct order of thinking steps.

These meta-cognitive frames and practices are essential to support students to tackle higher levels of challenge. Learners will be much clearer, and make far better progress, when their teacher has spent a few minutes requiring them to think about how they will approach the task in hand and why some approaches will be more effective than others. Such tasks focus the learners on process as well as product and invite them to consider what the task is really asking of them.

Here are some useful meta-cognitive questions for you to use:

- What's the key information you'll need to look out for when you're reading?

- What are the different ways you might go about this activity?

- What is this question/task really asking of you?

- Which approach do you think might be the most effective?

- What's the first thing that you'll need to do? Why?

- How might you help yourselves if you get stuck?

- Where might you go for more information?

- Given you have X minutes to work on this, how much time do you think you need to spend on each task?

THE ART OF TEACHER QUESTIONS

Surely, one of the key aspects of a teacher's job is to push learners harder than they would otherwise push themselves. Artful questions are one of the great ways of doing just that. Some teachers are black belts at asking questions that encourage learners to think more deeply than they might otherwise have done. Unless challenged by quality questions – for example, the meta-cognitive ones above – it's all too easy for some learners to think superficially or get away with doing just enough to get by.

By asking questions that provoke learners to become more focused and enquiring, teachers are pushing learners to close gaps and generate proof about whether or not they have achieved their learning goals. Whenever learners are unable to answer, or when they respond to these challenges unsatisfactorily, it suggests that there are gaps that need to be addressed, gaps that might not have come to light without the rich feedback that these meta-cognitive questions generate. Of course, it is necessary to bear in mind that the choice of questions will depend on what evidence you are seeking to uncover in each different context.

LARGE LEARNING

Challenge frameworks lend themselves well to what we call 'large learning'. Large learning is any activity in which we specifically require our students to make their thinking transparent as they work. Put learners into small groups, give them flip chart paper or sheets of lining paper, and ask them to organise and record their thinking processes on these during the activity. This technique is useful for two reasons. First, it enables learners to compare how their own thinking differs from the thinking of others, and to examine why that might be. The divergence in thinking might well prompt learners to consider other points of view. Second, it gives the teacher immediate feedback about how the class is really progressing and which learning gaps still remain to be closed.

HOW TO CREATE CHALLENGE

In this chapter, we'll describe a range of challenge frameworks that we've either used successfully ourselves or observed others using successfully in lessons over many years. We've chosen these particular frameworks for two very good reasons. First, because we've seen them used in many outstanding lessons where challenge was maintained throughout at an engagingly high level. Second, because of their adaptability. We have seen them working effectively at all the key stages, both at primary and secondary level, and across a range of different subjects. We feel that if they aren't already in your planning toolkit, then they should be.

BUT IS IT THE RIGHT FRAMEWORK?

The choice of which framework to use should, if you are teaching backwards, be based on the following question: will this activity help learners to close the gap between their starting points and their destination? If the answer to this question is no, then you need to consider a different activity. Otherwise, there is the danger of falling into the GLA trap! As you read on, why not look through one of your current units of learning and see where you could level up challenge by using one or more of these frameworks.

For each of the six challenge frameworks, we've provided an explanation of how it works, how to use it, and how it will stimulate learners. We've also suggested a list of possible (though not exhaustive) applications and supplied some suggestions relating to the CATER framework, as well as some meta-cognitive questions to get you started.

1. CREATING DILEMMAS USING PMI

Edward de Bono developed an excellent thinking tool called PMI (plus, minus, interesting).[3] It can be used when learners need to consider two or more opposing viewpoints, such as around contentious issues or decision-making. This simple activity is astonishingly useful because it challenges learners to consider a dilemma from different perspectives. Many learners find looking beyond their own immediate opinions and values both startling and eye-opening. Indeed, this easy-to-use process takes them way beyond simplistic analyses based on nothing more than unthinking prejudice or gut feeling. PMI is a tool that can be very productive when preparing learners for writing essays in which, for example, they have to compare and contrast ethical or moral issues, or differentiate between two items.

Here is an example of PMI in use. An author in his late thirties (OK, early forties) is interested in reconnecting with his youthful love of skateboarding. What might a PMI look like for making a wise decision about its viability?

P – Plus	M – Minus	I – Interesting
Possibility to make new friends. Adrenaline and nostalgia boost. Chance to wear clothing that hasn't been worn for 25 years. Opportunity to get more exercise.	Risk of losing existing friends. Risk of physical injury. The recovery time from injury will be much longer than when the author was 14. Threat of ASBO for skateboarding in the local shopping centre. Cost of purchasing any new skateboard equipment and clothing.	What will be the reaction of the author's children? Will they hate the idea of dad having a midlife crisis or join him? What will be the reaction of the author's wife and family? Will the tired body of the author remember how to skateboard? Will the author's old skateboard cope with the additional (ahem) ballast of the middle-aged author? Will the author have the time to skateboard? What will the author look like now in skateboarding clothing?

3   PMI was first described by Edward de Bono in *De Bono's Thinking Course: Powerful Tools to Transform Your Thinking* (London: BBC Active, 2006 [1982]), although he also employs the tool in his later work.

There may be elements of the interesting column that can be researched further so that these issues become pluses or minuses. For example, if the reaction from the author's children is overwhelmingly negative, that would become an additional minus point.

HOW TO USE PMI CHALLENGE IN LESSONS

Task: To challenge learners to think more deeply about a specific issue.

Organise the class into small groups and ask them to come up with three to five plus and minus points and two or three interesting points around that issue. This framework will force learners to think more deeply about the issue. You could also ask groups to consider only one aspect of the issue (P, M or I) and then bring them together to debate the pros and cons. At the end of these activities, you can get the learners to record their points on a PMI template which will provide them with a summary that can be used to write an essay.

PMI IN ACTION

Context: Mixed-ability GCSE religious education class.

Task objective: Kerry Burns, the class teacher, wanted her learners to evaluate the issue of abortion. Is it always wrong or can it be acceptable in certain circumstances? She also wanted them to consider how those with different religious beliefs perceive the issue and how these beliefs can affect people's decision-making processes about it.

Learners, working in groups of three, moved around three workstations in turn. Each station had a different scenario. The scenarios are related to three women, of different religious faiths, who are facing the choice of whether or not to have an abortion. Here is an example of one of the three scenarios:

Seeta has just found out that she is eight weeks pregnant. She is devastated as she has just qualified as a hospital doctor. She feels that now would be the wrong time to interrupt her career as she would miss out on important professional opportunities. Seeta lives with her husband who is very keen for her to have the baby. They have been married for five years. Seeta, her husband, and both their families are Muslim.

Learners spent 10 minutes at each station, reading the scenario, discussing it, and then agreeing on the P, M, and I points as to whether or not she should have an abortion. Each group recorded their points on a large PMI template (see example below). The teacher reminded the learners that they needed to explain in writing why they were putting each point into a particular category.

Photo: Kerry Burns.

Provide a summary sheet about each religion for learners who have knowledge gaps. If they don't know the Muslim, Anglican, or Roman Catholic positions on abortion, they won't be able to adequately PMI the scenarios.

Provide ready-made points on cards that learners then classify into plus, minus, or interesting.

Differentiate the content of the scenarios – simplify or make them more complex. Making them more complex will provide additional challenge to learners by making the decision less clear-cut.

Invite learners to adapt the scenario so that the weight of the argument might shift completely to the other side. For example, you could change the circumstances of Seeta's situation so that her Anglican family might support an abortion, especially if the pregnancy might be life threatening for her.

The teacher followed up this activity by asking learners to discuss a range of differentiated questions in small groups. The learners chose which level of challenge they took on. Some questions required them to apply their knowledge of the stance different religions take towards abortion, whereas other questions were more challenging and pushed learners to analyse and evaluate the decision from different perspectives – for example, from the viewpoint of Seeta's husband or from their own personal perspective.

These learners, having been challenged by the structure of the activity to explore beyond their own personal or cultural viewpoints, began to develop more of an understanding about why others had legitimate views which differed from their own. They were also able to explain and justify the stance different religions would be likely to adopt in each of the scenarios, as well as the extent to which the circumstances of the woman might or might not influence the religious viewpoint.

USEFUL TEACHER/LEARNER QUESTIONS WHEN USING PMI

- Why have you considered that factor to be a plus one?

- What would need to change in the scenario to change the balance of your PMI?

- Which do you think is the strongest/weakest argument in that category? Why?

- Which factor caused the most disagreement in your group about whether it was a plus or a minus?

- How does … tie in with what we know already?

- How has using PMI changed your initial feeling about this decision/choice/dilemma, if at all?

- Which of the plus/minus factors would you consider to be the strongest argument?

- What extra information would you need to help you to make a better decision? Where might you get that information from?

- Which of the points from the PMI would be most useful to use in your essay?

 Let's be magpies … Why not get groups to compare and contrast their PMI sheets with those of others? They could then 'steal' ideas that they hadn't initially thought of. A great example of cooperative learning.

OTHER GREAT LESSONS WE'VE SEEN WHERE PMI HAS BEEN USED

■ Considering which of the two candidates in the 1932 US presidential election was most electable.

■ Considering the strengths and weaknesses of different renewable energy sources.

■ Considering the relative strengths and weaknesses of a location for an industry, in geography or business studies.

■ Considering what choice a character in a story or play could or should make.

■ Deciding between different modes of transport to school.

■ Deciding between contemporary moral issues in PSHE, such as drug use, crime, healthy eating, and so on.

Where could you use PMI to raise the level of challenge in your lessons?

If this is a tool you could use regularly, why not print out class sets of PMI templates on A3 paper? If you got them laminated they would be reusable.

Get learners to summarise each point on a separate sticky note. Then they could move the point from one category to another more easily if they change their minds.

2. LIVING GRAPHS AND FORTUNE LINES

Living graphs provide an excellent challenge framework. They are an appropriate choice when learners need to learn about sequencing and/or factors that cause change over time. They are particularly helpful in challenging learners to better understand the information provided in a graph, especially turning abstract content into something more real and tangible.

Living graphs work like this. The learners are given a pre-prepared bar or line graph together with a set of statements which they have to place accurately on the graph. They then have to justify their reasons for placing the cards where they have.

Given the linear nature of graphs, living graphs are particularly suited to situations and contexts where information changes over time. For example, in business studies, a living graph could plot labour turnover in a firm or company over a period of time. Labour turnover is the rate at which staff enter and leave the organisation .

Living graphs provide the teacher with opportunities to include cards that might expose any misconceptions the learners might have. In other words, they are excellent activities to encourage learners to show what they know and prove they have achieved their learning goal.

LIVING GRAPHS IN ACTION

Here is a living graph which was used with a Year 10 BTEC PE class who were learning about the characteristics that affect the fitness of a rugby player. It is followed by a list of factors, some of which have a positive impact on fitness whereas others cause fitness levels to decline.

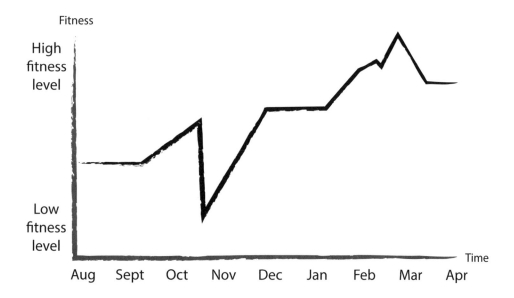

1   Injury to the carpals/metacarpals.

2   Bad weather means no games.

3   New gym membership increases the motivation to train.

4   The rugby season ends.

5   A prolonged time is spent on the substitutes' bench.

6   A semi-final cup match goes to extra time.

7   Training methods used are getting boring.

8   A more specific training programme is introduced.

9   A change in diet aids recovery.

10   Add a factor of your own …

The teacher, Tony Threlkeld, put the learners into small groups and gave each of them a set of cards. The task involved placing each of the cards accurately on the graph. The groups were told to justify their reasons for the placement of each card in writing. This enabled the class to compare and contrast their findings and justify the reasons for their choices.

The learners were absorbed by the challenge. Tony was explicit about the method they needed to follow. First, they organised the cards into two groups: the positive and negative factors that would cause the fitness of the rugby player to improve or decline. Next, the learners were asked to rank the cards according to how much each factor would affect the fitness of the player. Finally, they mapped the cards onto the living graph.

Given the ambiguity that Tony had built into the exercise, there were ample opportunities to test the learners' understanding to breaking point. There was heated debate in each of the groups as they refined their thinking. For example, there was discussion around whether the semi-final going to extra time would raise or lower fitness levels. Some learners argued that playing extra time might lead to improved fitness whereas others pointed to the fatigue and risk of wear-and-tear injuries.

This activity provided excellent feedback to the teacher on the learners' depth of knowledge of the factors that affect fitness. Learners took photos of the graphs, cards, and justifications and these provided excellent notes for them to write up as a piece of coursework.

For more advanced learners, the statements on each card could be made more ambiguous. As a consequence the challenge level would be higher.

Challenge learners to identify the assumptions they are making when putting each card on the graph.

Give learners a blank set of cards. The learners then have to write a statement on each card and identify where they would place it on the graph.

Provide a glossary of key terms to help those learners unfamiliar with any technical vocabulary (e.g. metacarpals).

Provide a flow map that helps learners to be clear on the thinking steps/methodology required to support the activity.

USEFUL TEACHER/LEARNER QUESTIONS WHEN USING LIVING GRAPHS

■ Would the information on that card cause the line to rise or fall?

■ Tell me more about why that card is there.

■ Where else could that card go?

■ What are you assuming for that card to go there?

■ Where couldn't that card go? Why would it be a poor choice to put it there?

■ Which of those cards would have the biggest positive impact?

■ What else could cause the line to rise/fall/remain unchanged?

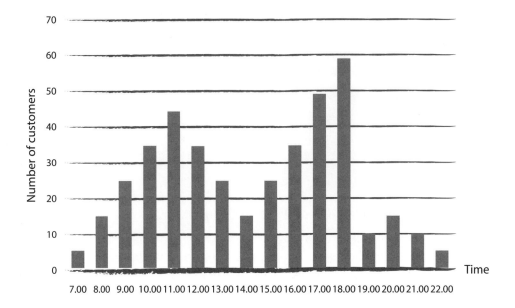

In this example, a day in the supermarket, learners were asked to interpret the information in the bar chart and place the cards where they believed each of the events would most likely have taken place.

1   Anita, a shop assistant, arrives to help open the store.

2   The shop manager asks, 'Do you want to go and have your lunch? It's quite quiet now.'

3   The queues at the tills are getting longer.

4   There are no loaves left on the shelves.

5   Mary is in a panic as her 3-year-old daughter has wandered off somewhere in the busy store.

6   All the shelves are full of food.

7   A delivery driver struggles to get past all of the parked cars in the car park.

8   Leon starts work to refill the shelves for the next day.

9   Anna drops into the shop on her way to work to buy a sandwich.

10   There are plenty of spaces in the car park.

11   All the tills are open and there are long queues at each one.

12 'Mum, Mum, can we get some sweets?' say the children on their way home from school.

OTHER GREAT LESSONS WE'VE SEEN WHERE LIVING GRAPHS HAVE BEEN USED

- Recounting the sequence of events during a school trip or in a story using photographs and statements.

- How blood sugar levels vary during the course of a day.

- The weather and the seasons.

- Changes in tension, attitude, relationships, and so on in a novel or play – short passages or quotes might be written on the cards.

Living graphs can be used whenever learners have to make sense of information that has been or can be presented in graph form. Where could you use a living graph to raise the level of challenge in your lessons?

FORTUNE LINES

Fortune lines help learners to extract information from living graphs and plot their own line showing the change over time of information or opinion. Whereas living graphs already contain visual information, fortune lines only provide the learners with the labelled axes – no data appears on the graph. Learners have to plot their own graph line using either information they gather themselves or that they're provided with.

Fortune lines are an extremely useful tool for getting learners to sequence events, make links between events, rank the impact of these events, and justify their reasoning. The activity provides an excellent level of challenge as there is a degree of ambiguity that promotes high quality discussion between the learners and requires them to engage in several important skills, including interpreting information, comparing and contrasting, justifying, explaining, sequencing, and link-making.

We've seen fortune lines used successfully in subjects such as drama, English and history, where they can inspire learners to get to grips with how characters, relationships, values, and events change over time. For example, in a lesson on Roald Dahl's story, *Danny, the Champion of the World*, the class might be asked to plot Danny's fear rating at different points in the book. To raise the level of challenge and deepen the learners' appreciation of writing skills, the class might then look at how the author conveys that sense of fear to the reader. What techniques does he use to indicate that Danny's fear level is increasing or decreasing?

HOW TO USE FORTUNE LINES

Provide the learners with a blank graph with only the axes labelled. The horizontal axis represents time. The vertical axis should represent something quantifiable – for example fear, hope, satisfaction, or power. Then give the learners a set of images or statements linked to the story or sequence of events they are studying, and challenge them to sequence these items in the correct order. This task can be done individually or in pairs. Once completed, the remaining task is for the learners to decide where each of the statements should go on the graph and place a cross where they wish to locate it.

The learners can then compare the fortune line they've plotted with those of others, explaining and justifying the reasons behind their choices. This discussion can provide learners with a richer, deeper understanding of characters and narrative.

It's possible to plot more than one line on the graph when learners need to compare the fortune of several different characters.

FORTUNE LINES IN ACTION

In this fortune line, the learners were asked to plot the change in Hitler's power during the 1930s. First, they had to arrange a series of events into chronological order, and then plot the changing fortunes of Hitler from 1930 to 1938. The teacher challenged the class to analyse and evaluate those events that were the most significant in Hitler's rise to power. He also urged them to seek out key interdependences between certain events. For example, how important was the Reichstag fire in terms of enabling Hitler to effect the ban on the Communist Party?

Power

Time

1   Following the death of Hindenburg, Hitler becomes Führer and Reich Chancellor.

2   As a result of the General Election the Nazi Party now have 107 representatives.

3   Britain, France, and Italy sign the Munich Agreement giving the Sudetenland to Germany.

4   Crystal Night. Thousands of Jewish shops are destroyed and hundreds of synagogues are burnt. It is orchestrated by the Nazi Party who also kill many Jews and send 30,000 to concentration camps.

5   The Communist Party is banned.

6   The Night of the Long Knives. Hitler destroys all opposition within his party.

7   German forces take control of the Sudetenland.

8   Peace treaty with Russia agreed with the Molotov–Ribbentrop pact. Hitler then invades Poland.

9   Hitler announces that the Nazi Party is the only political party permitted in Germany. Other political parties and unions are banned.

10 Anschluss. The German army occupy Austria and the two countries become unified.

11 Hitler becomes a German citizen. He is therefore allowed to stand against Hindenburg in the presidential election.

12   The Enabling Act gives Hitler the power to enact laws without involving the Reichstag. This effectively makes him a dictator.

13   Hitler is appointed chancellor of a coalition government.

14   The Reichstag is gutted by a fire. The Nazis blame the communists. Hitler uses the opportunity to hold fresh elections and win a larger share of the vote.

15   Hitler challenges Hindenburg for the presidency but fails to win.

16   Germany withdraws from the League of Nations. Afterwards, Hitler drastically increases the size of the German army and shuns the arms restrictions imposed by the Treaty of Versailles.

> One drama teacher we worked with discovered that using fortune lines made a huge impact on raising the level of challenge in her lesson. The class were studying Federico García Lorca's play, *Blood Wedding*. The class were asked to create a fortune line to plot the changes in tension during key scenes. The class then examined which techniques the playwright had used to heighten or lessen the tension. She was delighted – so much so that she created a class set of laminated A3 blank graphs so she could use them regularly without needing to produce new resources each time.

3. MYSTERIES

A mystery usually takes the form of a jumbled information exercise which challenges learners to solve a problem or organise information in a meaningful way. Through the process, learners develop their skills and knowledge across a number of key skill sets, including working cooperatively, sorting and classifying information, making links, and forming hypotheses. The key to an effective mystery is to give the learners enough space to work through the challenge by themselves – that is, without teacher intervention. Each learner is given some of the information necessary to solve the problem, but none of the learners have enough information to solve the problem on their own. The information may come in the form of a series of statements or, alternatively, there could be a mixed range of props, such as maps, photographs, and sounds.

HOW TO USE MYSTERIES

A good mystery usually has a question at its heart – a question that learners have to collaborate on in order to find the answer. The teacher can ask the question at the outset of the activity or the question can be included within the information itself. A simple example might be a short story that can be divided into 12 sentences and which contains a problem. In groups of no more than four, each learner gets three sentences written on a card. One sentence might say: 'How did the Sultan discover the identity of the thief?' The learners have to piece together the original sequence of the story and then use the information in the story to solve the problem. A narrative sequencing activity like this works best if two rules are applied: no showing and no writing. This forces everyone to be engaged in the activity as each individual has responsibility for a vital part of the whole.

With more complex information, such as in the A level business studies example on pages 204–205, divide the information into small pieces (between 15 and 30) and give each learner in the group an equal number of statements. Provide all the facts the group need to solve the mystery. Be sure that there are no individual clues which give away the answer. The activity is more challenging and beneficial if a large number of pieces of information must be combined to arrive at the solution. You might also add some red herrings in the form of irrelevant or misleading information, but ensure there are clues that will explain or discount them.

Learners tend to become absorbed in this type of challenge. They also understand that if the group is to succeed, they must each assume responsibility for a number of things that have traditionally been the teacher's responsibility. One of these is the task of getting everyone in the group to contribute, because each person has at least one piece of important information.

Avoid the temptation to jump in, help, or guide too much. Give the learners time to work things through for themselves – they'll find it much more satisfying when they succeed. If you do have to step in to move the process on, here are some helpful strategies:

- Give the group a limited number of 'question tokens' that they have to surrender each time they ask you a question.

- Drip feed more information as the lesson progresses in an intriguing way (e.g. police have found a CCTV 'still' of the scene).

- Provide a time-out midway through the activity where learners can ask questions and perhaps receive more information.

- Hold a 'brains' trust' at which the learners have to refine the information they've gathered. You can prompt them with questions such as, what are the five most important pieces of information you've uncovered so far?

■ Use hot seating – for example, you could ask a teaching assistant to role play the part of an eyewitness or suspect. Learners could compile a set of questions to ask them.

MYSTERIES IN ACTION

Here's an example of a mystery designed to challenge learners in a business studies class to develop a better understanding of the interrelationship between profit, costs, and sales revenue. The activity focuses on Buckenham Bikes, a bike shop which has had a bad year – its profits have fallen by 20%. Working in small groups, the class have to analyse the information below and decide what they think is the *one* most likely cause for the loss in profits.

1   The firm has no stock control system.

2   George rides to work each day as part of his training.

3   Buckenham Bikes Ltd has been trading since 1998.

4   Paul usually goes to lunch at 11.30 a.m.

5   Terry works in the warehouse on his own.

6   Norwich City Council have put £50,000 into making cycling safer in the city centre.

7   George has been working long hours in the shop to ensure the business remains solvent.

8   The government introduced the Cycle to Work scheme in 2005. This means that employees can claim back the VAT on bicycle purchases.

9   Sales of Trek bikes have been dogged this year by technical problems.

10 Terry usually has a late lunch so that he can visit Ladbrokes on his way back to the warehouse.

11 Cycling has become more popular since the gold medal-winning performances of Team GB at the London Olympics.

12 Buckenham Bikes is the registered dealer for Trek bikes in eastern England.

13 The Buckenham Bikes website deals with customers nationwide.

14 The shop has limited parking outside.

15 Unemployment is rising and is forecast to peak at 2.5 million.

16 The Halfords chain has recently been advertising heavily nationwide.

17 The warehouse is five miles from the shop.

18 Michael is a learner who works in the shop at weekends.

19 Buckenham Bikes has a good reputation with local cyclists.

20 This is the first recession that Buckenham Bikes has experienced.

21 Internet sales are up 70% for the firm compared to last year.

22 The Buckenham Bikes shop is located in Norwich city centre.

23 Buckenham Bikes Ltd has two shareholders, George, and his wife, Helen.

24 Paul and George share responsibility for repairing bikes brought in by customers.

25 Buckenham Bikes sells new bikes, equipment, and clothing. It also offers a repair service.

26 Halfords' stock control system has won a business award this year.

27 Norwich Retailers' Association have recently complained about the effect of traffic jams on trade. The jams are being caused by repairs to water mains pipes which have closed some roads to cars.

28 George's wife, Helen, had a baby six months ago. This has meant she has been unable to track the finances of the firm as she did before.

The teacher gave each group a visual organiser to help them to collate their thinking. With its help, the learners quickly identified that the shop's good reputation with local cyclists could not, in all likelihood, have caused either costs to have risen or sales to have fallen.

Profits fall by 20% compared to last finacial year Profit = sales revenue - costs	Causes of sales revenue falling	Causes of cost

Questions we have …

Not causes:

The answer to the puzzle, and it's based on a true story, is that Terry was selling stock on eBay to fund a gambling habit. His lack of supervision (working alone at the warehouse five miles from the shop) and his awareness that there was little oversight of stock control due to Helen's absence on maternity leave, meant that he had the opportunity to steal for a significant period of time without attracting attention. It took the arrival of the auditors to discover that stock was missing.

This mystery helped the learners to clarify some of the complex interrelationships that exist between profits, costs, and sales revenue. It helped them to grasp that some of the factors which create profit or loss might be external (e.g. competition, the economy), internal (e.g. poor organisation or management), or a mixture of both. In addition, they were able to develop their social communication skills, such as attentive listening, questioning, and turn-taking.

THE MYSTERIOUS CASE OF THE MISSING JELLYFISH

A mystery should bring together the powerful motivational triggers of fantasy, challenge, and competence in one compelling activity. For one group of learners, the mystery began in Min's reception class when one of the children noticed that Jess the jellyfish (Jess was a toy, not a real jellyfish!) had disappeared. Where could she be? For these children, one of whom was close to tears at the shock of Jess's disappearance, it was imperative that Jess be found. The children quickly assembled on the carpet and a small group were selected to lead the search. They took turns to suggest places where she could have gone or who might have taken her. All of the children were captivated. The mystery was almost undermined by one boy who pointed out, 'Jess can't have walked off, as jellyfish haven't got legs!' The faces of the teacher and teacher assistant were a picture as they tried to stifle smiles of admiration for this 5-year-old zoological expert.

The search party were each given a map of the school and, accompanied by their teacher, embarked on their quest to find Jess. The first clue led them to the chicken coop. But there was no sign of their gelatinous friend there. Instead there was a small box. The children excitedly opened the box. Inside there were pictures of a register, a telephone, and the school secretary. After two minutes of heated debate, the intrepid sleuths decided that this meant that their next move was to head for the school office.

When they got there they explained to the staff that Jess had gone missing. The school secretary, in a performance that was worthy of an Oscar, feigned disbelief and offered them a package which contained a further set of clues. Two more stops later and the children were delighted to find Jess, sitting bandaged in the medical room. Their delight was exceeded only by that of their teacher, Min, who had discovered how effective a mystery could be in developing the speaking and listening skills of her young learners, as well as their vocabulary.

USEFUL TEACHER/LEARNERS QUESTIONS WHEN USING MYSTERIES

- Which information is not relevant? Why do you say that?
- What's the question we're trying to solve here? (Useful when learners are struggling for direction.)
- What extra information might you need?
- What questions would you like to ask that might help you to solve the mystery more quickly?
- How are … and … linked?
- What makes you say that?
- What evidence can you give to back up what you've just said?
- What else could that mean?

Raise the level of challenge by adding red herrings.

Lower the level of challenge by drip feeding essential information so they don't get overwhelmed.

Use a visual organiser, as in the business studies example on page 204–205, to help learners to organise their thinking.

Offer additional support *resources*, such as glossaries or timelines of events, that might be appropriate.

MORE MYSTERIES IN ACTION

Why not use some of the following ideas to create your own mysteries?

- Which country is the murderer hiding in? – Geography mystery.
- Why is the Maori boy crying? – A human geography mystery exploring racism and inequality in New Zealand.
- Who killed our plant? – Biology mystery exploring what supports or hinders healthy plant growth.

■ Why did the product get rejected? – A design technology mystery (which works equally well in food, textiles, and resistant materials technology) where learners try to work out the reasons why a shop sent a product back to the supplier.

■ Why did this person die? – A Year 12 health and social care lesson about the neglect of an elderly person.

■ What's the mummy's code? – A Year 3 numeracy class using information from previously learned skills to discover the code that opens an Egyptian sarcophagus.

An English teacher we worked with simply took the plot from a Roald Dahl story, changed some of the names and details, and bingo!, there was a perfectly constructed mystery.

4. TRANSLATE NEW LEARNING

The learners walked into the classroom and received the shocking news. Their maths teacher, Lucy Bull, revealed that the head of maths had been murdered – repeatedly stabbed in the back with a set square. At this point, the class began to smell a rat. One of the learners piped up, 'But I've just seen her in the dinner hall.'

However, Lucy persisted in role. She informed them that their job was to help unmask the culprit. They were to apply their knowledge of speed, distance, and time to work out who could have been at the crime scene at the time the murder took place.

There were six suspects – all members of staff at the school. The learners were supplied with information about each of the suspects to enable them to work out which of the teachers could have been at the murder scene at the time in question.

We've worked with many maths and science teachers who've found it invaluable to challenge learners to apply their new learning in real and experiential contexts as a way of deepening their understanding and exposing any misconceptions. One maths teacher reflected on the problem of simply teaching to the test: 'My class all failed to complete the question on ratios in the last exam. They all knew ratios and could confidently do all of the questions I set in class. However, the wording of the exam question was slightly different from previous exam papers and it threw them totally.' His conclusion was brutally honest: 'If a small change in the question meant they couldn't do it, clearly they didn't understand ratios well enough. Which means that maybe I didn't teach it clearly enough!'

Challenging learners to apply their learning to other contexts has provided a valuable area for teachers of many subjects to explore. We mentioned biology teacher Steve Cullen and his Year 8 class earlier in this chapter. His aim was to extend and deepen the learning of his class so that they could describe how breathing is affected by damage to alveoli and to explain some of the effects of poor oxygen supply to cells.

He put his learners into the role of trainee doctors. They were told that a patient had been rushed in for treatment. Their task was to apply their knowledge and to analyse and evaluate the available evidence, before deciding on the cause(s) of the patient's condition. They were told that the individual had been admitted with a number of symptoms: tiredness and lethargy, chest pains, persistent coughing, and the production of dark phlegm.

There were three workstations around the classroom offering 'evidence' that learners, working in pairs, had to analyse. One was an experiment showing a sample of cells from the patient's blood, another station comprised the patient's heart (don't panic, it was a sheep's heart bought from the local butcher!), and the final station was a set of X-rays showing the patient's lungs. Steve also provided an 'NHS helpdesk' in the corner of the room with resources for those learners who needed additional support.

The quality of analysis was first class and the learners were in flow throughout. The medical reports they produced and their diagnosis of the causes were excellent. Many demonstrated a level of analysis pushing up towards AS level.

THE MYSTERY BOX

A Year 1 teacher, Rachel Armstrong, had been working with her learners on the use of the senses in creative writing. She created a fantastic challenge which required them to apply their learning to a new context. At the start of the lesson she unveiled a mystery box (like the one opposite). She told her class that there was something in the box and that she would read out clues, one at a time, to help them guess what it was. The children had to think carefully about their answers and ensure that every answer fitted with what had already been established about the 'thing' in the box.

Photo: Mark Burns.

Once the class were familiar with the game, Rachel sent the learners back to their tables. On each table was a mystery box, each one containing a different animal. The learners on each table looked in their own box to identify their animal. They then had to write sensory-based clues that would help other learners to guess what was in their box. In order to provide them with additional challenge, the more able learners were discouraged from writing clues that told others what the creature looked or sounded like. Instead, they had to use the senses of smell and touch to describe the animal.

The plenary saw each table read out their clues one at a time. The rest of the class were captivated by the task of trying to identify the mystery animal. All the time, Rachel was delighted as the learners were developing their descriptive writing.

How could you challenge learners to apply their knowledge or skills to a different context? As Daniel Willingham points out: 'It is virtually impossible to become proficient at a mental task without extended practice.'[4] Consequently, the more opportunities we, as teachers, create in lessons for learners to apply their new learning, the better. Over time, practice leads to better recall, shifting short-term to longer-term memory. Practice also enables learners to achieve a level of mastery that enables them to do things almost without thinking. For instance, when Mark's 6-year-old daughter, Ruby, gets dressed each morning, she has to concentrate totally to do up her shirt buttons. The level of concentration can be seen by her tongue poking out of the corner of her mouth. Andy's daughter, Anna, 17, on the other hand, can get dressed while eating toast and texting! Those extra 11 years of practice have led to mastery.

Here are some other examples of creating challenge through application:

- A teacher got his Year 9 English class to write and perform the voiceover for a film trailer to practise their presentation skills.

- Teacher Peter Moss invited his Year 7 music class to use everyday classroom items to collaboratively create a musical composition that resembled the sounds and rhythms of factory machinery.

- A Year 5 maths class applied their knowledge of area and space to design the layout of the shop floor and car park for a new supermarket which was to open next to the school.

- A reception class applied their subtraction skills to a game of ten-pin bowling. After each throw, the children had to calculate how many skittles had been knocked down and therefore how many were left standing.

---

4   Willingham, *Why Don't Students Like School?*, p. 107.

5. RANKING

Ranking is an activity that develops the learners' appreciation and understanding that, in any given context, different factors, concepts, and ideas are likely to have higher value or greater significance than others. Ranking challenges learners to work together to discuss and make judgements about the relative importance of different items. This importance may depend on a range of different factors.

Ranking develops several important skills, such as evaluating, justifying, reasoning, negotiating, and establishing hierarchies of relative importance. It can be very useful in helping learners to explore the idea that the top-ranked criterion in one context may not be the same in another. It is best if the criteria learners work with are precise. It's not particularly helpful to give them criteria such as 'best to worst' or allowing them to choose their own, as this simply promotes vagueness. Ranking activities are very good at promoting learner–learner discussion as the learners evaluate, justify, reason, and negotiate their way to a solution.

For example, history teacher Matt Heywood wanted his class to assess which of Prime Minister Harold Wilson's cabinet colleagues posed the greatest threat to his position. He did this by providing his learners with background information on each of his ministers. The class, working in small groups, had to analyse the information and complete a summary card for each individual (as in the example on page 212). By structuring the analysis in this way, Matt was able to ensure that his class considered the threat level of each minister based on a precise yet wide ranging set of clear criteria. This prevented learners from making superficial judgements. It also helped them to appreciate the range of factors they might consider when writing an essay on this topic.

Barbara Castle	
Score	Justification
Personality and background	
Vision	
Popularity	
Calamity	
Unreliability	
Overall threat	

The exercise ensured that the class were fully prepared for the debate in the second half of the lesson during which they discussed which of the ministers they felt posed the most threat to Harold Wilson and why. The success of the debate was entirely due to the quality of the preparatory work done in the ranking activity. It also gave Matt the reassurance that he could give out the written homework assignment safe in the knowledge that he would get back high quality work.

Physical education teacher Paul Brett really challenged his A level PE class with a highly creative ranking exercise. The class were learning about theories of arousal. Paul showed his class video clips of the four leading golfers from the final hour of the British Open Golf tournament of 2012. The class watched their tee shots, observed where each ball landed, and took note of the reaction of each player and the response from the crowd. Then Paul set them to work. Their challenge was to use their knowledge of theories of arousal, together with other relevant prior learning, such as theories of social facilitation, to correctly identify the finishing order of the golfers.

Working in groups of three the class set to work. Paul observed, assessed, and, where necessary, challenged their thinking with pertinent questions. It was one of those rare lessons in which when the bell rings the class want to carry on working. They were determined to solve the task before they went to lunch.

USEFUL QUESTIONS FOR TEACHER/LEARNERS

■ What are the strengths and weaknesses of …?

■ How did you decide that?

■ What made you choose that order?

■ Can you justify that decision?

■ Why do you think others ranked that differently?

■ What evidence can you give to support this point of view?

■ Might it be possible for someone else to rank these differently? Why might they do this?

■ How did you go about deciding on the ranking?

■ What other information would help you to make a better decision?

Add additional complexity to make ranking more challenging – for example, by providing additional information or by increasing the range of factors that learners have to assess.

Provide support materials that explain the thinking process necessary to complete the ranking more clearly for those who need it.

Find three specific instances where you could you use ranking to raise the level of challenge in your lessons.

6. VISUAL ORGANISERS

We're big fans of visual organisers. They're a fantastic tool to help learners structure their thinking before a writing task. In addition, they provide opportunities to refine understanding, particularly when learners see that certain information could go in more than one category. They also enable teachers to get richer feedback about whether learners have closed their gaps or not.

Visual organisers come in many flavours, shapes, and forms which can be used to encourage learners to sort, classify, sequence, and rank. From simple Venn diagrams to much more elaborate designs, we've seen them help teachers to raise significantly the level of challenge presented to learners.

You can download a range of organisers that you can adapt for your classes at:

http://osiriseducational.co.uk/TB/resources/

VISUAL ORGANISERS TO DEVELOP SORTING AND CLASSIFYING SKILLS

Visual organisers require learners to organise items into discrete groups based on their similarities and differences. This is a skill that learners have to develop from the Early Years onwards. Grouping items based on their similarity and recognising the differences between various groups enables learners to develop a deeper knowledge and understanding of the properties of those items. The process can enrich their appreciation of the full extent to which one item belongs to one group and not another.

The most common way to use visual organisers to sort and classify is to provide learners with a collection of cards printed with either images or words related to an area they have been studying. With younger learners this might include props. Then ask them to group the cards as they see fit. Providing words or images that could fit into more than one category can encourage impassioned and energetic discussion!

SORTING AND CLASSIFYING IN ACTION

The example opposite is from a science lesson. It shows a template to make a set of cards associated with acids and alkalis. First, the teacher asked the learners to sort the cards into those related to acids and those related to alkalis. Having done this, the class were challenged to subdivide the cards in each category into further subcategories. The learners came up with a creative range of new categories which included uses in real life, disadvantages, and characteristics.

Child cries because he got soap in his eyes	Litmus unaffected	NaCl	David unblocked the drains with strong bleach
Water	Stomach digesting food	Vinegar	Lemon juice
Rust on cars	PH7	PH2	Oven cleaner
Bleach	NH_3NH_4OH	Tooth decay	Can burn the skin
Indigestion	PH10	Baking powder	Sour taste
Bitter taste	NaOH	Turns litmus red	Soapy to touch
Milk of magnesia	Turns litmus blue	H_2SO_4	Black coffee
Often react with metals to leave a salt	Batteries	PH2	HCl

The activity encouraged the learners to identify the similarities and differences of acids and alkalis in more depth and breadth than they otherwise might have done. Indeed, they saw that the differences extended far beyond the PH values.

The information from this activity could be arranged in a visual organiser such as the one below. This framework invites the learners to classify the information into three categories: information unique to acids, information that acids and alkalis share, and information unique to alkalis. The teacher also challenged learners to add additional information to this visual organiser based on their learning in previous lessons.

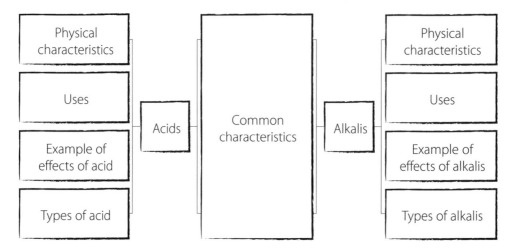

This visual organiser enables the learners to arrange all their knowledge about acids and alkalis into a format that facilitates easy retrieval. It also provides immediate feedback to the teacher on whether the learners fully understand the material. If they still have gaps, it's much easier for the teacher to pinpoint where those gaps are.

SORTING AND CLASSIFYING DIFFERENT TYPES OF BOOKS

During one lunchtime, teacher Katy Wren set up an excellent challenge for her Year 3 class to deepen their understanding of the characteristics of different kinds of books. It was an experimental lesson that convinced her of the importance of challenge in lessons. She put all the books in her classroom on the floor in the middle of the room and 'staged' a class mess. When the children came in from play and saw their books scattered around, she acted as though it was a surprise to her. 'Oh my goodness, what's happened? What would the head teacher say if he saw this mess?'

She asked the children for their help. They were only too keen to do so. She invited them to take books back to their table and sort them for her into different types, which they did with lots of discussion. She didn't give any criteria to the class – she let them decide this for themselves. The teacher was amazed at the quality of discussion among the children. They sorted them into picture books, fiction, and non-fiction. She then asked them if they were sure that all the titles were in the right piles. The learners all agreed that the picture books and fiction books were in the correct piles. Katy asked them to put these on the correct shelves at the back of the classroom.

The teacher noticed that there were still some fiction books on the tables among the remaining non-fiction books, so she gave the children large sheets of paper and asked them to look at all the non-fiction titles on their table and decide what they had in common and in what ways they were different. The outcome was astonishingly good. They correctly identified the remaining fiction books and came up with a list of features for non-fiction. She finished the lesson by asking the class what they had learned. The feedback was amazing. The whole class proved to her that they could describe the different characteristics of fiction and non-fiction books.

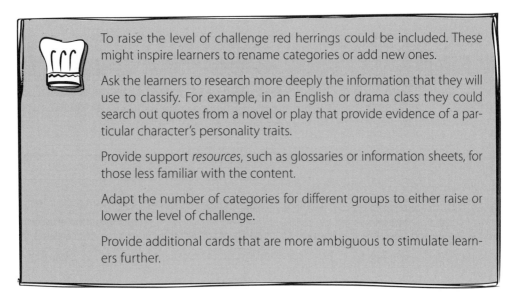

To raise the level of challenge red herrings could be included. These might inspire learners to rename categories or add new ones.

Ask the learners to research more deeply the information that they will use to classify. For example, in an English or drama class they could search out quotes from a novel or play that provide evidence of a particular character's personality traits.

Provide support *resources*, such as glossaries or information sheets, for those less familiar with the content.

Adapt the number of categories for different groups to either raise or lower the level of challenge.

Provide additional cards that are more ambiguous to stimulate learners further.

CAUSE–EVENT–EFFECT VISUAL ORGANISERS

This type of visual organiser challenges learners to organise information according to whether it's about an event, the causes of the event, or the effects of an event. The organiser on page 218 was created to help a class understand the differences between causes and effects. The teacher found that learners sometimes got confused when answering a question and often wrote about the causes of an event when the question was asking about the effects. She set her class the challenge of classifying the following information about migration from Mexico to the USA.

■ 850,000 were caught in 1995 and were deported.

- Mexican culture has enriched the US border states with food, language, and music.
- Adult literacy rates in Mexico of 55% because of poor education.
- Mexican migrants provide cheap labour for US firms.
- Excellent medical facilities in USA – 400 patients per doctor.
- Migrant workers keep wages low, which affects Americans.
- Harder for Mexican women to find a partner due to migration of young men to USA.
- Migrants send US$12.1 billion a year back to Mexico.
- High cost of patrolling the borders and deporting illegal immigrants.
- More than one million Mexicans migrate to the USA each year.
- High unemployment in Mexico.
- Plentiful low-wage job opportunities in USA.
- Illegal migration costs the USA millions of dollars for border patrols and prisons.
- Poor medical facilities in Mexico.
- Illegal migration is a huge problem for both countries.
- Racial tensions are high in some US cities.
- Incidences of TB are rising in the USA.
- Shortage of workers in rural Mexico.
- Life expectancy is 72 years in Mexico.
- Some Mexican villages have lost two-thirds of their population.
- Life expectancy is 76 years in the USA.
- The border between USA and Mexico is 2,000 km long.
- Most jobs in Mexico are low paid.
- US patrols guard the border to prevent illegal immigrants from crossing.
- Young people tend to migrate, leaving behind the old and the very young.

The learners used the following visual organiser to sort the information. Their teacher asked them to sub-classify the causes into push and pull factors. They also discussed which of the causes and effects were more important than others.

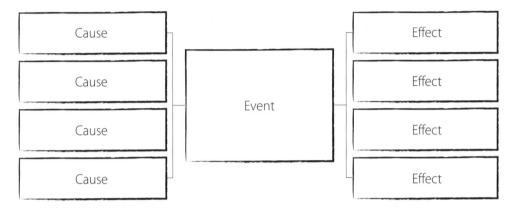

SEQUENCING WITH VISUAL ORGANISERS

This type of visual organiser is particularly useful when studying sequences or stages in a process. This is a common challenge in subjects such as history, the sciences, geography, and English. For instance, it could be a process like glaciation or stages in the flow of a story as in the example below.

Learning to put events into a logical order is a key skill in story-writing and the development of argument. In this case, the teacher wanted his class to develop their story structuring skills. He gave them a challenge which really got them into flow and helped them to see the power of a well-organised structure. He gave each learner a set of the cards above. Working individually, they had to sequence the cards in any order to make a storyline. They then stuck their cards onto the template below and wrote the story's plot underneath.

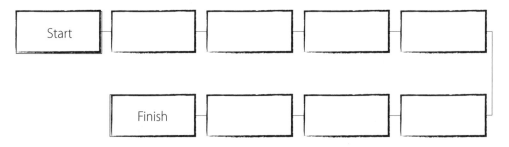

The teacher also pointed out, for those learners who wanted to explore the option, that they could also organise the cards non-chronologically by starting with a card later in the sequence and using 'flashbacks' in their stories.

This pair of visual organisers helped the teacher to realise just how valuable they could be in developing the clarity of the learners' thinking processes. As a result, the quality of their writing, in particular its inner coherence and structure, came on in leaps and bounds.

Provide more information or more ambiguity to increase the level of challenge.

Encourage learners to create their own subcategories.

Provide descriptions on the visual organiser to help support those learners who need them.

Provide a list of prompt questions that will help guide learners to categorise information.

USEFUL QUESTIONS FOR TEACHER/LEARNERS

- Why have you put that card there? Where else could it go?
- If you could have a new category, what would it be?
- Could you come up with another example that would go into that category?
- Which categories could that card definitely not go into?
- How are … and … linked?
- What makes you say that?
- What evidence can you give to back up what you've just said?
- How are those two categories similar?
- How will you remember the differences between the categories?
- If you had to summarise that category in one sentence or a picture, what would it be and why?
- How is the information in your visual organiser different to theirs?
- Can you explain the differences between your organiser and theirs?

Are you convinced by now of the usefulness and adaptability of visual organisers? If you are, create some class sets of the visual organiser templates that you would use most regularly. They could be laminated so that learners can use whiteboard pens or sticky notes to organise their thinking.

FAQS

Does this mean I have to completely re-plan schemes of learning?

Not at all. But what is essential is that you test the scheme against the backward planning steps. Does the planning open gaps for *all* learners based on their starting point? Are there sufficient challenge opportunities for you, the teacher, to get accurate feedback throughout the block of lessons? Based on previous experience, is there sufficient challenge to expose the misconceptions that usually arise?

Many teachers we've worked with have found that complete re-planning is rarely necessary. What they find instead is that there are usually particular areas of their schemes of learning that require both more challenge and more effective ways to differentiate learning.

What might happen if I pitch the level of challenge too high?

We've found this to be a common fear among teachers when experimenting with making their lessons more demanding. Typically, their experience (and ours) is that learners can cope with much more challenge than they think. We recall a PE teacher, Rob, who discovered his bottom set Year 7 learners were able to complete a task he wouldn't normally have given them until they were in Year 9! While we need to remember that too much challenge without adequate support can lead to anxiety, we want our learners to embrace demanding tasks and not to fear failure. Therefore, it's important for teachers to model courage in the face of challenge as we learn more about our own teaching and learning strengths and our current limitations.

What would you recommend doing first?

Why not take a look at how other teachers in your school create high levels of challenge. Our experience of working in hundreds of schools around the UK is that where teachers actively collaborate, share resources, and discuss planning together, the teaching and learning in those schools is more vibrant and teacher motivation is higher. Often, the best ideas come from someone who teaches a completely different subject or year group to yourself. Ask yourself, for example, how you can adapt an activity given to a Year 5 class for a Year 1 class. Why reinvent the wheel every day? Time to stop working harder and start working smarter! Or, see if you can arrange a 'swap shop' in your school where every teacher brings along their own top 10 challenges to share.

IN A NUTSHELL

Challenge lies at the heart of effective learning and it is the essential fifth step in the teaching backwards process. Without challenge, learners won't have the opportunity to stretch their potential or get excited about developing their knowledge, understanding, and skills to reach their learning destinations.

As learners grapple with the task in hand, carefully designed assignments offer the teacher the opportunity to gather accurate feedback about which aspects of the new learning their class have mastered and which parts they still need to improve. Challenge helps the teacher to expose any learning gaps the class may still have.

Research shows that high levels of challenge raise standards, get learners into flow, support them to apply their learning across different contexts, and remember it more deeply and for longer.

Challenge frameworks are a very useful and adaptable tool for engaging students in their learning while also providing deep levels of enjoyment and satisfaction.

TEACHING BACKWARDS CHECKLIST

Challenge (micro – module of learning)	This is always part of my practice	I sometimes do this	I never do this
I create opportunities in lessons to get rich feedback through the challenges I plan in lessons.			
The challenges that are planned in lessons are directly linked to the knowledge, understanding, and skills that learners are aiming to develop.			
I plan challenges that are appropriately stretching for all learners.			
I use questioning to deepen and extend learning.			
I model effectively the planning and thinking process skills that learners need to consider *before* they work on a challenge.			

Challenge (micro – module of learning)	This is always part of my practice	I sometimes do this	I never do this
I model effectively the planning and thinking process skills that learners need to consider *during* their work on a challenge.			
I use questioning to challenge all learners to provide proof of their learning.			

Download this checklist from:

http://osiriseducational.co.uk/TB/resources/

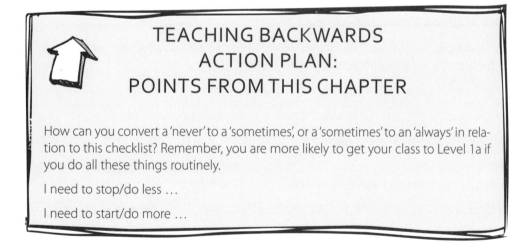

TEACHING BACKWARDS ACTION PLAN: POINTS FROM THIS CHAPTER

How can you convert a 'never' to a 'sometimes', or a 'sometimes' to an 'always' in relation to this checklist? Remember, you are more likely to get your class to Level 1a if you do all these things routinely.

I need to stop/do less …

I need to start/do more …

FOR MORE INFORMATION ...

When you know what you are looking for, there are many websites with ideas that can be adapted to create high levels of challenge in lessons.

For maths teachers, we highly recommend our colleague Darryn Robinson's website and the resources he shares:

www.richermaths.weebly.com/

For secondary school maths we suggest a visit to:

http://www.nationalstemcentre.org.uk/elibrary/collection/1160/durham-maths-mysteries#collection-resources/

For mysteries for Key Stage 1 and 2 maths, this site is well worth trying:

http://teacher.scholastic.com/maven/

For languages teachers at all key stages we recommend the following website, particularly as the authors are very generous in sharing resources:

http://www.sunderlandschools.org/mfl-sunderland/

For geography teachers our recommendation is this excellent collection:

http://www.sln.org.uk/geography/

This is a really useful blog entry by Alex Quigley on how to improve the quality of teacher questioning and push classroom discussion to a deeper level:

http://www.huntingenglish.com/2013/12/26/disciplined-discussion-easy-abc/

This is an excellent article on the importance of thinking carefully about planning so that learners think deeply about the 'right' things in lessons:

http://www.aft.org/newspubs/periodicals/ae/summer2003/willingham.cfm

Shaun Allison's thought-provoking blog reinforces the importance of high levels of challenge for all learners:

http://classteaching.wordpress.com/2014/03/02/raising-the-bar/

This is another really useful blog post from Andy Tharby on strategies to support learners to overcome challenge:

http://reflectingenglish.wordpress.com/2014/03/01/the-everest-writing-scaffold/

David Didau's blog entry on differentiation reinforces the message that, when planning, focusing on the destination is crucially important:

http://www.learningspy.co.uk/english-gcse/building-challenge-differentiation -thats-quick-and-works/

REFERENCES

Mihaly Csikszentmihalyi, *Flow: The Psychology of Optimal Experience* (New York: Harper and Row, 1990).

Edward de Bono, *De Bono's Thinking Course: Powerful Tools to Transform Your Thinking* (London: BBC Active, 2006 [1982]).

John Hattie, *Visible Learning for Teachers: Maximizing Impact on Learning* (Abingdon: Routledge, 2011).

Daniel Willingham, *Why Don't Students Like School? A Cognitive Scientist Answers Questions About How the Mind Works and What It Means for the Classroom* (San Francisco, CA: Jossey-Bass, 2009).

FURTHER SUGGESTED READING

Maths teachers working at Key Stage 3, 4, and 5 may like to invest in an excellent book, *Mathematical Team Games* by Vivien Lucas (St Albans: Tarquin Publications, 2003). The puzzles are already prepared for you!

We also recommend David Leat's *Thinking Through Geography* (London: Chris Kington Publishing, 2001) and David Leat and David Kinninment's *More Thinking Through Geography* (London: Chris Kington Publishing, 2005).

Chapter 6

FEEDBACK

'Can I come back after school to finish closing my gap please Miss?'

Sharon stormed into the feedback session, slamming the DVD of her lesson and her scribbled self-reflection notes onto the table. Either she'd been on an assertiveness course since we'd last seen her or this was going to be a tricky feedback session!

'Those lazy little so-and-sos [exact words modified to avoid a parental advisory label!]. Just look at their exercise books! Do they think I'm going to work myself into the ground? *They've* only got to do Year 5 once. *I* might have to teach it 30 more times!'

At this point a smile of relief crept over our faces. Like many other teachers before her, watching her own lesson on video had opened Sharon's eyes to the gap between where her class actually were and where she wanted them to be: Level 1a. Sharon had realised that her class were not in the habit of listening to and acting on the high quality verbal feedback she gave them. At least they were consistent! They weren't taking a blind bit of notice of her written feedback either. Our subsequent feedback session with her was extremely productive as we helped her to plan how to teach backwards and push her class up towards Level 1a. In particular, by getting her learners to pay attention to and act on feedback.

Willingness to act on feedback, both for teachers and learners, is critically important, but by itself it's not enough to achieve Level 1a. Something else needs to happen too. For example, in a Year 7 gymnastics lesson, we heard the teacher tell a group of boys that there was one particular gap they still needed to close in their gymnastics routine: 'Please work on making it more aesthetically pleasing, boys. I'll come back in a few minutes and see how you're getting on.'

The feedback was spot on, but it left the boys shrugging their shoulders. They had no idea what the teacher meant and were questioning each other about whether they had mis-heard him. 'Aesthetically? Doesn't he mean athletically?' commented one puzzled gymnast.

Needless to say, when the teacher returned five minutes later no progress had been made in closing the gap. The feedback was ineffective because the learners and their teacher weren't speaking the same language.

- Do you have learners who ignore or don't know how to work with feedback?

- Does your feedback have as much impact as you would like it to have?

- Do you and your class speak the same 'feedback language'?

- Do your learners have the skills to give quality feedback to themselves and to each other?

This chapter describes some of the inspiring journeys that Sharon and other teachers we've worked with have taken their classes on. These are journeys where teachers and their students have overcome the barriers that can get in the way of effective feedback and the resistance that often occurs when feedback is not offered in appropriate ways. These are teachers and students who have learned to share the same feedback language so they can quickly move onwards and upwards towards Level 1a.

WHAT'S IN THIS CHAPTER FOR ME?

Most teachers tend to run their classrooms using well-developed habits and routines, which can be very effective. Consciously and assiduously built up over time, they can enhance learning and the skills required to achieve it. However, there are also habits and routines that are unhelpful, that get in the way and slow learning down. This chapter will challenge you to reflect on your current feedback habits and routines and consider whether you're maximising the full power of feedback in your classroom.

The right kind of feedback, offered with real awareness, can have a massive impact on learning. Note the use of the word 'can'. We've observed thousands of lessons where teacher feedback has been utterly ineffective, and in some cases even detrimental to learning. Many of these teachers have simply been unaware of how to give quality feedback and what the key ingredients of excellent feedback are. How would you rate yourself in the art and science of giving feedback? Whatever your skill level in this critical pedagogical area, this chapter will enable you to develop and enhance your existing feedback skills.

As usual, we'll refer to gaps. It's a word that many teachers who've attended our programmes have adopted when they discuss how to develop and improve their classes. They talk about 'closing gaps' and the actions that are required to achieve this. The power of this concept is that it invites learners to stop comparing their performance with that of their peers and asks them instead to focus on their own personal gap – the one that exists between their current level of performance and the model or destination they are working towards.

WHAT'S THE THINKING BEHIND THIS CHAPTER?

In Chapter 5, we explored the importance of the judicious use of challenge when teaching backwards. Unless lessons are appropriately demanding, learners won't be sufficiently motivated or stretched to develop their newly acquired knowledge, understanding, and skills so that they can learn how to close their own gaps. However, challenge alone, important though it is, is rarely enough to help learners close the gap between their starting point and the model they're aiming for. What they also need is the magical ingredient of excellent feedback to support and guide them along their gap-closing journey.

We both remember the trial of learning to drive. In common with most novice drivers we had real issues with hill starts. So much so that we would sometimes study Ordnance Survey maps to try to plot a flat route for our driving lessons! Clutch pedal down: left foot; accelerator pedal down: right foot; listen to the engine revs; release the hand brake with the left hand, while holding the steering wheel in the right hand. It was all too much. Particularly when we're being hooted, flashed, and overtaken by impatient car drivers as we alternated between stalling and violently bunny-hopping forwards.

Without timely and useful feedback from our instructors, it's unlikely that we'd ever have mastered this tricky and crucially important driving skill. Without effective feedback, it can be hard to identify the root causes of whatever problems we're having as we try to learn a new and challenging skill, especially when we're not yet sufficiently aware to give accurate feedback to ourselves.

As novice drivers it would have been very easy to mistakenly blame our lack of mastery on our clutch foot when the real problem lay with our accelerator foot, or vice versa. If the feedback we got at the time from our instructors had been ineffective, we might well have ended up labelling ourselves as inept and useless car drivers and resigned ourselves to a life of bicycling! Then the Ordnance Survey maps really would have come in useful!

As it turned out, the effective feedback we received helped us to identify the gaps in our skill and knowledge, and to see how we could close them quickly to reach the smooth proficiency to which we aspired. The aim of feedback is to lead the learner towards mastery, a level of proficiency that enables them to recognise when something is going wrong and to know what to do to correct the problem in real time, just as when a competent driver, sensing the car is about to stall, with an almost unconscious adjustment of the foot, presses down ever so lightly on the clutch to prevent the engine from dying.

Finally, there's one more point we want to make about the relationship between challenge and feedback. In our experience, when learners don't need any feedback to close their gaps it's usually because they've been given insufficient challenge. And this usually means that no real learning is taking place because there's no stretch.

In this chapter, we'll identify the key factors and ingredients that underpin the high quality feedback that takes place in classrooms that operate at Level 1a, and we'll make available to you some of the most effective tools and strategies that enable teachers and learners to achieve this.

LEVEL 1A FEEDBACK

Level 1a feedback has three key ingredients, which we will explore in detail below:

1 Feedback is timely.

2 Learning adapts as a result of feedback.

3 Reflecting on feedback is a habit.

1. FEEDBACK IS TIMELY

In our previous book, *Engaging Learners*, we wrote about the importance of flow in the process of effective learning. One of the key ways that learners get into flow, and stay in it, is that they are able to give themselves, and each other, immediate quality feedback in real time. In this way, they can continue working effectively even when the teacher is engaged elsewhere in the classroom. The speed with which learners can act on feedback is essential here. As Doug Lemov and colleagues highlight in their excellent book, *Practice Perfect*, 'the speed of feedback is critically important – maybe the single most important factor in determining its success.'[1]

In classes where learners haven't been exposed to the discipline of effective feedback, and remain dependent on their teacher's input, two potentially damaging scenarios can occur while they wait in turn for their teacher to give them feedback. First, some learners waste valuable learning time waiting for their teacher to come to their desk to 'check' that what they're doing is correct. Others even follow their teacher around the room, trying to push their work under his or her nose for more immediate attention. This is highly ineffective. Waiting long periods for feedback is a clear reminder to these learners of their depen-

---

1 Doug Lemov, Erica Woolway, and Katie Yezzi, *Practice Perfect: 42 Rules for Getting Better at Getting Better* (San Francisco, CA: Jossey-Bass, 2012), p. 117.

dence on the teacher. The second scenario is that some learners will continue with their work while they wait for feedback. But in doing so, it's quite likely that they will continue to make the same mistakes and develop bad habits in the process. It's precisely these mistakes and bad habits that will negatively reinforce their feelings of incompetence.

The challenge for teachers is that it's not unusual for them to have a class of 30 learners or so to whom they want to give individual attention. How can they possibly give timely feedback to each one? It's nigh on impossible to tour the room giving and receiving bespoke feedback on this ratio without feeling highly stressed by morning break! So what can teachers do? The way the best teachers get their classes to Level 1a is by investing time in training learners to accurately identify where their gaps are and how they can close them. And not just in their own work but in each other's too! As a result, learners are able to give themselves and each other effective feedback in real time while they continue to work and stay in flow. If you consider this aim too lofty, just take a moment to think about what happens when your learners nervously enter the exam hall. As they proceed through the exam, they will have to rely solely on the feedback they give themselves in order to maximise their chances of success. Any other form of feedback in this context is called cheating! The exam results will give feedback not only on the effectiveness of the students' learning but also on the quality of the teaching they received.

As we stated in Chapter 5, every module of learning that a teacher plans should provide opportunities for teachers to give quality feedback to learners and to develop their learners' feedback-giving and feedback-receiving skills. We also argued that teachers need to insert opportunities for their students to give them high quality feedback too, so that the teachers themselves can learn to respond more effectively to the actual needs of each particular class.

Ensure that you set aside the time to observe, listen, question, and invite challenge from your students. Unless you do this, you'll miss the opportunity to receive timely feedback from them for your own development.

2. LEARNING ADAPTS AS A RESULT OF FEEDBACK

Several years ago, a maths teacher at one of our in-school training sessions admitted that he didn't see the point of marking books. 'I'd rather devote the time to planning my lessons,' went his argument. 'The only point of marking books is to keep Ofsted and the head teacher happy.' His colleagues were shocked by this admission. For us, it was a tell-tale sign that this teacher was teaching forwards not backwards. He was wedded to a delivery model of teaching which was not being adapted by feedback from his learners. The Level 1a teachers we've worked with highly value the opportunity to get feedback from their learners when they mark their written work because it provides them with the essential information they need about which gaps have been closed and which still remain. They also use questioning techniques to get feedback about what continues to cause problems for their learners and to gauge what and how they need to teach them next.

A primary school head teacher who we greatly admire put it perfectly. 'I don't want to see a week's worth of lesson planning from each teacher on a Monday morning. It's pointless doing this because that planning will be out of date by Wednesday. The feedback from learners during Monday's and Tuesday's lessons should cause the planning to be reworked.'

Similarly, an A level business studies teacher used the feedback summary sheet below to note down the gaps he identified in his learners' work while marking their essays. It helped him to summarise valuable feedback that he would use to plan subsequent lessons.

Feedback summary sheet	
Name	Gap identified

Feedback from learners, both written and verbal, enables teachers to adapt their teaching within lessons as well as modifying their plans for future lessons.

3. REFLECTING ON FEEDBACK IS A HABIT

The pace of modern life seems to be getting faster and faster. This can pose potentially huge dangers in the classroom. One of these is that time to reflect on the quality of our own and our learners' work can get squeezed. Many passionate and growth-minded teachers sense that the fast-paced culture of achievement in their schools paradoxically inhibits them from improving what they do in their classrooms. Indeed, some schools operate at such a frenetic pace that there seems to be no time available for either teachers or learners to reflect on the quality of their work. This is absurd because the relationship between active learning and reflective learning is well documented as key to transferring shorter to longer term memory, and to the process of critiquing and improving what one is doing. In his book *Thinking, Fast and Slow*, Daniel Kahneman explores the limitations of thinking fast.[2] He argues that our thinking is controlled by two systems which respectively produce fast and slow thinking. He repeatedly makes the point that failure to do enough slow thinking is counterproductive. Fast thinking has its place, but used inappropriately it can lead to decisions based on instinct and assumption which often turn out to be incorrect. Fast thinking can lead to poor decisions that could have been avoided by taking more time to think through the implications and consequences of what we were about to do.

One teacher we worked with recently reflected on the drawbacks of her fast thinking. 'I use Twitter extensively for ideas to improve my teaching. However, I think I'm trying to cram too many new ideas into my teaching, so that I'm not sure which ones are working and which ones are stopping me from levelling up.' Our advice was to slow down and take more time to reflect on which gaps she was going to prioritise and to work on closing those first. We also suggested that she only experimented with one or two new ideas at a time so she could really pay attention to whether they added value or not.

Despite current trends, it's perfectly possible to create a school culture that puts reflection and feedback at its core with startlingly effective results. Andy visited the inspirational Sandringham School in Hertfordshire, where being reflective is part of the staff's DNA. The quality and depth of discussion among the teachers was clearly the result of building a culture with reflection and feedback at its core. Staff collaborate extensively and many run action research projects designed to help them refine the quality of their teaching and learning, pushing their boundaries ever further. They actively live the concept of that

2   Daniel Kahneman, *Thinking, Fast and Slow* (London: Penguin, 2012).

brilliant sports performance coach, Sir Clive Woodward, who once famously made the point, 'Better never stops.'

As teachers, like it or not, we are the models that learners look to for direction and inspiration. If we don't show that we value reflection, then we can't reasonably expect our learners to do so either. If we don't stop to reflect in real time, then it's unlikely that our learners will develop the habit either. On too many occasions, we've seen fantastic opportunities for learners to make progress through timely feedback missed by teachers in a hurry. On just as many other occasions, we've seen learners miss great learning opportunities because they'd never been taught the discipline of pausing to reflect and then take action on the feedback they'd received.

HOW TO LEVEL UP TO LEVEL 1A FEEDBACK: CREATING A CULTURE WHERE FEEDBACK CAN THRIVE

So, how do teachers whose classes operate at the lofty heights of Level 1a do it? Have they just been lucky? Our experience tells us that luck plays no part whatsoever. What we've noticed is that these teachers teach backwards: they work hard to improve the attitudes of their learners towards feedback (which we wrote about in Chapter 1); they train their learners to give high quality feedback to themselves and their peers; and they make routines habitual and transparent in their lessons. As you read the rest of this chapter, consider your class(es) and how the suggestions we offer might help you to close the gap between your learners' current level and Level 1a.

DEVELOPING LEVEL 1A FEEDBACK SKILLS

We caught one teacher looking wistfully out of the window on one of our training days. She was considering all the benefits that could come with the skills we were talking about – skills that she and her learners currently didn't have. Our theme was how to turn a learner into a mini-me. A mini-me is a learner who has the skills and confidence to take over certain teacher roles and functions, in particular the giving of high quality feedback to themselves and their peers.

If we're to reach the Holy Grail of achieving Level 1a feedback, it's essential that we train our learners to look at a piece of work and provide the same gap-closing feedback that a good teacher would, as in the example below. Students had first been given a written assignment in class to answer an exam question, which was followed up by the challenge of critiquing their partner's answer.

Photo: Kerry Burns.

Here we can see the feedback that one young learner, Reece (a pupil at Broadgreen International School), gave to one of his peers. The quality of detailed feedback for a learner in Year 8 is excellent, so much so that his teacher is unable to add anything to improve it. In other words, at Level 1a learners are using the same feedback language and skills that their teacher would use. Given that we don't have the time each lesson to give every single learner live feedback, we need to commit to training our classes so that they can give themselves and their peers high quality feedback.

We've worked with many teachers who've successfully trained their learners so they can give themselves Level 1a feedback. We've seen the impact this has had both on teachers and their learners. Teachers notice that this process empowers their learners to move towards clarity and self-confidence. One teacher commented: 'The most powerful feedback is invisible in classrooms. It's rarely seen or heard. It's the internal voice in a learner's head.' When learners are able to give themselves high quality feedback, their increasing sense of competence and confidence is tangible. Suddenly they find themselves able to get into flow, absorbed by the challenge of closing their own gaps. Instead of being told by their teacher to work on particular gaps, these learners are now seeking gaps they can close independently. As a result, learner performance improves rapidly as they take greater responsibility for their own learning; time is saved because learners no longer have to wait for feedback from their teacher; and the teacher herself finds she has more time on her hands to give support to those learners who really do need individual attention.

Essential to success in developing Level 1a feedback is first to teach the skills, and second to give learners a chance to practise, practise, practise! It takes time to learn how to give accurate feedback to yourself and others – do not underestimate how much. As John Hattie makes clear, 'Learners get 80% of their feedback on learning from their peers and 80% of that is wrong.'[3] The fact is that feedback takes place between learners all the time. It also continually goes on inside their heads. It doesn't just happen when the teacher organises a peer or self-assessment activity. For these reasons, it's necessary to teach our learners proper feedback skills from the outset to counteract Hattie's prognosis; otherwise we leave it to chance.

In the section that follows, we've collected some of the most effective activities we've observed across more than a thousand lessons where teachers have not left feedback to chance. They've taught backwards. Instead of being satisfied with a low level of learner achievement, they've carried out a plan to develop their learners to Level 1a. These learners have developed the skills to give high quality feedback to themselves and each other on what next steps are required to close their own gaps.

---

3   Hattie, *Visible Learning for Teachers*, p. 131.

PLANNING THE JOURNEY

Teaching backwards from Level 1a requires a plan to close the gaps that learners currently have in their feedback-giving skills. Joanne Philpott, in her excellent book *Captivating Your Class*, aimed at Key Stage 5 teachers, details a structured calendar of development for peer and self-assessment from September to July so that the class can move together towards Level 1a.[4] The calendar of events develops the skill and culture of peer feedback over time, so that as the class progress towards the summer exams, they take progressively more ownership of assessment. This calendar is shared with the class in September so that they understand the plan for development and the reasons why it is important for them to work on it. Clear explanation of these reasons at an early stage prevents learners from asking, 'Why are we marking our own work? Isn't that your job?'

Crucial to the plan is a progression starting with the agreement of protocols in September. This ensures that all feedback given in class meets the three key feedback requirements of being *kind*, *specific*, and *helpful*. The teacher then gradually extends the scope and complexity of the critique until the class are providing high quality feedback to their peers immediately after they have completed a practice exam question. In this way, feedback is delivered much more quickly than it would have been if the class had had to wait for the teacher to mark it, and without any diminution of quality.

STEP 1: INDUCTION

If we want to build a culture where feedback can thrive, we'll need a step-by-step plan for achieving it. Ideally this will start during the induction period in September. But if you're already mid-term don't let that stop you starting as soon as you can.

SHARE THE FEEDBACK INGREDIENTS

Taking a class from Level 2b to Level 1a in terms of giving and receiving feedback to close gaps requires the same process of backward planning as does a module of learning. In Chapter 3, we emphasised how important it is that learners are clear about their destination and that they understand what is necessary to give great peer assessment. So, how should peer feedback, or any feedback for that matter, be given? Several years ago we were greatly impressed by Ron Berger's recipe for giving high quality feedback. Berger

---

4   Joanne Philpott, *Captivating Your Class: Effective Teaching Skills* (London: Continuum, 2009).

argues convincingly that there are three ingredients that support high quality feedback. It should be kind, specific, and helpful.[5]

When we critique others' work and give them advice it is important that we

Be Kind, Be Specific, Be Helpful

Source: Emma Lord.

It's important for feedback to be kind so that the receiver doesn't personalise it and experience it as an attack. When this occurs, and learners feel that their identity or their ability is being criticised, there is a natural tendency for them to become defensive and close down to the gift of feedback. When feedback is kind, the receiver is much more likely to open up to the benefits of listening to and acting on it.

Feedback must also be specific. It has to identify exactly what the learner has done well or failed to do well, so that the receiver clearly understands what he or she has to reproduce or avoid in subsequent work. The feedback should also pinpoint the specific steps that still need to be taken for the learners to close their gaps.

Finally, feedback has to be helpful. It has to help the receiver to improve in the context of the current piece of work. There is no point giving feedback that is simply a list of positive strokes without the necessary descriptive feedback on the successful or unsuccessful behaviours or actions of the learner. The feedback also needs to be given using language the learners understand. Excellent teachers find ways to check this understanding by asking questions or by scrutinising their learners' next piece of work.

Good feedback needs to be given using all three of these qualities. Kindness without specificity and helpfulness tends to lack rigour and clarity; specificity without kindness and helpfulness can feel too direct and intrusive; helpfulness without kindness and specificity can seem vague and undirected. In Level 1a classrooms, the teacher and the learners are aware of this and offer each other feedback accordingly.

Our experience in primary and secondary classrooms where learners are not working at Level 1a is that feedback is generally kind but neither specific nor helpful, as in the example below.

---

5   Berger, *An Ethic of Excellence*.

Photo: Mark Burns.

Learners tend to want to say nice things to each other about their work. Perhaps they fear reprisals in kind or that they won't be liked if they're more specific. It takes courage and training to know how to give feedback that is also specific and helpful. Even when learners are taught to use feedback scaffolding such as WWW (What Went Well) and EBI (Even Better If) they often fail to get beyond kind. They make general comments about improvement that are too vague for the receiver to do anything useful with. Unless feedback is kind, specific, and helpful, it will be of little use in helping the receivers to close their own gaps.

PEER MARKING AGREEMENTS

It's essential to establish clear protocols such as kind, specific, and helpful *before* introducing peer marking. This ensures that learners don't have to guess what is expected of them. Here's an example of a really effective peer marking agreement from a Year 4 class. Its strengths lie in two things: the clarity it offers the learners for giving feedback and the high expectations of the teacher who drew up the agreement. The ideal time to introduce this is in September, as part of the induction process, when each learner should commit to and sign the agreement.

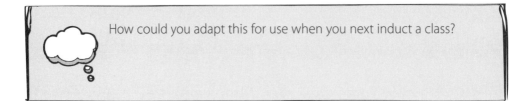

Peer Marking Agreement

When I mark my partner's work, I will always:
★ Read their work carefully.
★ Remember that it is their work and if I write in their book, my handwriting must be my best.
★ Think carefully about what I can say to help them.
★ Say what I like about their work.
★ Give them helpful and positive comments so that they can improve their work next time.
★ Think about what I can learn from them.
Signed..A.T.Smith..Date 23.05.13

Source: www.teachingessentials.co.uk *Photo:* Natalie Packer.

How could you adapt this for use when you next induct a class?

FEEDBACK TOP TRUMPS

The next step is to ensure that there is clarity around what we mean by high quality feedback. Several teachers we've worked with have adapted the format of top trumps cards to encourage their classes to understand what high quality feedback looks, sounds, and feels like, especially the requirement that it be kind, specific, and helpful.

Ask the class to work in pairs and give them a piece of written work to read. Then give each pair four different examples of feedback on this piece of written work. Ask the learners to decide which example of feedback is the best, working with the criteria of kind, specific, and helpful. To help the class in their analysis, provide them with a top trumps card for each one (see the example opposite). Ask the learners to award marks out of 10 for each of the criteria and to colour code the four texts identifying where each of the criteria is present. Tell them that if they identify feedback of low quality in any of the examples, they should use the space given to suggest improvements.

FEEDBACK A	
Kind	/10
Specific	/10
Helpful	/10
Improvements	

After the activity, the class can share their analyses – which feedback they thought was best and why. They can also discuss what gaps exist in the other examples and how these gaps could be closed. Finally, the learners can rewrite the other three examples ensuring that the qualities of kindness, specificity, and helpfulness are incorporated.

Whenever they are giving each other feedback, gently remind learners from time to time to be mindful of the three protocols. And if you really want to walk your talk, invite them to critique you on whether your feedback always conforms to the three criteria too!

STEP 2: BUILDING FEEDBACK SKILLS – HOW TO CRITIQUE LEARNER WORK

Having established a shared understanding of what good feedback consists of, the next step is to model the process of how to critique work. This is a skill so it will take practice. It's essential to set aside time for your learners to get better at it. If you don't give them time to practise, don't expect them to improve.

We've been really impressed by the way the iPad app, Explain Everything, can be used to enable classroom work-in-progress to be critiqued in real time (for more see Chapter 4). It can work for whole class or small group feedback. The app enables the teacher to import photographs or videos of the learners' work and then to project it, and even annotate it, in front of the class on the whiteboard or on a wall.

If you haven't got access to an iPad in your classroom, there are cheaper and less technical resources available. A visualiser can be used equally effectively for the same purpose and can be purchased for less than £40. Either way, unless you've got a way of projecting work onto a wall so that you can collectively assess and critique it, you'll find it extremely difficult to develop the Level 1a feedback skills of your class.

The key to modelling the process of how to critique student work is to talk through your thinking with the class, using the app or visualiser, as you assess an exemplar piece of work and provide feedback on it. As well as demonstrating *what* you're doing, it's just as essential to explain *why* it's important and for them to know *how* to do it for themselves. Making this explicit helps novice learners to think more like expert assessors when they evaluate a piece of work and give quality feedback on it. It will also help them to transfer their learning to different feedback situations as they start giving peer assessment to each other as the year progresses.

Make sure that each learner has a copy of the work that's going to be assessed so they can annotate it in the same way that you do. At each step, make sure they understand why the feedback is being given and that it's kind, specific, and helpful.

It's a really good idea to build up a bank of exemplar work for you and your learners to critique. Remember, your class cannot become expert assessors unless they practise regularly. Many teachers we've worked with have become avid collectors of examples of work for learners to evaluate in order to develop their assessment and feedback skills.

STEP 3: PRACTICE

The following three activities develop the peer assessment skills that learners will need to be able to share high quality feedback. They also help them to feel much more comfortable about the process. The usefulness of these activities partly derives from the fact that learners tend to find them very engaging. As we've said before, when learners step into a flow state, higher quality learning can take place.

BE THE TEACHER

This activity puts learners into the role of teacher – more particularly, into the teacher role of 'assessor'. The responsibility of this role can build a strong sense of competency within the class as they recognise that over time their assessment of their own work, and that of their peers, can approach the same level of quality as that of their teacher. In this activity, learners are given an exemplar piece of work to assess. The teacher asks the learners to grade the work using the previously established and explained success criteria. The 'assessors' should focus on giving feedback on what the candidate needs to do to close the gaps and to score full marks. This is done by carefully studying the piece of work, identifying which elements of the success criteria are present and which gaps remain. Learners tend to thrive on the responsibility they are given and take their role very seriously. Sometimes they can even be overheard making critical comments about the quality of teaching the candidate must have received to be making such mistakes!

Photo: Kerry Burns.

This activity tends to be most successful when the whole class are working on the same example. In this way, the feedback the teacher receives means that they can easily notice and point out any aspects the learners may have overlooked. The activity not only allows the class to reflect on the candidate's mistakes but also enables them to identify mistakes that they themselves have been making when critiquing. This is an excellent activity for developing a shared language of feedback with a class, and provides instant feedback to the teacher on the level of clarity learners have achieved about feedback success criteria.

A Year 1 teacher used the same principle with her class in the example opposite. She told the children that the head teacher was coming to check that all her learners' books were up to date with the marking. She explained that she'd found some work she'd forgotten to mark and asked them if they would help her. Of course, being Year 1 learners they were very keen to help and readily agreed. The children took to their task diligently, checking the work for finger spaces, capital letters, spelling, and full stops. Once they'd marked all the work, they checked in with the teacher before writing final versions of their feedback. Just as they finished, the head teacher arrived. Putting on a performance worthy of a BAFTA, she set about theatrically checking all the work – with a magnifying glass, no less! – and praised the class teacher for her excellent marking. When the head teacher left the room, the teacher congratulated the children for doing such a good job and saving her from getting into trouble.

Photo: Wendy Brown.

SPOT THE MISTAKE

Challenging learners to spot mistakes is an excellent way of developing feedback skills. One French teacher used this to good effect. He was seeking to improve learners' attention to detail – too many of the class were dropping marks by sloppy conjugation of verbs and poor use of tenses.

He provided his Year 10 class with five examples of written work. Each example had a different number of mistakes. One example had five mistakes, another four, and so on. The teacher challenged the class, working in pairs, to correctly identify the number of mistakes in each of the examples. This activity saw learners carefully scrutinising each example in turn. When they'd decided on the number of mistakes in a particular instance, they got immediate feedback from the teacher on whether they were right. However, if they were wrong, he wouldn't tell them which mistakes they had overlooked. The class became very competitive. They wanted to be the first pair to identify all the mistakes correctly, yet the need for attention to detail meant that each pair needed to take the time to be sufficiently rigorous.

After the activity had concluded, the class discussed the different mistakes that had been made in the examples and how they themselves could avoid falling into the same traps. The teacher then set the class the target of proofreading their future written work for these same mistakes before they handed it in for marking.

> How clear are your learners about the feedback improvement advice they are given?
>
> Are they able to give high quality feedback to their peers?

GUESS WHOSE FEEDBACK?

This is a really effective activity for challenging learners to develop greater clarity about giving and receiving high quality feedback. It also encourages learners to think more deeply about the feedback offered by the teacher and to learn from each other's feedback. Use it when handing back work that you've already assessed, but instead of providing written feedback in each learner's workbook, write your comments on separate slips of paper. For each piece of work, write three key feedback comments – the points that the learner should pay most attention in order to close their gaps. Next, arrange the class into groups of three or four. Return the books to each learner and give the group all of their combined feedback slips in a shuffled pile. Thus, for a group of four there will be 12 slips. Their task is to match each feedback slip to the piece of work to which it applies. This demanding activity encourages learners to identify and assess the gaps that exist in each of their pieces of work, and then to assess and identify the feedback advice that aims to close those gaps.

Initially, this exercise can be done with all the learners using the same exemplar work and feedback comments. This enables the class to compare their decisions and identify any lack of consensus. With practice, learners become better at correctly matching the feedback to the appropriate piece of work. We've also seen teachers create more challenge by leaving gaps so that learners have the opportunity to add to the feedback given.

STEP 4: LEARNER AUTONOMY

When the teacher has proof that learners are able to give Level 1a feedback they can be given more autonomy. Remember, the emphasis is on proof not assumption. One teacher we worked with was very clear about this. She argued persuasively that she needs to see a learner give accurate feedback at least three times for her to be convinced that he or she is an expert on that piece of learning.

LEARNER-LED CRITIQUES

When learners have achieved this level of skill, critiquing can be learner-led, although the teacher might still act as a hands-on observer, as was done in a GCSE history lesson we observed. The teacher began by distributing the success criteria for an A* written answer that the class had co-constructed with him during the previous lesson. The teacher wanted the learners to critique an exemplar answer before working on improving their own essay writing. Each learner was given a photocopy of the exemplar answer and, after 10 minutes of silent assessment, the teacher invited them to share their views. One of the class acted as a scribe and collated their observations. The feedback was projected onto a screen through an iPad, and the feedback was then annotated with comments about the changes that could be made, and why, and where they could be inserted into the exemplar text. The class skilfully identified the gaps that were preventing the answer from gaining an A* grade. The teacher was delighted with the quality of their analysis. Satisfied, he sent them off to write up their own answer in silence. As they commenced the task, he turned to us and whispered, 'That's great. This will mean I'll need to spend less time marking their answers.' He had successfully trained his learners to know how to work with success criteria and apply them as feedback to a real piece of work. His experience was that when his class were able to identify gaps in the work of others, they'd be much less likely to leave the same gaps in their own work. They would also be able to see more clearly the steps they'd need to take to reach their A* destination.

As learners become more proficient, critiquing can be done by groups of learners working independently of the teacher. The teacher is then free to work either with particular learners or to circulate the classroom, monitoring and advising on the quality of the feedback.

One PE teacher we worked with used his iPad to great effect in a lesson on high jumping. He videoed the approach and take-offs of his learners as they worked to improve their jumping technique. Then he stopped the activity, called the learners over and played the video clips back to them, pausing at key points. The learners used the high jumping success criteria that they'd worked on previously to unpick which parts of their own performances needed to be adapted. Seeing was believing. Up till then, they'd all been convinced they were using gold medal standard techniques. Two minutes of reflection with an iPad showed them where their personal gaps were and what they needed to do to improve.

FEEDBACK GALLERY

Once learners have developed the skill of giving and receiving quality feedback, they can deepen their work by using feedback galleries. These enable learners to give and receive feedback on several pieces of text or learner work at the same time.

In the photograph below, learners in a sixth-form psychology class have stuck up their essay plans around the classroom in feedback galleries. Working in pairs, the learners visit each essay plan in turn. They have two tasks. First, they note down on sticky notes any suggestions they may have for improvements. Second, and hence the reason for the mobile phone in camera mode, they act as 'magpies', stealing ideas they think would improve their own plan.

Photo: Andy Griffith.

There are many ways to adapt feedback galleries. One Year 6 English teacher, for example, gave different feedback tasks to her learners working in groups. Each group was asked to respond on just one specific aspect of the success criteria (e.g. use of punctuation, sentence structure). To help distinguish each group's feedback, they were given different coloured sticky notes. After 15 minutes of work in the feedback gallery, each learner had received kind, specific, and helpful feedback on the five aspects of writing that they were working to improve. All the while, the teacher circulated the classroom, monitoring the accuracy of the feedback and ensuring it conformed to the three criteria.

In this activity, feedback was provided more quickly than if the class had had to wait for their teacher to mark their work between lessons. Furthermore, there was still time during the lesson to put the feedback to good use, so the class worked in silence closing the gaps that had been identified for them by their peers.

Give different groups of learners the responsibility for identifying, assessing, and giving feedback on particular aspects of the work, instead of on all of it. Give the more complex aspects of the work to those learners who are working at higher levels of challenge.

Provide a checklist for those learners who need more guidance on which aspects of the work to provide feedback on.

Particular groups of learners can be invited to work with the teacher, or a teaching assistant, to focus on a particular gap that they're struggling to close. This could be an advanced group just as well as a less advanced group.

One teacher we observed, who realised the impact of using a feedback gallery with his classes, now has clothes pegs neatly glued around his walls ready and waiting for the next set of work to be displayed in his feedback gallery.

Are your learners better at peer and self-assessing now than they were at the start of the school year? If not, what are the barriers preventing this class from levelling up?

Do you create enough time to build your learners' KASH for giving high quality feedback?

DEVELOPING LEVEL 1A FEEDBACK HABITS

Would it be a problem in your classroom if your learners completely ignored your instructions – for example, if they refused to stop talking when you asked them to? Whenever we pose this question, teachers always confirm that, of course, it would be a problem. A major one! If this situation was actually to occur then no meaningful learning could take place. It would mean that productive classroom norms had broken down. It's at these times, when the dialogue between teacher and learners breaks down, that problems occur. As Sharon discovered at the start of this chapter, this is what happens when learners don't listen to and act on the feedback they're given.

STAMPS

We're passionate advocates for insisting that learners do more with the feedback they receive. Working in a Year 6 class one day, we saw a teacher using a feedback stamp whenever she delivered verbal feedback to learners. She would stamp the learners' books to show that she was regularly giving verbal feedback in lessons. This was not only for the learners but also for those occasions when the school's leadership carried out their regular book scrutinies (or 'book tyrannies' as one exhausted teacher described them!). We felt she was missing a trick and, after discussing this with her, she now takes a slightly different approach.

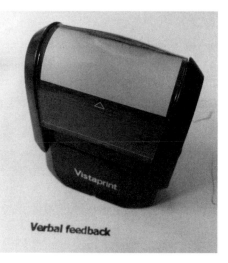

Photo: Mark Burns.

She still uses her stamp whenever she gives verbal feedback, but now she makes an extra demand of the learner. The learner has to summarise her feedback in one sentence in the margin of their workbook beneath the stamp. The great advantage of this is that it provides the teacher with immediate feedback about whether or not the learner has received the feedback and then understood it. This strategy gives the feedback much more impact without requiring any additional work from the teacher.

The teacher's stamp and the learner's summarising sentence become a visible reminder to the learner about the changes they need to make to their work to close their gaps. With

10 minutes of the lesson to go, the teacher reminds those learners who have received a verbal feedback stamp that they must act on the feedback in their written work to show they've understood it. Just before the end of the lesson, these learners are asked to underline all the instances in their work where they've addressed this feedback. This teacher has high expectations of her class. They know she'll refuse to mark their work if they haven't taken the time and care to address the issue and underline the relevant passages.

The feedback stamp reinforces for learners the importance of acting immediately on the feedback they're given if they want to improve. And there are other advantages too. When the teacher sits down to mark the learners' work, she'll get immediate pointers about whether the gaps she identified earlier have been closed or not. And let's be honest, it's not uncommon for teachers to have completely forgotten about some of the individual verbal feedback they've dispensed during the course of a hard day's teaching. Consequently, the stamp provides teachers with a useful reminder of the gaps they've pinpointed.

Try using a feedback stamp or a similar routine in your own teaching. Notice how this improves learner attention to, and utilisation of, the feedback you give them.

Art teacher Paul Fife has developed a clear process for giving and receiving feedback with his GCSE classes. Whenever he offers feedback, Paul stamps the border of the learner's work with a verbal feedback stamp. His learners know this means they have to write down the feedback Paul has just given them straightaway before it gets forgotten. Before Paul will have any further discussion about improvement with a particular learner, he'll ask them whether or not the previous piece of feedback has been understood and addressed. If it hasn't, he'll ask the learner to act first on the original feedback before he gives any more. In this way, he's pushing his learners to take more responsibility for closing their own gaps with the feedback they've been given.

Paul has also created spaces around the classroom where learners can leave feedback for him about their work. This feedback might take the form of a question they have about their work, a request for particular help in the next lesson, or a request for more resources. The boards provide a useful forum for Paul to maintain a constant dialogue with his learners about their ongoing improvement.

TARGET LOGS

Over the last three years, we've noticed that both the quantity and quality of written feedback to learners has increased. Ofsted's sharper focus on learners' books and evidence of progress over time has led school leaders to check more regularly that books are being marked.

Date	Target identified	Action taken	Completed		
	1.				
	2.				
	3.				
	4.				
	5.				
	6.				

However, we often feel that this relentless drive for the marking of books is, in some schools, missing the point of why we devote so many hours to this important task of assessment and feedback. Unless learners engage with and act on the written feedback that teachers provide them with, marking is an utter waste of time. When asked, many teachers say that the most frustrating and thankless part of their job is writing feedback that is consistently ignored by learners.

That said, we're also pleased to say that marking is an area where many of the teachers we've worked with have made a transformational difference to their learners' progress. One particular strategy that we've seen in action has enabled teachers to offer their learners impactful and timely feedback without having to work any harder. Like most great ideas, it's deceptively simple yet highly effective. The secret is a simple piece of paper stuck inside the cover of learners' books. We call it a 'feedback target log'. Its purpose is to ensure that learners get into the habit of acting on their teacher's written feedback.

One of the problems with the kind of written feedback that teachers have traditionally written in learner books is that it's frequently skimmed over and easily forgotten. For both learners and teachers, it's often out of sight, out of mind. And, to state an obvious fact, learners are generally not in the habit of flicking back through their workbooks to look up past feedback comments. It's hardly surprising that a common teacher moan is about having to mark the same mistakes from the same learners week in, week out.

Here is a copy of a learner's book, showing their target log, from the wonderful Isleworth Town Primary School in West London. As you can see, the target log flips up from the inside front cover of the exercise book. It's a constant in-the-face reminder of the targets that the learner is required to focus on.

Photo: Mark Burns.

HOW TO MAKE TARGET LOGS WORK

There are four key steps to making target logs work well:

Step 1. As soon as the learners get their marked work back from the teacher, they should read and then copy the 'target' that the teacher has given them into their target log. This provides a record of each target given to a learner over time. Typically there are no more than three targets for a learner to work on, depending on the age and competence level of the individual. Too much feedback tends to be counterproductive.

Step 2. When the learners embark on their next piece of work, the teacher directs them to flip up their target log from the inside cover of their books. The teacher asks them to have a brief discussion with their partner about how they're going to address this target in the next piece of work. This discussion acts as a powerful reminder about the importance of addressing their targets and closing their gaps. Given the high visibility of the log, learners have a constant reminder of the gap they should be focusing on and closing as they work.

Step 3. After completing the piece of work, each learner has to underline or highlight precisely where in their work they have addressed the target. If they have more than one target, then they indicate each one using the number indicated in the 'target identified' column. This is an important step as it provides feedback to the teacher about whether or not learners have understood the targets they've been set. If the teacher finds that a learner is not addressing the target correctly, they will make time as soon as possible to talk through the problem with that learner

Step 4. When the teacher marks each newly completed piece of work she can quickly check whether the existing targets have been met. If this is the case, the teacher signs off one of the boxes in the 'Completed' column. You might be wondering why there are three boxes in this column. Hitting a target once does not prove mastery. We recommend, therefore, that the learner demonstrates that they've hit the target at least three times before it's signed off. Once a target is signed off, an additional and more challenging target should be added.

Used effectively, the target log transforms the learner's book into a story of how they have closed successive gaps over time using the feedback their teacher has given them.

Several teachers we've worked with now use learners' books and target logs at parents' evenings. When parents ask how their child is progressing, these teachers ask the learners themselves to explain. The learners use their target logs and the successive pieces of annotated work in their books to show their parents how they're incorporating their teacher's feedback to make progress. Impressive, eh?

Getting learners to act on feedback to close their gaps can sometimes be nothing more than an aide-memoire. In the example below, teacher Caroline Creaby simply gives her A level learners a nudge before they sit down to complete a written answer.

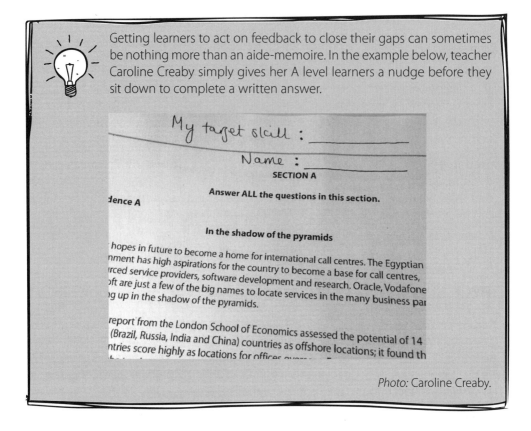

My target skill : _____

Name : _____

SECTION A

Answer ALL the questions in this section.

dence A

In the shadow of the pyramids

hopes in future to become a home for international call centres. The Egyptian nment has high aspirations for the country to become a base for call centres, rced service providers, software development and research. Oracle, Vodafone oft are just a few of the big names to locate services in the many business par ng up in the shadow of the pyramids.

report from the London School of Economics assessed the potential of 14 (Brazil, Russia, India and China) countries as offshore locations; it found th ntries score highly as locations for offices overs

Photo: Caroline Creaby.

Are your classes in the habit of acting on written and verbal feedback?

How could you use or adapt the ideas in this section to increase the impact of your feedback?

REFLECTION TIME

'Teaching can be a wasteland of missed opportunities,' we mused as we observed a teacher completely lose the plot from the outset of her lesson. The lesson began with the learners' marked homework being given back to them. With hardly a pause for breath, the teacher asked the class to put the work into their folders and write down the day's date. It was time to move on. This was a stunningly wasteful missed opportunity. Her learners had hardly any time to take note of the feedback she'd given them. All the hard work she'd put into marking their work the previous evening looked like going to waste.

Worse still, because they'd only had time for a brief glance at the grades she'd given them, and only a few moments to look at and consider her feedback, there was a depressingly predictable learner response. There was a minute or so of furtive comparing followed by various disparaging, whispered, and unhelpful learner exchanges such as, 'You're thick', 'Loser', and worse. As we reflected back to her after the lesson, her desire to move on, to teach forwards, to apportion no time for the thoughtful integration of feedback, was simply encouraging learners to ignore her useful suggestions for improvement and focus instead on comparing themselves with each other. There was a real risk that she was unwittingly creating a fixed mindset culture in her classroom.

Fortunately, this teacher was able to see how her classroom habits were getting in the way of the learning of her class. She now teaches very differently – it is more considered and there is much more time for reflection. We're passionate advocates for 'slow thinking' in the classroom. Our experience with teachers who teach backwards to achieve outstanding results is that they change gears frequently to make their interactions more interesting and to slow down their classes. At key points in their lessons they ask learners to pause, listen to, and then act on feedback. This slowing down for reflection, contemplation, and action reconnects learners with one of the most important purposes of their work: the necessity of closing their gaps so they can move towards mastery. Without these pauses to survey where they've come from, where they currently are, and where they need to go next, some learners will experience school as endless work with little purpose. And with some justification!

Slowing down not only provides learners with opportunities to gain greater clarity about what their gaps are and how to close them. It also provides a valuable opportunity to reflect on what has been learned and how. This enables learners to appreciate the progress they've already made so they can connect with their potential to continually grow and develop. In other words, effective time for reflection sows the seeds for growth mindsets to take root and flourish.

We shouldn't assume that learners view their progress through the same eyes as we do, especially if we've fallen into the trap of unwittingly fostering a fixed mindset culture in our classrooms by not giving learners enough time or opportunity to monitor and experience their development. We remember talking to one lad in a Year 8 English class about his work. He explained that he was finding it really difficult and felt that English was a subject he wasn't much good at. His teacher was shocked to hear this. She described the progress he had made during the year as 'phenomenal'. How could such a disconnect occur between a teacher and her learner? Carol Dweck's work on mindsets has shown beyond doubt that learners with fixed mindsets are less accurate in their self-judgements than those with growth mindsets. Learners like this one can easily fall into the trap of being overly negative about their current position and experience their gaps as bigger than they really are. This can be easily remedied when teachers regularly find time for reflection. Reflection helps learners to see the progress they've made so far, what steps are necessary to move them beyond where they currently are, and how they can progress towards their destinations.

WHO IS FEEDBACK FOR?

In his influential book, *Embedded Formative Assessment*, Dylan Wiliam really cuts to the chase: 'I often ask teachers whether they believe that their students spend as much time utilising the feedback they are given as it has taken the teacher to provide it.'[6] When we run our training days, most teachers confess that they seem to work far harder giving feedback than their learners ever do acting on it. If this is also the case for you, the following section should provide some practical tools to ensure that you can radically re-balance this workload. One teacher cheekily commented on an INSET day, 'If I give up marking, great. I'll be doing less work than my learners.' However, we want to make it clear that this certainly isn't what we're advocating! We want to free up your time and energy by developing your own and your learners' feedback skills, so you can focus your attention on really helping learners to close their gaps and reach their destinations.

---

6   Wiliam, *Embedded Formative Assessment*, p. 129.

GAP TASKS

So, let's return to the teacher who had omitted to give her learners any time for reflection on feedback. When we returned to work with her two months later, we were mightily impressed with the changes she'd made. When she returned the learners' work, she put up this gap task slide on her whiteboard. She confessed later that the slide was there just as much to remind her to slow down and value quality feedback time as it was for her learners. The point is that it worked. The slide, we should mention in passing, came from Tom Brush (http://tombrush1982. blogspot.co.uk/) an innovative PE teacher at Wheelers Lane Technology College in Birmingham, who applies the same principles to his subject.

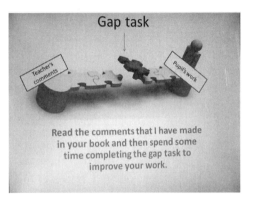

Photo: Mark Burns.

The teacher instructed the class to work on closing their own gap that she had identified in their work. Note the term 'own gap'. The teacher was making it as difficult as possible for learners to compare their own performance with that of others. Indeed, she had created a new culture in her classroom where beating your personal best prevailed over doing better (or worse) than others. The learners spent 10 minutes conscientiously reading and acting on the feedback given. During this period of quiet reflection we had the opportunity to have a quick word with many of them. They were unanimous in valuing this quiet time to improve their work using the feedback their teacher had provided. One learner typified the prevailing mood when he commented, 'I get cleverer more quickly now that I'm in the habit of reading feedback from my teacher.' We also observed the teacher making much more effective use of the valuable time she had gained to speak to individual learners about specific points for improvement.

What was also noticeable was that the quality of the teacher's written feedback had also changed. In our previous observation her comments had tended to be summative in nature. Now they posed a direct challenge or question for learners to act on. This was, she reflected, because she now expected them to take direct action on an important task within a specific time frame. It was disciplined and it was rigorous. The teacher had even coined a name for this part of her lesson. She called it her 'just review' time.

In some teachers' classrooms that we've observed, learners are asked to use different coloured pens to update their work based on their teacher's feedback. In others, learners write updates in the margin or on sticky notes. Whichever way works best for you, and them, the key is to be able to quickly get feedback from learners about whether they are clear on the gap identified and how to close it.

JUST REVIEW LESSONS

In some modules of learning, it makes sense to devote considerably more than 10 minutes to reflecting on existing work, reviewing progress made so far, and identifying gaps that still need to be closed. Indeed, many teachers we've worked with are now in the habit of building into their planning just review (JR) lessons. These often take up a whole lesson or a significant portion of it. Here is one example which focuses exclusively on time for reflection and gap closing.

THE SUM OF THE PARTS

Purpose: To identify and close any gaps remaining at the end of a module of learning.

Before the lesson, the teacher divides up the content of the module into sections. Learners, working in pairs, are then given a section each to work on. These may be allocated according to levels of challenge, or based on a particular gap a pair have struggled with during the module in order to check their mastery of it, or the sections could just be distributed in the form of an old-fashioned lucky dip.

The learners are allocated an amount of time to organise their section into a revision or review aid. The format they will present it in could be a physical model, a digital creation, a video performance, an audio recording, or a summarised script on a sheet of A4.

As we advocated in Chapter 3, skilful *Blue Peter* teachers, in this case the students themselves, will have an exemplar to demonstrate the finished products, the ingredients, and the level of quality that will be required. This might include worked examples, useful mnemonics to aid recall, or a particular focus on tricky or confusing areas.

This process can take up to two lessons, depending on the age and stage of the learners, and the finished products can become resources that are collated into a physical or virtual revision pack so that every learner in the class can have access to them. One maths teacher, commenting on how well JR lessons enabled his class to identify and close their remaining gaps, went on to say that he believed that just one JR lesson could make a significant difference in terms of his learners' mastery of each specific topic.

REVIEW THEIR PERSONAL BESTS

ONE-TO-ONE REVIEWS

Making time for in-depth, one-to-one reviews with learners is an invaluable way to get them to reflect on their own progress. It is particularly important for those with fixed mindsets. Good one-to-one reviews force learners to slow down, reflect on their learning, and unpick any misconceptions that might be preventing them from closing their gaps.

Of course, given the usual 1:30 ratio in a classroom, this isn't going to be a weekly event, particularly for secondary teachers who teach multiple classes. However, setting aside quality time to reflect with learners individually about the progress they're making and the gaps they need to be closing is key to personalising feedback. Sitting down with learners individually to review their learning offers a powerful opportunity for you and them to take stock. In particular, it enables learners to realise how far they've progressed since last term, and it enables the teacher to monitor how well they've understood the feedback they've received and what the next steps in their development should be. Through this process, learners can begin to appreciate the value of pausing to reflect. This is a habit we really want to encourage and develop in our learners. However, it can be difficult to make this happen if we're running a classroom that operates at a hundred miles an hour.

We worked with one passionate secondary school teacher who told us his aim was to speak to every single learner at least once in each lesson. He believed this approach would help him to develop good relationships with his learners. We recorded a video of him at work with his class before discussing the advantages and disadvantages of his approach. When we talked with him after he had watched himself on video his beliefs had already begun to shift. He saw himself rushing around his classroom like a bat out of hell in his determination to speak to each learner. Our shared reflection with him was that it would probably be better to provide higher quality, more detailed feedback to a smaller number of learners during each lesson. In this way, he would avoid spreading himself too thinly. He accepted this immediately, realising that his current way of giving feedback was providing no real value at all.

SMALL GROUP REVIEWS

Another excellent strategy we've seen used that creates time for high quality feedback is the small group review. One teacher referred to it as a politer version of the board meetings in the TV show *The Apprentice*.

In a secondary school ICT classroom, one particular teacher we've worked with sets up a 'project meeting' table. As each learner project progresses, the teacher organises regular planning meetings with small groups of learners. These meetings are calendared in advance so learners know that they need to be organised and ready to present their progress, discuss whatever challenges they are currently facing, and compare their progress with the action plan they developed at the start of the project. The teacher, who used to work in the IT industry, is keen to ensure that her subject accurately reflects best practice in the world of work. By incorporating group reviews into the day-to-day norms of her lessons, she is developing her learners' KASH so that they can move effectively into this work environment, as well as experiencing its routine professional behaviours and procedures.

The aim of the review is to provide focused feedback on their current project. Each learner leaves the review with greater clarity on how they will close their own gaps using the review sheet opposite. This kind of quality in-depth discussion would not be possible through the short informal chats that might occur if the teacher just circulated around the class. Another teacher told us that since she had adopted the use of group reviews, several important pedagogical changes had happened in her classroom. She has greater clarity about the progress each individual learner in her class is making; her learners are clearer on her expectations in terms of their progress, the quality of their work, and the deadlines they have to meet; and she has been able to give much higher quality verbal feedback that has had made a massive impact on her learners' progress.

Review sheet		
Name		
Start doing ...	Keep doing ...	Stop doing ...

Sometimes issues that have arisen in one group review are shared with the whole class. This could be because there is useful learning for other groups that will help them to avoid a particular pitfall, or it could be to recommend a more effective way of proceeding.

> Do you have well-developed routines that ensure learners have time to act on feedback?
>
> How often do you review learning with individuals in your class(es)?

FAQS

Wouldn't these ideas be best addressed when I induct a new class at the start of September?

Of course, you're right. In a perfect world it would make absolute sense. Teachers who have embraced the power and principles of teaching backwards naturally introduce these skills and techniques during the induction of any new class. However, it's never too late in the school year to make a start. We've seen plenty of examples of teachers in primary and secondary schools who've picked a seemingly non-descript Monday morning to introduce a new norm into their classrooms. They've found that when learners see the reason for the new behaviours they've been able to adapt surprisingly quickly. And when learners notice the improvements they can make as a result of listening to and acting on quality feedback, and how quickly and easily they can close gaps that before seemed insurmountable, they're motivated to pay attention even more. Teachers too can become more motivated to persist, even with the most reluctant learners, because they never want to return to the dispiriting world of giving feedback that never gets acted on.

I'm really struggling to get all of my class to act on feedback. What can I do?

Getting learners' attitudes right, and getting their heads in the optimal place, are necessary skills to acquire if learners are going to be able to receive and then give high quality feedback to themselves and others. Unless they see hard evidence of the benefits that feedback can give them, some learners will be reluctant to buy in. It's worth remembering that some of your learners might well have developed negative attitudes over many years at school, and even had them reinforced by their parents, so these habits can be a challenge to change.

However, it's important to persevere. Encouraging a learner to get into the habit of listening to and acting on useful feedback might well be one of the most valuable things we can teach them before they leave school. In the long term, whether in the context of work or personal relationships, the ability to give and receive quality feedback is both an important life skill and a significant predictor of success.

As teachers, we need to have a growth mindset about our ability to influence and change our learners' KASH. The ideas in this chapter might not change every learner you teach straightaway. Yet just because the challenge might seem substantial, it is crucial to the life chances of our learners. We believe you'll find many of the ideas and activities that we've described in this chapter really useful in effecting these changes and giving your learners a good grounding in the uses of effective feedback and a grasp of how to make it happen.

Aren't these issues whole-school ones that I can't tackle on my own?

What impresses us most is when we go into schools where results are poor and see the outlier teachers at work. Despite the poor norms of learners, including fixed mindsets, these teachers' classrooms are oases of Level 1a feedback. This convinces us that taking your class on this journey is not impossible. Of course, it's more difficult to create this kind of change when you're working alone. But when you start to succeed, and level up your class to Level 1a, don't be surprised if the school leadership team soon comes knocking at your door to find out how your classes have been transformed by the power of feedback.

IN A NUTSHELL

The final step in teaching backwards is feedback. This is the feedback that helps learners to close whatever gaps exist between where they currently are and the destination they are aiming for.

At Level 1a, teachers are able to give learners timely feedback to help them close these gaps. Given a classroom ratio of 1:30, giving and receiving such feedback might seem impossible. Yet teachers who teach backwards achieve it by training their classes in the necessary skills and habits so that learners are able to give high quality feedback to themselves, to each other, and to their teacher.

If feedback is to be effective it has to be accurate, but it also has to be delivered and received well. Making time to develop this skill step by step is essential. The first of these steps is to model how to give high quality feedback. Another is to ensure that feedback is kind, specific, and helpful.

As learners' skills develop, the teacher can introduce activities such as 'be the teacher' to give learners more responsibility for assessing the work of others. Finally, in the context of today's fast-paced world, it's also essential to develop the habit of slowing down in the classroom so that learners can benefit from the pedagogical necessity of pausing and reflecting on the verbal and written feedback they receive, and on the overall progress they are making.

TEACHING BACKWARDS CHECKLIST

Feedback (macro – course/ academic year)	This is always part of my practice	I sometimes do this	I never do this
I model explicitly how to critique work and give kind, specific, and helpful feedback.			
I create time for learners to practise critiquing exemplar work so they develop a better understanding of the gaps in their own work.			
I train learners to improve their skills so they know how to give high quality feedback.			
I work to develop a community of learners who value feedback as a way of improving.			
I provide opportunities for learners to critique their own and others' work and discuss how it could be improved.			

Feedback (macro – course/ academic year)	This is always part of my practice	I sometimes do this	I never do this
I encourage learners to take responsibility for checking to ensure that they have addressed previous feedback.			
I have developed well-established habits with my class where they pause to reflect and then act on *verbal* feedback.			
I have developed well-established habits with my class where they pause to reflect and then act on *written* feedback.			
I deliberately build time into my planning of modules of learning so that learners can pause and reflect on the feedback they are given.			
I create time at the end of modules of learning for learners to review their progress and identify remaining gaps.			
I schedule time to conduct small group and one-to-one reviews about progress with my learners.			

Download this checklist from:

http://osiriseducational.co.uk/TB/resources/

TEACHING BACKWARDS ACTION PLAN: POINTS FROM THIS CHAPTER

How can you convert a 'never' to a 'sometimes', or a 'sometimes' to an 'always' in relation to this checklist? Remember, you are more likely to get your class to Level 1a if you do all these things routinely.

I need to stop/do less …

I need to start/do more …

FOR MORE INFORMATION …

Caroline Creaby at Sandringham School exploring ways to get her class to act on feedback:

http://sandagogy.co.uk/learning/index.php?q=blog/carolinecreaby/effort-deliberate-practice-exams-responding-feedback

Tom Sherrington's blog is always thought-provoking. This is a gem on feedback:

http://headguruteacher.com/2012/11/10/mak-feedback-count-close-the-gap/

CONCLUSION

Teaching backwards or teaching forwards?

We hope that you've enjoyed this book. Maybe *Teaching Backwards* will be a once-only read or perhaps it may be something that you dip into again and again. Hopefully, we've convinced you that teaching backwards is the way forward towards outstanding lessons and results.

To fully embrace the spirit of teaching backwards you must hold two beliefs. First, you must believe in the merits and importance of learner autonomy. We believe the aim of any good teacher is like that of a good parent: to increasingly encourage our children to become more autonomous and to make their way in the world by themselves. Of course, we'll be around to guide and advise them when they need it or ask for it, and if we play our part well they'll value what we have to say. Second, you've got to have a PB or personal best mentality – the desire and curiosity to become a better teacher year after year. This can only come from being a good learner who believes the journey towards excellence never ends.

Many teachers who have attended our courses have seen the quality of their teaching transformed when they have embraced the principles of teaching backwards. Some have recognised the importance of building high expectations with their classes. Others have stopped guessing the starting points of their learners. Still more have ceased being vague about the destinations they want them to reach and lax about how they will get proof of their learning. Instead, they've started to become more challenging, more disciplined in their planning, and more precise and skilful at getting feedback from their learners. They do less guessing and more investigating. They've got more empathy but they accept fewer excuses.

The beauty of teaching backwards is that it applies equally to teachers as it does to learners. You may find it useful to ask yourself some challenging questions based on each of the chapters.

First, how could you stretch your own self-expectations even higher than the ones you currently hold? You've already got this book in your hands, so our guess is that you already have the desire and curiosity to become a better, more effective teacher, and you've got the humility to want to read a book about how you might do just that. Some teachers have never done this. But you have.

Second, are you really confident that you know what your own starting points are? Some teachers are confused about how to judge the quality of their own teaching. We hope that the ideas, descriptor levels, and checklists in this book will give you a chance to assess where you currently are across a range of criteria, so that you can evaluate more accurately your own current starting point.

Third, how can you set about defining and demystifying the destination that you want to achieve as a teacher? Hopefully, you're someone who's come into this job to make a positive difference to the lives of children. Reflecting on the level descriptors in this book will help you to appreciate the KASH that's required to get your classes up to Level 1a. It's here that learners make the most progress. Thoughtful reflection and subsequent practice will enable you to identify whatever gaps may exist in your own KASH, as well as the KASH of your learners.

Fourth, how do you begin looking for proofs of learning? This time it's the proof of your own learning as a teacher. What will be the evidence that demonstrates to you that you've truly levelled up? We'd expect that you will see improved and more rapid progress from your learners, more engagement from them too, and that your level of job satisfaction will be on the rise.

Finally, how do you work with the last two stages of teaching backwards – challenge and feedback? We hope you are ready to set yourself undertakings that open gaps for your own development and then seek feedback that helps you to close them. This encourages a virtuous cycle: as you close one set of gaps, you see the value in opening new ones in a continuous process of personal and professional self-development.

Our hope is that this book makes a positive impact on your teaching, and that your teaching makes an even bigger impact on the learning of your classes, both the ones you have now and the ones you are yet to meet.

We know that there's lots of pressure out there, but there's still room for learning and enjoyment too. Sadly, a small number of colleagues spend too much of their time teaching forwards, delivering information in a manner that fails to light that spark of enthusiasm that excites and motivates their learners. In doing so, they frequently fail to make the maximum impact on their learners, while learning little or nothing new themselves.

The alternative is to teach backwards. If you regularly follow the teaching backwards steps for yourself, then the very least that will happen is that you become a more reflective teacher who is always looking to set a new personal best, and probably does. At the other end of the scale, you'll be supporting your learners to transform themselves into highly motivated, self-confident individuals who can rise to challenges with enthusiasm and apply their learning across a range of contexts. And when you see that happening, it will very likely mean that you've transformed yourself too. Now, that really would be outstanding.

Appendix

THE BIG FOUR OR FACE

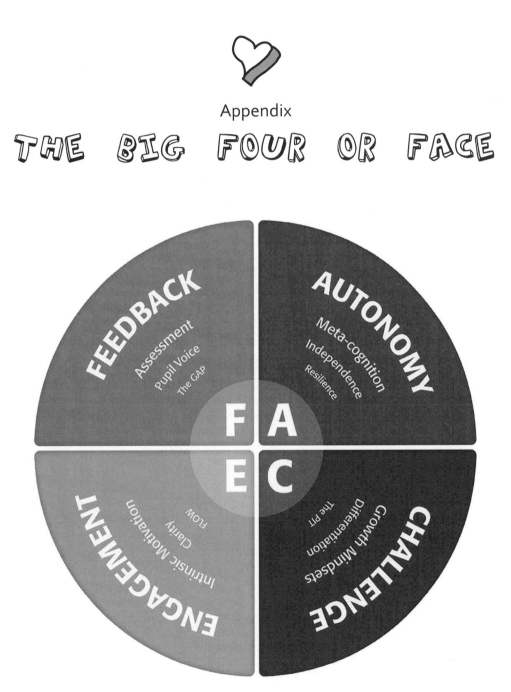

Big Four FACE and contents © Andy Griffith and Mark Burns.
Design © Osiris Educational Woodhall Spa Ltd

1   Feedback. From a teacher perspective, learning needs to be structured to provide opportunities to get frequent feedback on the progress of the learners. It's this feedback that informs the direction of the rest of the lesson and all future planning. From a learner perspective, as they move through the education system they need to become increasingly adept at judging the quality of their learning against success criteria and then applying effective strategies to constantly improve the quality of their work.

2   Autonomy. We believe that the purpose of education is to equip young people to thrive in an ever-changing world. This is the thread that runs through all of our work. Unless children are literate, numerate, and have the 'right' KASH when they leave school they will face significant barriers. These barriers are likely to affect their economic, social, and emotional well-being.

3   Challenge. Challenge lies at the very heart of learning. Everything in science, human understanding, and knowledge began with a question or problem that needed solving. Challenge in lessons is crucial. Teachers need it to assess understanding, give more accurate feedback, and prompt learners to think more deeply about key concepts. Learners need it to help them to understand and remember what they have been taught, to motivate them, and to give them a sense of achievement for having overcome obstacles that at first sight may have seemed daunting.

4   Engagement. Engagement is characterised by flow – a profound sense of being fully absorbed in whatever it is we're doing. Without this deep kind of engagement, it will be very tricky to get learners to step up to the challenge of learning. Engagement is essential if they're to become more independent in their learning, develop the confidence and courage to give themselves and each other quality feedback, and rise to the challenge of stretching themselves to the limit.

The concept of the Big Four, by the way, hasn't just come from our own experiences in the classroom and the training room. It also corresponds with the work of John Hattie.[1] The conclusions of his work are very clear. The most effective teachers set challenges based on the starting points of learners and make it clear what they need to do to overcome any obstacles. They create open and engaging learning environments where sharing mistakes and misconceptions is welcomed. Teachers promote high expectations and hold the belief that, with the right teaching and feedback, *all* learners can succeed.

---

1   John Hattie and Gregory Yates, *Visible Learning and the Science of How We Learn* (Abingdon: Routledge, 2013).

BIBLIOGRAPHY

Berger, Ron (2003). *An Ethic of Excellence: Building a Culture of Craftsmanship with Students* (Portsmouth, NH: Heinemann Educational Books).

Berger, Ron, Leah Rugen, and Libby Woodfin (2014). *Leaders of Their Own Learning: Transforming Schools Through Student-Engaged Assessment* (San Francisco, CA: Jossey-Bass).

Bjork, Robert (2013). 'Desirable Difficulties Perspective on Learning', in Harold Pashler (ed.), *Encyclopedia of the Mind* (Thousand Oaks, CA: Sage Reference). Available at: http://bjorklab.psych. ucla.edu/pubs/RBjork_inpress.pdf.

Claxton, Guy, Maryl Chambers, Graham Powell, and Bill Lucas (2011). *The Learning Powered School: Pioneering 21st Century Education* (Bristol: TLO Ltd). Available at: http://www.wikispaces.com/file/ view/TheLearningPoweredSchool_Extract_TLOLimited_2011.pdf/241982374/TheLearning PoweredSchool_Extract_TLOLimited_2011.pdf.

Csikszentmihalyi, Mihaly (1990). *Flow: The Psychology of Optimal Experience* (New York: Harper and Row).

de Bono, Edward (2006 [1982]). *De Bono's Thinking Course: Powerful Tools to Transform Your Thinking* (London: BBC Active).

Dweck, Carol (2000). *Self-Theories: Their Role in Motivation, Personality and Development (Essays in Social Psychology)* (Philadelphia, PA: Psychology Press).

Dweck, Carol (2007). *Mindset: The New Psychology of Success* (New York: Ballantine).

Einhorn, Stefan (2010). *The Art of Being Kind* (London: Piatkus).

Gilbert, Ian (2010). *Why Do I Need a Teacher When I've Got Google? The Essential Guide to the Big Issues for Every 21st Century Teacher* (Abingdon: Routledge).

Gladwell, Malcolm (2008). *Outliers: The Story of Success* (New York: Little, Brown and Co.).

Griffith, Andy and Mark Burns (2012). *Engaging Learners* (Carmarthen: Crown House Publishing).

Hargreaves, Andy and Michael Fullan (2012). *Professional Capital: Transforming Teaching In Every School* (Abingdon: Routledge).

Hattie, John (2011). *Visible Learning for Teachers: Maximizing Impact on Learning* (Abingdon: Routledge).

Hattie, John and Gregory Yates (2013). *Visible Learning and the Science of How We Learn* (Abingdon: Routledge).

Heath, Chip and Dan Heath (2008). *Made to Stick: Why Some Ideas Take Hold and Others Come Unstuck* (London: Arrow).

Hymer, Barry (2009). *Gifted and Talented Pocketbook* (Alresford: Teachers' Pocketbooks).

Jensen, Eric (2008). *Super Teaching: Over 1000 Practical Strategies* (Thousand Oaks, CA: Sage).

Kahneman, Daniel (2012). *Thinking, Fast and Slow* (London: Penguin).

Leat, David (2001). *Thinking Through Geography*, 2nd edn (London: Chris Kington Publishing).

Leat, David and David Kinninment (2005). *More Thinking Through Geography* (London: Chris Kington Publishing).

Lemov, Doug, Erica Woolway, and Katie Yezzi (2012). *Practice Perfect: 42 Rules for Getting Better at Getting Better* (San Francisco, CA: Jossey-Bass).

Lucas, Vivien (2003). *Mathematical Team Games: Enjoyable Activities to Enhance the Curriculum* (St Albans: Tarquin Publications).

Marzano, Robert (2007). *The Art and Science of Teaching: A Comprehensive Framework for Effective Instruction* (Alexandria, VA: Association for Supervision and Curriculum Development).

McQuillan, Jeff and Gisela Conde (1996). 'The Conditions of Flow in Reading: Two Studies of Optimal Experience', *Reading Psychology: An International Quarterly* 17: 109–135.

Nottingham, James (n.d.). 'Encouraging Thinking Skills', *Teach Primary*. Available at: http://www.teachprimary.com/learning_resources/view/encouraging-thinking-skills.

Nottingham, James (2010). *Challenging Learning* (Berwick upon Tweed: JN Publishing).

Nuthall, Graham (2007). *The Hidden Lives of Learners* (Wellington: NZCER Press).

Owen, Nick (2001). *The Magic of Metaphor: 77 Stories for Teachers, Trainers and Thinkers* (Carmarthen: Crown House Publishing).

Owen, Nick (2004). *More Magic of Metaphor: Stories for Leaders, Influencers and Motivators and Spiral Dynamics Wizards* (Carmarthen: Crown House Publishing).

Owen, Nick (2009). *The Salmon of Knowledge: Stories for Work, Life, the Dark Shadow, and OneSelf* (Carmarthen: Crown House Publishing).

Philpott, Joanne (2009). *Captivating Your Class: Effective Teaching Skills* (London: Continuum).

Pink, Daniel (2012). *To Sell Is Human: The Surprising Truth About Persuading, Convincing, and Influencing Others* (New York: Riverhead).

Rogers, Carl (1961). *On Becoming a Person: A Therapist's View of Psychotherapy* (London: Constable & Robinson).

Rosenthal, Robert and Lenore Jacobson (2003). *Pygmalion in the Classroom: Teacher Expectation and Pupils' Intellectual Development* (Norwalk, CT and Carmarthen: Crown House Publishing).

Rowling, J. K. (2008). 'The Fringe Benefits of Failure, and the Importance of Imagination', Commencement Address at the Annual Meeting of the Harvard Alumni Association, June. Available at: http://harvardmagazine.com/2008/06/the-fringe-benefits-failure-the-importance-imagination.

Tomlinson, Carol Ann and Marcia B. Imbeau (2010). *Leading and Managing a Differentiated Classroom* (Alexandria, VA: Association for Supervision and Curriculum Development).

Waters, Mick (2013). *Thinking Allowed: On Schooling* (Carmarthen: Independent Thinking Press).

Wiggins, Grant and Jay McTighe (2005). *Understanding by Design* (Alexandria, VA: Association for Supervision and Curriculum Development).

Wiliam, Dylan (2011). *Embedded Formative Assessment* (Bloomington, IN: Solution Tree Press).

Willingham, Daniel (2009). *Why Don't Students Like School? A Cognitive Scientist Answers Questions About How the Mind Works and What It Means for the Classroom* (San Francisco, CA: Jossey-Bass).

Willshaw, Steve (31 May 2013) 'Flow and Reading for Pleasure', *Steve Willshaw*. Available at: https://stevewillshaw.wordpress.com/tag/rooted-in-reading/.

Wragg, Edward and George Brown (1993). *Explaining (Classroom Skills)* (London: Routledge).

ACTIVITIES

INDEX

S

T

V

W

Y

Osiris Educational is the UK's leading independent provider of professional development for teachers.

Osiris believes that every child should receive a world-class education. Helping teachers in their continuous development is the crucial step to achieving this. We work at the forefront of innovation in education providing pioneering, challenging and effective training solutions.

More than 400 presenters work with Osiris Educational to help teachers improve their ways of thinking and their approaches to teaching.

Some of the most renowned trainers from across the world work with Osiris Educational including: Professor John Hattie, Professor Barry Hymer, Bill Rogers, Professor Viviane Robinson, Professor Carol Dweck, Andy Griffith and Mark Burns.

Our five crucial paths to CPD training cover everything from Early Years through to Key Stage 5.

Day Courses:
- Leadership and Management
- Teaching and Learning
- Pastoral and Behavioural
- SEN and Gifted and Talented
- Curriculum
- Ofsted

In-School Training:
- Early Years
- Primary
- Secondary

Teacher and Leadership Programmes:
- Outstanding Teaching Intervention
- Visible Learning
- Mindsets

Conferences and Keynotes:
- Leading Speakers
- Key Issues and Policies

Fast Updates:
- Twilights
- Policy Briefings

FOR MORE INFORMATION CALL 0808 160 5 160
OR VISIT OSIRISEDUCATIONAL.CO.UK